CHURCH

American Society of Missiology Series, No. 33

CHURCH

Community for the Kingdom

John Fuellenbach

ORBIS BOOKS

Maryknoll, New York 10545

The Catholic Foreign Mission Society of America (Maryknoll) recruits and trains people for overseas missionary service. Through Orbis Books, Maryknoll aims to foster the international dialogue that is essential to mission. The books published, however, reflect the opinions of their authors and are not meant to represent the official position of the Society. To obtain more information about Maryknoll and Orbis Books, please visit our website at www.maryknoll.org.

Library of Congress Cataloging-in-Publication Data

Fuellenbach, John.
    Church : community for the Kingdom / John Fuellenbach.
        p. cm. — (American Society of Missiology series ; no. 33)
Includes index.
    ISBN 1-57075-416-0
    1. Church. 2. Kingdom of God. 3. Mission of the church. 4. Catholic Church—Doctrines. 5. Vatican Council (2nd : 1962-1965) I. Title. II. Series.
    BX1746 .F84 2002
    260—dc21   2001008346

Contents

PART 2
MODELS OF THE CHURCH

Preface to the ASM Series

The purpose of the ASM (American Society of Missiology) Series is to publish—without regard for disciplinary, national, or denominational boundaries—scholarly works of high quality and wide interest on missiological themes from the entire spectrum of scholarly pursuits relevant to Christian mission, which is always the focus of books in the Series.

By *mission* is meant the effort to effect passage over the boundary between faith in Jesus Christ and its absence. In this understanding of mission, the basic functions of Christian proclamation, dialogue, witness, service, worship, liberation, and nurture are of special concern. And in that context questions arise, including, How does the transition from one cultural context to another influence the shape and interaction between these dynamic functions, especially in regard to the cultural and religious plurality that comprises the global context of Christian mission?

The promotion of scholarly dialogue among missiologists, and among missiologists and scholars in other fields of inquiry, may involve the publication of views that some missiologists cannot accept, and with which members of the Editorial Committee do not agree. Manuscripts published in the Series reflect the opinions of their authors and are not understood to represent the position of the American Society of Missiology or of the Editorial Committee. Selection is guided by such criteria as intrinsic worth, readability, and accessibility to a range of interested persons and not merely to experts or specialists.

The ASM Series, in collaboration with Orbis Books, seeks to publish scholarly works of high merit and wide interest on numerous aspects of missiology—the study of mission. Able presentations on new and creative approaches to the practice and understanding of mission will receive close attention.

The ASM Series Editorial Committee
Jonathan J. Bonk
Angelyn Dries, OSF
Scott W. Sunquist

Preface

My fascination in theology has always been the kingdom of God, the symbol Jesus consistently used to explain his life and mission. Thus this book aims to present a vision of the church that understands itself wholly from the standpoint of the kingdom, finds its identity in the presence of the kingdom now, and sees its mission entirely in the service of the kingdom.

The title, *Church: Community for the Kingdom*, encapsulates this purpose. First, the church is the community in which the kingdom is now experienced and celebrated and where the future fulfillment of God's great design for creation already dawns. It is the community where the future life with the Triune God is already happening in hidden but real signs, for the church is an icon of the Trinity. Second, the church is *for* the kingdom because its mission is totally geared to witness and proclaim it. As Jesus saw himself charged to proclaim the kingdom and to bring it to all cities and towns (Lk 4:42), so the church, following his footsteps, has to understand its very essence and mission in the service of the kingdom as well. That is how Jesus instructed his disciples: "As the Father has sent me, so I send you" (Jn 20:21).

There are many possible approaches to the mystery of the church. The one presented here tries to capture Jesus' vision of the kingdom, which he threw like fire into this world and which he wanted to see burning everywhere (Lk 12:49). This fire he entrusted to the community of his disciples who, after they had received it as the great gift of the Risen Lord on Easter (Jn 20:22) or on Pentecost (Acts 2:3-4), went out and preached what they themselves had received.

I am pleased that *Church: Community for the Kingdom* has been selected for the American Society of Missiology Series. It finds its place alongside the monumental *Transforming Mission* by David Bosch and *The Church in Cultures* by my confrere in the Society of the Divine Word, Louis J. Luzbetak. A word on why an ecclesiology book such as mine finds a home in a *missiological* series is appropriate. First, the reader should note that *Church: Community for the Kingdom* is organized and draws upon Roman Catholic principles. The mission theme may seem underemphasized to scholars who identify themselves as missiologists. More to the point, though, the way it is dealt with here exemplifies the preference of Catholics to do theological mission studies within branches such as ecclesiology and Christology rather than principally in books that wear the label missiology. As a member of the Society of the Divine Word, which has committed so many resources to advance the discipline of missiology, it is not that I do not see the importance of mission studies being done as a distinct academic theological branch. Rather, I also believe that questions concerning the mission of the church should be of concern to the *whole* church and need to permeate the entire theological curriculum. I hope this book helps its readers think new thoughts about the church's mission and that it will be useful to men and women who are not professionally interested in missiology as a formal branch of theology.

The term *mission* itself has become—at least in the popular imagination— synonymous with religio-imperialistic activity carried on by Europeans and North Americans in the Global South. Specialists, of course, know that this is far too crude a judgment. The more one studies mission in relation to the colonial enterprise, the more one realizes how many forms the Christian mission–colonialism relationship took. Some were in direct opposition to one another. In many others the accusation that they were two aspects of one corrupt enterprise can be proved beyond doubt. In many cases, according to the thesis of scholars associated with Professors Lamin Sanneh and Andrew Walls on the history of mission from the North, Christian mission has been one of the most important forces animating the struggle to preserve local cultures.[1] *Mission* is, in other words, a highly ambiguous term.

Whatever one's views of the past, Christian mission has entered a new era. Nevertheless, I sometimes have the impression that—even if the majority of missionaries today are Asians, Africans, and Latin Americans—our thinking about mission resembles the habit of mind Marshall McLuhan once called, if I remember his words correctly, "moving forward while looking through the rearview mirror." That is to say, our thoughts are so dominated by the past we are unable to examine what is really happening in the present. To partake in the Christian mission in the world, I suggest in *Church: Community for the Kingdom*, we need to break out of such patterns and drink deeply from the waters of the symbol Jesus used to crystallize his own mission and that of his disciples. By this I mean that Jesus embodied and pointed to the kingdom as that which God was bringing to fulfillment in sending himself and the Spirit. The community that was created on earth was born when the disciples let God's love and power transform them—it was a community for the kingdom.

I am conscious of the ecumenical nature of the American Society of Missiology Series. Yet my book is Roman Catholic in its sources and tone. I see this quality as both a limitation and an asset. The missionary movement gave rise to the ecumenical movement, as we all know. And the classic ecumenical movement is in at least as great a crisis as mission. To return to health, both need continually to root themselves in the earth of living tradition in which concrete communities grow. I hope that the limits of taking a specifically Roman Catholic

[1] See Lamin Sanneh, *Translating the Message: The Missionary Impact on Culture* (Maryknoll, New York: Orbis Books, 1989); Andrew F. Walls, *The Missionary Movement in Christian History* (Maryknoll, New York: Orbis Books, 1996); and Andrew F. Walls, *The Cross-Cultural Process in Christian History: Studies in the Transmission and Appropriation of Christian Faith* (Maryknoll, New York: Orbis Books, 2001).

approach to explicating theologically the nature of the Christian mission will help in that process. In being Catholic, may it be no less catholic.

The Roman Catholic Church, at the Second Vatican Council (1962-65), realized the necessity of returning to the sources to open itself to the fire of the Master's love so that the world may come to believe. The council presented a vision of the church as a church-in-mission that remains a permanent challenge. In the meantime, the church as a pilgrim people has to move on. New challenges arise and new models of how to conceive church have to be sought and developed if it wants to remain faithful to its Master's message. As Jesus learned the way of the kingdom through circumstances in which he was put (Mk 7:25-29), so the church will come to understand its very being and mission afresh if it remains open to the times and the Spirit of Jesus. Today the church faces two big challenges: (1) how to make the kingdom of God understood in the different cultures of the world; and (2) how to live Jesus' own life principles of love, justice, and compassion in a world where the poor are getting poorer and the rich few are getting richer.

The approach to understanding church in this book is presented accordingly: first, Jesus's message of the kingdom and the church; second, the vision of the church itself as presented in Vatican II; and third, the challenges to the church in the present world, with an attempt to outline some models of church in response to these challenges.

This book is about the church, its very being, purpose, and goal today, written not from some neutral viewpoint but from my experience and that of others who are deeply engaged in its life. The reflections that emerge affect our own life and self-understanding as priests, religious, or lay people who belong to the community called church.

Far from attempting to achieve a level of "objective" discourse about church, we speak as people who live in it, celebrate it, and take part in its mission. To get a better understanding of church, therefore, means to enter more deeply into our own identity. This is not just any topic that we discuss, investigate scientifically, observe critically, and propose to correct and resolve in view of today's pressing problems. Our investigation is neither neutral nor detached, as if its outcome bears no consequences for our vocation as Christians. For us the church is an object of faith, because as believers we pray: "We believe in the one, holy, catholic, and apostolic church." Accessing and understanding our topic requires, besides purely scientific methods, an engagement of faith.

The Jewish philosopher Martin Buber was once asked by Ben Gurion, first prime minister of Israel, "Why do you believe in God at all?" Buber responded: "If God would be one about whom we could talk, I would certainly not be a believer. But since God is one with whom I can talk, I believe."

Our conversation about the church will be holistic. That means that it seeks to be, first, objective—rational and theological; second, pastoral—witnessing, creating, and strengthening our faith; and third, spiritual—nurturing, enhancing, and vivifying our own faith.

Our aim is an understanding of church that will renew our reasons for being part of it and reanimate our joy and love for this church that Jesus loved by laying down his life for it (Eph 5:25). More than ever before we must come to love what often seems a hopeless, overaged, and scandal-ridden church. Otherwise we cannot live in it with the joy and enthusiasm needed to carry on our vocation to proclaim the joyful news of God's kingdom in this age.

Hans Urs von Balthasar coined the phrase "kneeling theology," which many theologians have since picked up. Balthasar regards it as "literally being one of the saddest chapters in the history of theology that at one point there came the change from a kneeling theology to a sitting theology."[2] For him, good theology is always praying theology. Serious theology cannot be content with being a sitting theology; it must remain a kneeling theology. J. B. Metz puts it another way: "The talk about God originates from talk with God, and theology originates from the language of prayer."[3]

Yet, we have to add still one more dimension: good theology needs practice as well. It must be based on pastoral involvement and therefore be a critical reflection on the church's pastoral actions. The situation, the circumstances, and the cultural context are means through which the Spirit speaks to us. We must live and experience these realities against the background of our faith commitment before we explore the question of which way God calls the church today. "Theology starts at sundown, not earlier," to use a phrase from Hegel who applied it to philosophy.

To fathom the church we cannot just talk *about* it. We must talk *with* it, since we are part of it. Only in this way can we come to sense the divine mystery behind the phenomenon we call church, a mystery that goes beyond all human comprehension.

My wish is that all who read this book will come to understand the church a little better but ultimately that they come to love it in a new way based on an experience of it. This can only happen to those who have been touched by the fire that Jesus came to throw on the earth, the Holy Spirit whom, according to Luke, the heavenly Father will give to those who ask him (Lk 11:13).

---

[2] Hans Urs von Balthasar, "Theologie und Heiligkeit," in *Deus: Verbum cavo. Shizzen zur Theologie* (Einsiedeln: Benzinger, 1960), 1:224.

[3] Johann B. Metz, *Gotteskrise. Versuch zur "geistigen situation der Zeit"* (Düsseldorf: Patmos, 1994), 79.

Introduction

Every theological topic presupposes a "horizon of understanding" against which it projects its findings and synthesizes them into a comprehensive view. Most of the time this background is taken for granted and not explicitly reflected upon. Clarifying this horizon, however, allows the central thought underlying the topic to be understood more readily. To this end we will look at four basic presuppositions underlying our study of the church as well as at the essential relationships of Jesus to the kingdom, to the church, and to Israel.

PRESUPPOSITIONS

The Distinction between Individual Salvation and the Necessity of a Church

God desires the salvation of all people not only theoretically but effectively (1 Tm 2:4-5; Ti 2:11). Every human person, no matter what his or her faith and religion, may effectively be saved by following his/her own religion and conscience.

Salvation must be held possible outside the Church. The Second Vatican Council (1962-65) has reaffirmed this doctrinal stand in unambiguous terms in its Dogmatic Constitution on the Church (*Lumen Gentium*, nn. 16-17), as well as in its declaration on the relationship of the Church to non-Christian religions *(Nostra Aetate)*, its Decree on the Church's missionary activity *(Ad Gentes)*, and its Pastoral Constitution on the Church in the Modern World *(Gaudium et Spes)*. A celebrated passage of the last document, after stating how Christians come in contact with the paschal mystery of the death and Resurrection of Jesus Christ, affirms clearly that the same applies—"in a way known to God"—for members of the other religious traditions. It says: "All this holds true not for Christians only, but also for all men of goodwill in whose hearts grace is active invisibly. For since Christ died for all, and since all men are in fact called to one and the same destiny, which is divine, we must hold that the Holy Spirit offers to all the possibility of being made partners, in a way known to God, in the paschal mystery" (*Gaudium et Spes* 22).[1]

---

[1] Jacques Dupuis, "Religious Plurality and the Christological Debate," *Sedos Bulletin* 28 (1996), 330.

1

It will be helpful to consider in greater detail several of the points expressed in this rich text.

First, the council looks at God's universal salvific will not as an abstract possibility but as a concrete reality, actually operative among all people. God's ultimate aim with creation is the salvation of all people. This purpose was present in creation right from the beginning.

The Bible begins not with the election of the people of God, but rather with the creation of the world. The first figure is not Abraham, but the *adam*, the human being, and in the first chapter of Genesis *adam* refers not to a particular individual but to humanity as a whole. The Bible begins with humanity. This observation has serious theological import; it makes clear that everything the Bible goes on to describe is not only an action between God and a chosen people but is directed toward the nations, the world, the universe. God's concern is not first of all for Israel but for the whole world. God did not create religion but the world.

As universally as the Bible begins, so does it end. Its first image is the creation of the world out of chaos. The last great image is God's new world, God's new creation, in which all creation finds its goal and its perfection. This last image of the Bible spread before us is John's prophetic vision in Revelation 21:1—22:5. John deliberately connected his great closing vision to the opening chapters of the Bible. The scriptures open with "In the beginning . . . God created the heavens and the earth" (Gn 1:1) and chapter 21 of Revelation echoes this with "Then I saw a new heaven and a new earth; for the first heaven and the first earth had passed away" (v. 1).[2]

What is important here is the universality of God's plan of salvation, which embraces the entire human race and the whole of creation. This broad understanding of God's plan of salvation and of God's loving concern for all people and every aspect of their lives enjoys widespread acceptance today. The mission of the church is understood as being first and foremost part of God's turning toward the world in creative love, redemptive healing, and transforming power. This turning takes place in ordinary history and is not confined to the activity of the church. The activity of the Holy Spirit is universal, not limited by space or time (*Redemptoris Missio,* no. 28). The church is called to participate in a project that comes from God and belongs to God. In participating in God's plan the church never starts from scratch. The church encounters human beings and a world in which God's Spirit is already operative.

> [It is not] as if every person is to be thought to exist in a profane and secular world bereft of the presence of God's Spirit, and it is into this graceless world that the Spirit descended through the supernatural and sacral ministry of the church, just as the Spirit descended upon Jesus at his baptism, and just as the Spirit descended upon his disciples at Pentecost.[3]

---

[2] Gehard Lohfink, *Does God Need the Church?* (Collegeville, Minnesota: The Liturgical Press, 1999), 21.

[3] William V. Dych, S.J., *Thy Kingdom Come: Jesus and the Reign of God* (New York: Crossroad Publishing Company, 1999), 90.

The Spirit does not descend into a profane and graceless universe. Rather, the Spirit's descent is "coextensive with the entire history of the human family," because God created this family with the sole purpose of letting it share in his divine life. We must assume that God's Spirit resonates and resounds in the hearts of all people because the Spirit is the innermost dynamism of the world and of history. In consequence the church is not necessary to initiate a person into the supernatural world where the Spirit dwells.[4]

Second, within God's plan of salvation for all humanity and the universal presence of the Spirit, the concrete possibility of salvation available to all men and women of goodwill is through Jesus Christ and his paschal mystery. The uniqueness and centrality of God incarnated in Jesus Christ remains the basic foundation of all salvation.

Third, this salvation for all reaches out to everyone through the universal action of the Holy Spirit, released through the death and resurrection of Jesus Christ. His action "affects not only individuals but also society and history, people, cultures and religions," as Pope Paul II affirms in *Redemptoris Missio* (no. 28).

Fourth, the manner in which salvation in Jesus Christ is made available outside the church through the working of the Holy Spirit remains mysterious to us. This last point does not amount to saying that the "how" of salvation outside the church lies altogether beyond the scope of theological investigation, but rather indicates that whatever theological explanation may be given has to preserve the reference to Christ and his Spirit. God's saving grace or the faith that justifies has a christological and pneumatological dimension even outside the church.

If we hold to this conviction, we have to conclude that membership in the church is not necessary for personal salvation. "Personal salvation, in other words, is not inextricably linked with one's membership or non-membership in the Church. It is existence within the kingdom of God, not within the Church, that finally determines our relationship with God and our reception of salvation."[5] But this view, commonly held today, does not mean the church is not needed at all for the salvation of humankind. The issue is not "Outside the church no salvation"; rather, the question is, "Without the church, could there be salvation for humanity at all?"

An initial answer would be: The church is necessary for the world at large as a sacrament, an efficacious sign and instrument of God's redemptive activity in Jesus Christ, leading toward the final kingdom of God. For those who are called by God to profess the Lordship of Christ and to collaborate with him in the coming of the kingdom for the salvation of all, the church is definitely necessary for their personal salvation as well.[6]

William V. Dych insists that the church's necessity must be seen in the total response that God's presence in the world demands rather than in bringing his presence into the world. As Dych puts it:

---

[4] Ibid., 90.

[5] Richard P. McBrien, *Catholicism* (London: Geoffrey Chapman, 1981), 772.

[6] Ibid., 721-722.

What is lacking in the world is not the descending moment of the presence of God's Spirit; or, to transpose this into nonspatial images, what is lacking is not God's initiative in the offer and the call of God's Spirit, who is universally present in all times and in all cultures. What is lacking is human response to this call, and this is the "ascending" moment or the human side of the divine-human relationship. The existence of this relationship requires two freedoms, human response as well as divine initiative. Because human existence takes place in time and in history, this response has to take place in time and in history. The real importance and the real necessity of the church, then, lie not in the first instance in its quality as a "divine" institution in an otherwise profane world, but in the quality and measure of its human response to the Spirit of God, who is always already present by the time the church arrives on the scene.[7]

Salvation as Bound to Community

God's saving action is historically bound up with a community rather than with individual persons unrelated to the community they may live in. Why did God choose Israel? The element of choice is underived and remains a mystery, much like the mystery of why one falls in love with this particular person and not with someone else.

But the concept of election is always combined with a mandate. God's choice fell on Israel for the sake of the nations. God needs a witness in the world, a people in which God's salvation can be made visible. That is the reason the burden of election rests on the people of Israel. Israel's being chosen is not a privilege or a preference *over others*, but an existence *for others*, and hence the heaviest burden in history.

The idea of election is central and fundamental in scripture, but it is not a concept very much appreciated today. The concept crystallizes Israel's knowledge that God desires to liberate and change the entire world but for that purpose needs a visible place and living witnesses. This has nothing to do with preference, advantage, elitism, or being "better than," but it has a great deal to do with God's respect for human dignity and human freedom. God's omnipotence consists not in being able to do what God wants but rather in the fact that God's plan for the world will succeed. The problem here is human freedom. Human beings can oppose God's plan. They can refuse to be a people of God. They can say, "I reject all of it."[8]

The message of Jesus is not addressed to scattered individuals but to a community. Even if God addresses the individual and calls him or her to conversion, God always sees that person as an integral part of the community in which individuals live and come to understand their salvation. As Joachim Gnilka remarks, "If Jesus' offer of salvation were understood in terms of individualized

---

[7] Dych, *Thy Kingdom Come*, 91.
[8] Lohfink, *Does God Need the Church?*, 31-39.

salvation, it would be grossly misconstrued."[9] To understand the church, the communitarian aspect of salvation must be fully grasped and understood. Otherwise we see no need for a church at all.

Finally, and most fundamentally, the ultimate reason why salvation is conceived as communitarian is rooted in the Triune God. God is "family" and the ultimate goal of creation is to participate in the communitarian life of the Triune God.

Being a Christian as a Call to Mission

We need to distinguish between one's personal salvation and being called into the church through baptism. To be "called by God" means to be drawn into God's own plan and into the mission of the Son, which extends into the mission of the church. Because of this call a person chosen by God is "holy, consecrated, set apart." But that happens for a specific purpose: to be "sent out" (Mk 3:13-15), to engage actively in God's mission, to become a co-worker with God for the salvation-transformation of the world into God's final design. Mission is, therefore, the ultimate aim of any call by God. We are not called to occupy a place of honor or to receive personal advantages. To be called by God means that we are on an assignment for God. To be a Christian means being called to mission by the sacrament of baptism. Baptism is not a passport to heaven or a ticket for entering eternal life; it is, above all, a call to mission. Most people will find eternal life without being baptized. The privilege of being a Christian consists precisely in having been called to participate in a special way in the mission of Christ, which continues in the church and is meant for the salvation of all.[10]

However, the correct understanding of what it means to be a Christian in terms of mission should not lead us to look at the church in purely functional terms. The church community itself is a sacramental anticipation of God's final plan with the whole of humanity. It is the celebration of God's plan of salvation initially already achieved in the here and now. This gives meaning and joy to those invited to share God's own mission for the world. Those called by Christ into his mission should perceive of themselves as Paul did:

> This mystery, as it is now revealed in the Spirit to his holy apostles and prophets, was unknown to humanity in previous generations. . . . I, who am less than the least of all God's holy people, have been entrusted with this special grace, of proclaiming to the gentiles the unfathomable treasure of Christ and of throwing light on the inner workings of the mystery kept hidden through all the ages in God, the Creator of everything (Eph 3:3-11).

---

[9] Joachim Gnilka, *Jesus of Nazareth: Message and History* (Peabody, Massachusetts: Hendrickson Publishers, 1997), 190.

[10] John Fuellenbach, *Throw Fire* (Manila: Logos Publication, 1998), 85-101.

The Meaning of "the Keys of the Kingdom" Given to Peter (Mt 16:18-19)

Jesus gave to Peter, upon whom he has built his church, the "keys of the kingdom of God" (Mt 16:18-19). Therefore the church has an important role to play concerning the kingdom in history. The keys let the church unlock the secrets of the kingdom and proclaim God's terms for entry into or exclusion from the kingdom of God. The meaning is not that only those who join the Catholic Church will enter the kingdom. The church does not decide to whom the kingdom will ultimately be granted or who ultimately will be excluded. In this context the words of Jesus, "Many will come from east and west and will take their places in the kingdom of God while the presumed heirs of the kingdom will be thrown out" (Mt 8:11-12), are very significant for the members of the church as well.

ESSENTIAL RELATIONSHIPS:
JESUS AND THE KINGDOM, THE CHURCH, AND ISRAEL

Jesus and the Kingdom

The central message of Jesus was the kingdom of God, which he came to "throw like fire into this world" (Lk 12:49). This "fire" is not to be understood as an abstract idea or as a worldview but as a world-transforming power. Its sole aim is to extend the life of the Trinity into the whole of creation, to draw all that exists into God's own communion and love. God's kingdom is therefore meant for the salvation of all human beings who ever lived and will live.[11]

The kingdom of God is that final state of creation in which God's being Abba will be the all-embracing and determining factor. All reality will be fully permeated by this love and fully respond to it. It is that state of creation that scripture calls the new heaven and the new earth. Both realities, kingdom and Father, though distinct and not simply interchangeable, complement each other. The kingdom explains God's being Abba, and the Fatherhood of God provides a basis for and an explanation of the kingdom. Everything Jesus said and did was said and done in the light of the kingdom of God, which was coming with him and through him.

> The reign of God is the key. Jesus without it is a disincarnated person—a person without a body. Jesus separated from it is a theological construct that does not correspond to reality. Jesus only loosely connected with it is a phantom that preoccupies the doctrinal interest of the religious authorities but haunts the hearts of people in the street. Jesus without the reign of God is an incomplete Jesus. Jesus whose life and mission are not shaped by it is not the way, the truth, and the life (John 14:6), to use that profound

---

[11] Ibid., 13-60.

expression in John's Gospel. Jesus is the way because his is the way of God's reign. Jesus is the truth because his is the truth revealed by it. Jesus is the life because his is the life empowered by it.[12]

The two terms *Abba* and *kingdom of God* embrace Jesus' vision, the vision for which he lived, suffered, and died.

God's Plan for the World

Jesus' vision has something to do with the ultimate meaning of every human being, the fulfillment of the deepest aspiration of every human heart, the plan God has for all of creation. It has something to do with what St. Augustine expressed in this way: "Restless is our heart, O God, until it rests in you." Or, in the words of Gandhi: "Man's ultimate aim is the realization of God. I live and move and have my being in pursuit of this goal."

The deepest desire of every human heart is complete union with God, a union that includes union with all of God's family and harmony with the universe. It embraces God, all human beings, and the world and nature as well. To the vexing question that has haunted millions of people, Why did God create the universe and human beings?, there is a simple answer that could be phrased as follows: God, the Triune One, said, "We enjoy life so much that we want to share it with other beings whom we will create for that purpose." God created us with the sole purpose of bringing us to share God's own life. But it is not only we humans that will participate in God's life; it is the whole universe that God's love wants to lead into the fullness of life, because God is a lover of life.

> Yes, you love all that exists, you hold nothing of what you have made in abhorrence, for had you hated anything, you would not have formed it. And how, had you not willed it, could a thing persist, how be conserved if not called forth by you? You spare all things because all things are yours, LORD, LOVER OF LIFE, you whose imperishable spirit is in all (Wis 11:24-26).[13]

Kingdom as Belonging to This World

There is a danger of seeing the kingdom as a totally transcendent, otherworldly reality that lies beyond this one, as if it had nothing to do with the labyrinth of this world. The consequence of such a view could be called the *trampoline effect*. Whenever life begins to become oppressive and troublesome, a person just leaps into the air with a bold kick and soars relieved and unencumbered into so-called eternal fields.

---

[12] C. S. Song, *Jesus and the Reign of God* (Minneapolis: Fortress Press, 1993), 7-8.
[13] Fuellenbach, *Throw Fire*, 71-72.

Jesus did not envision the kingdom that he preached as something that belongs totally and exclusively to the world to come. His kingdom vision leaves room for understanding it as belonging to this world as well as proclaiming a future that cannot be deduced from the circumstances of present history. The future, as the Bible understands it, is something qualitatively new. It lies beyond human planning and capability, something we can only allow to be given to us. While this symbol takes the world and human effort in history seriously, it does not surrender openness to a transcendent future in the fullness of God. Only God can ultimately guarantee the fulfillment of humankind's deepest aspirations.

> Our engagement in this struggle (to make the kingdom hope come true) can be without illusions because we know by faith that no human program by itself will bring in the eschaton. Our engagement can also be without ultimate despair, because we believe that, no matter how great our self-created horror becomes, God is faithful to his promise and he will bring the kingdom which has already drawn near to us in his Son.[14]

The kingdom of God is incarnated in history, in human society and in the world. Although it is not purely and simply identical with the world, it is "identifiable" in the world. We may also say that the kingdom shows itself in society and is encountered in society, but this society is not the kingdom.

> To discover the theme of the Reign of God is to discover the full dimension of the inevitable historical character of Christianity. Our God is the God of history, who has entered into history, has a purpose and a plan for history, and has shown these to us in Jesus. God's plan is the Reign of God. The Reign is the dream, the utopia God cherishes for history, God's overall design for the world, the arcane mystery hidden for centuries and now revealed fully in Jesus.[15]

The Dream of God for Creation

Marcus Borg described the kingdom of God as God's dream for creation in these words: "In a broad sense the Bible as a whole is the story of the dream of God, beginning in Genesis with paradise and ending with paradise restored in the great concluding vision of the Book of Revelation." The first paradise is two individuals in a garden, and the second paradise is communal and urban—the new Jerusalem, the city of God.

Yet the dream of God is not the whole of the biblical story, for the Bible also includes the nightmarish elements introduced by what happens in human history.

---

[14] Benedict T. Viviano, *The Kingdom of God in History* (Wilmington, Delaware: Michael Glazier, 1988), 28-29.

[15] Pedro Casaldáliga and José-Maria Vigil, *Political Holiness: A Spirituality of Liberation* (Maryknoll, New York: Orbis Books, 1994), 82.

The Bible speaks about the rejection of the dream as well as the dream itself. Thus, in a narrower sense, the dream of God is a social and political vision of a world of justice and peace in which human beings do not hurt, destroy, oppress, or exploit one another. It is the dream expressed with many images and by many voices in the Bible, for example, in Micah 4:3-4:

> [God] shall judge between many peoples, and shall arbitrate between strong nations far away; they shall beat their swords into plowshares, and their spears into pruning hooks; nation shall not lift up sword against nation, neither shall they learn war any more; but they shall all sit under their own vines and under their own fig trees, and no one shall make them afraid; for the mouth of the LORD of hosts has spoken.

The dream of God is a vision of *shalom,* a rich Hebrew word often translated "peace," but meaning much more than the absence of war. It means well-being in a comprehensive sense. It includes freedom from negatives such as oppression, anxiety, and fear, as well as the presence of positives such as health, prosperity, and security. Shalom thus includes a social vision: the dream of a world in which such well-being belongs to everybody. As the story of the interaction between the dream of God and the rejection of the dream through what happens in history, the Bible is a tale of two kingdoms: the kingdom of God and the kingdom of this world.[16]

This seems to have been the kingdom message Jesus came to proclaim. It is a vision of God, the world, humankind, and creation as a whole as well as of each individual human person. It is the most grandiose vision that the world has ever known. For this vision Jesus lived, labored, suffered, and died. This is the vision he entrusted to his disciples: "As the Father has sent me, so I send you" (Jn 20:21).

The final goal of creation can therefore be envisioned as the great gathering of all human beings that have ever lived, live, and will live, together with all creatures of any kind celebrating an eternal feast—the great banquet envisioned by Isaiah. Here everyone will know everyone and know each person intimately as an enrichment, a gift to be immensely enjoyed. The exclusion of some (hell) is possible and cannot be denied as a real possibility. However, if some really will be excluded from the banquet, it is not ours to know or to decide who they will be. Only God will make this decision. We will always have to remind ourselves of Jesus' own words: "What is impossible for human beings, God can still make possible" (Mk 10:27).

Jesus and the Church

This joyful message of salvation for all, however, is intrinsically bound to the unique person, Jesus of Nazareth. Jesus is the kingdom himself, and he

---

[16] Marcus J. Borg, *The God We Never Knew* (San Francisco: Harper, 1997), 133-134.

remains the radiating center from which its world-transforming power will accomplish the task for which he came. The kingdom cannot be separated from the person of Jesus of Nazareth if Christianity is to remain true to its name. As John Paul II says in *Redemptoris Missio*:

> The proclamation and establishment of God's Kingdom are the purpose of Jesus' mission: "I was sent for this purpose" (Lk 4:43). But that is not all. Jesus himself is the "good news," as he declares at the very beginning of his mission in the synagogue of Nazareth when he applies to himself the words of Isaiah about the Anointed One sent by the Spirit of the Lord (cf. Lk 4:14-21). Since the "good news" is Christ, there is an identification between the message and the messenger, between saying, doing and being. His power, the secret of the effectiveness of his actions, lies in his total identification with the message he announces: He proclaims the "good news" not just by what he says or does, but by what he is (no. 13).

But Jesus is gone. Since his death and resurrection he has entered into the new creation, which is neither visible nor tangible. How then will God's saving presence—intrinsically tied up with the one mediator Jesus Christ—be available to us in space and time? How will that saving person remain present until the day of the final fulfillment of his promises? Who will make Christ present now in our age and time?

The answers given to these questions differ. The traditional response is that Jesus founded a church that will make him and his message of the kingdom present throughout the centuries.

For the Catholic Church, therefore, it seems to be the visible and tangible community with its divinely willed hierarchy and magisterium, that guarantees the presence of Christ through the centuries.

For many Protestant churches the enduring presence of Christ and through him the presence of God, who wants to save all, is guaranteed through the word of God contained in holy scripture. God's saving presence is tangible and concretely accessible wherever the word of God is proclaimed. In the words of the Lausanne Covenant, "Christ is universal in the sense that he is available to all who hear his people's proclamation of the Gospel, but effective only to those who believe."[17] Therefore people ask: Is organized religion necessary, or should scripture not be enough to ensure the perpetual presence of Christ in history? Does he have to be tied to a particular group of people with a particular structure and way of making him present? Why church at all? Do we need a church? How necessary is the church for salvation?

Should we not let the word of God take care of itself? Can the Bible not vindicate its claim of alone possessing the absolute truth? As a Hindu once

---

[17] As quoted in Ralph Covell, "Jesus Christ and World Religions," in *The Good News of the Kingdom: Mission Theology for the Third Millennium,* ed. Charles Van Engen, Dean S. Gilliland, Paul Pierson (Maryknoll, New York: Orbis Books, 1993), 163.

asked me: "If you Christians are so sure that only your holy books contain the full truth, why don't you let these books themselves prove it instead of binding their truth to the interpretation of a magisterium and a hierarchical office?"

The answer to this pointed question is linked to the incarnation of God in Jesus Christ. Christ is the historically real and actual presence of the eschatologically victorious mercy of God (Rahner). He is God made visible and present to us with the aim and goal of communicating himself once and for all to us. God has bound himself to this person, Jesus of Nazareth, in a way and to a degree not done in any other religion. Only through him and in him is God's saving grace now available for all. In the words of Karl Rahner:

> From the moment the Logos assumes this human nature from out of the unity of mankind, as a part of it, redemption cannot be arrested or canceled. The fate of the world has been finally decided, and in the sense of divine mercy. Before Christ, the dialogue between God and humankind in the history of eternal welfare and loss was an open one. . . . Everything was still unsettled. . . . But now in the Word of God, God's last word is uttered into the visible public history of humankind, a word of grace, reconciliation and eternal life: Jesus Christ. The grace of God no longer comes (when it does come) steeply down from on high, from God absolutely transcending the world, and in a manner that is without history, purely episodic, it is permanently in the world in tangible historical form, established in the flesh of Christ as part of the World, of humanity and of its very history.[18]

The question now is this: How can this redemption accomplished in Jesus Christ become effectively present in time and space for every human being, since Christ is not physically present in the world in the way he was when he walked this earth? Or, how can we come in contact with him in a manner that is certain and reaches into our very world? Who represents him, the historically real and actual presence of the saving love of God? It is here that we have to seek to locate the church.

Jesus and Israel

Another related issue to consider before answering the above questions is that of Jesus and Israel. Jesus understood his mission first and foremost in the context of Israel's mission. He saw himself as being sent to the house of Israel and not to the Gentiles. His instructions to the disciples were: "Go nowhere among the Gentiles, and enter no town of the Samaritans, but go rather to the lost sheep of the house of Israel" (Mt 10:5-6). He came to restore Israel, to make it once and for all what it never managed to become, the true Covenant partner. In the words of Joachim Gnilka: "To formulate it pointedly, Israel was his

---

[18] Karl Rahner, *The Church and the Sacraments* (London: Burns & Oates, 1963), 15.

'church,' the people who were to be called out anew and ultimately into God's kingdom. By church *(ekklesia)* one first and foremost has nothing else in mind than the called-out people of God."[19]

The issue of Jesus and the church, therefore, can be raised in a double context: that of Jesus' preaching of the kingdom and that of the way he understood Israel's mission in God's plan of salvation. The community that evolved after Easter has to be seen and evaluated in the context of Israel's election and mission as presented in the Old Testament, since God's plan of salvation is one.[20]

> Jesus' relationship to Israel, the erstwhile people of God, which its rejection of him brings to an end but which is open to new beginnings, is preparatory for what is to unfold. The salvation Jesus proclaimed is focused on a people and can be realized only in a people. A people is to be gathered into the coming kingdom of God that is at hand. "People of God"/ "church" and "Kingdom of God" are corresponding concepts, not incompatible entities.[21]

OVERVIEW OF THIS BOOK

We will attempt to answer these questions in two ways. First, we go back to Jesus himself, as far as possible, and ask these questions: Did Jesus envision a church establishing itself after his death and resurrection? What did Jesus himself intend with the group he gathered around him? Since Jesus understood his mission in the setting of the old covenant, were his disciples to become the true Covenant people as the messianic age had promised? What were they to be, once he would not be in their midst any longer? Did he foresee a church in an organized form that would go on preaching his message until the end of time?

Second, we will ask the present Catholic Church how it understands and evaluates itself. Since Vatican II was the church's official contemporary self-evaluation, we will see how this assembly saw itself and how it understood and presented the essence and mission of the church for today.

We will examine both aspects: Jesus' own foresight of a future community to proclaim and carry on his vision as well as the church's self-understanding as it emerged in Vatican II.

Finally, we will have to look beyond the council's vision of the church. The early church came to understand its own identity and its mission in different ways, as the New Testament clearly indicates, depending on the different situations and cultures into which it planted the gospel of the kingdom of God. There is a great variety of church-images and conceptions of church organization present

---

[19] Gnilka, *Jesus of Nazareth*, 190.

[20] Gerhard Lohfink, *Jesus and Community* (London: SPCK Press, 1985), 75-148.

[21] Gnilka, *Jesus of Nazareth*, 198.

in the New Testament due to the context in which the church came into existence. Today, once again, the church has to find its identity and mission in the current context that is generally described as *globalization* and *inculturation*. It is in this context that we will present two models of church that seem to respond more adequately to the challenges the church faces at the present.

Part 1

THE CHURCH IN SCRIPTURE
AND IN VATICAN II

1

Jesus and the Church

RETURN TO THE JESUS WHO WALKED THIS EARTH

In dealing with our study of the church, it is essential that we go back to the Jesus who walked on this earth and have a fresh look at his vision. Only by returning to the Jesus as he "presents himself in the Gospels" (*Perfectae Caritatis,* no. 2) will we find anew a foundation for our self-understanding not only as individual Christians but also as church. As Johann B. Metz sees it, only the imagery of discipleship carries the capacity to call the church back to its origins, to its authentic life and mission:

> The Church . . . cannot solve the crisis of its historical identity and its societal legitimation in a purely interpretative or hermeneutical manner, but only by practical identification. The problem of her identity is fundamentally a theory-praxis problem. That praxis whose intelligible and identity-securing power cannot be replaced by interpretation is called discipleship. The Church's crisis is due to a deficit in discipleship and to difficulties in adapting to Jesus.[1]

The most salient sentence in this quotation is the last one concerning the crisis in the church today. As early as the mid-seventies the German Bishops Conference assessed the situation of the church in Germany. Looking for an appropriate response to the then emerging faith crisis in the country, they proposed a solution that echoed the words of Metz: "The way out of the situation in which we find ourselves today can only be once again a way into fellowship with Jesus the Lord." Today, thirty years later, the crisis has heightened and the response proposed at that time seems to be even more urgent now: "The *way out* . . . can only be a *way into* following the Jesus who walked this earth."

---

[1] Johann B. Metz, "For a Renewed Church before a New Council: A Concept in Four Theses," in *Toward Vatican III: The Work That Needs to Be Done,* ed. David Tracy with Hans Küng and Johann B. Metz (New York: Seabury, 1978), 139.

Looking at their churches, the bishops found it necessary to stress the following signposts of discipleship: the obedience of the cross, poverty, freedom, and joy, attitudes and behavior that counted so high in Jesus' own life. The bishops then confessed that their churches portray a religion of prosperity rather than a religion of the cross; a rich church rather than a church in solidarity with the poor and weak; a church anxiously holding back from the risk of the freedom of the gospel rather than going on the offensive; and finally, a church that looks anxiously inward rather than radiating the joy of the redeemed. They felt the urgent need to return to the root of the Christian commitment, to the Jesus who walked the earth and died for a vision the world today needs so badly.[2]

In the light of the image crisis of the church today, Avery Dulles proposed a new conception of the church that he calls community of disciples. Behind this image we find again an expression of the newly discovered realization that the basic vocation of any Christian is first and foremost to be a disciple, to follow the Lord as he walked over this earth. The emphasis here is on following the Lord rather than following the church, on being constantly on the road rather than having already reached the goal. The church must be seen as the community of those who have made it their lives' profession to follow the Lord and, as such, to build a community called church.[3]

Discipleship gives to the individual as well as to the Christian community a unique identity and purpose. But this should not lead it to withdraw into its own cocoon. As a notion that essentially relates Christian identity to the actions of Jesus, discipleship does not exclude the wider world but demands from Christians a commitment to mission in the world. Though disciples take their cue for action only from following Jesus, they are not exempt from acting in or on behalf of the world. On the contrary, this very independence provides them with a basis for criticizing and challenging the standards of the larger society. Being called to participate in God's own mission for the world demands that the baptized not withdraw from but engage vigorously in God's saving actions for all humanity and all human affairs.

BIBLICAL INSIGHTS INTO ISRAEL, KINGDOM, AND CHURCH

The Exodus Story: God's Election of a Contrast Society

The Exodus story in the Old Testament explains to us most clearly what God has in mind for God's creatures: God intends to lead all of humanity by choosing one particular people to be the sign and instrument to accomplish this goal. To understand the purpose and mission of the church as the newly chosen people

---

[2] "Unsere Hoffnung: Ein Bekenntnis zum Glauben in dieser Zeit," *Herder Korrespondenz* 30 (1976), 208-209.

[3] Avery Dulles, *A Church to Believe In: Discipleship and the Dynamics of Freedom* (New York: Crossroad, 1982), 1-18.

of God, it is essential not to lose sight of this foundational story of God's saving intervention in history.

The oldest historical summary of the faith that we have from Israel is Numbers 20:15: "Our forefathers went down into Egypt, and we lived there many years. The Egyptians mistreated us and our fathers, then we cried to Yahweh and he heard our cry. He sent an angel who brought us forth out of Egypt." But the official creed became Deuteronomy 26:5-9:

> Then you shall declare before the LORD your God: "My father was a wandering Aramean, and he went down into Egypt with a few people and lived there and became a great nation, powerful and numerous. But the Egyptians mistreated us and made us suffer, putting us to hard labor. Then we cried out to the LORD, the God of our fathers, and the LORD heard our voice and saw our misery, toil and oppression. So the LORD brought us out of Egypt with a mighty hand and an outstretched arm, with great terror and with miraculous signs and wonders. He brought us to this place and gave us this land, a land flowing with milk and honey."

This text is the quintessence of Israel's faith, and it is neither an accident nor an exaggeration that it is entirely subsumed under the theme of liberation.

> This central Old Testament text alone should silence anyone who finds it embarrassing for Christian churches to speak of an "option for the poor" and for a theology to call itself "liberation theology." This credo is above all a confession of God who led the poor into freedom. If the credo of the New Testament adds new dimensions, it certainly never falls short of this credo.[4]

This creed has the following scheme of action: (1) People are in distress; (2) they cry out to God; (3) God hears their cry and sees their distress; (4) God intervenes and alleviates the distress.

Israel shares these points with other religions around it. In these religions the gods are also concerned with the poor and listen to their cry, but for the Israelites the response of Yahweh was significantly different from that of other gods. First, in the Near East poor people would pray to their gods and experience help from them as individuals or as small groups. The social system, however, in which they lived and which might have been the source of their poverty, was not expected to be changed by the gods in favor of the poor. It would remain the same. There was never a large group in a given population that was recognized

---

[4] Norbert Lohfink, *Option for the Poor: The Basic Principle of Liberation Theology in the Light of the Bible* (Berkeley, California: Bibal Press 1987), 35-36. The concept of "contrast society" for the church—the term used in the title of this section—was coined by Norbert and Gerhard Lohfink. They developed this concept in various writings and against a host of critics.

as a group of poor and oppressed people and then rescued by a god from poverty and oppression. In the words of Deuteronomy 4:34: "Has any god ever attempted to go to a nation and take it himself from the midst of another nation, by trials, by signs, by wonders, and by war, by mighty hand and an outstretched arm, and by great terror, according to all that Yahweh, your God, did for you in Egypt before your eyes?"

Second, the misery of the Israelites in Egypt is clearly explained in the Credo of Deuteronomy 26 as the result of economic exploitation and social degradation. Poverty is recognized as the product of human action. It is not fate or the will of God or something deserved because of personal fault. It is created by the social system represented by Pharaoh.

Third, Yahweh does not intervene to lighten the suffering only to leave the system intact or even help it to get reestablished by integrating the poor again into society. Instead the poor are removed from the impoverished situation. This is a previously unheard-of message. God physically removes the poor from the world of oppression and takes them completely outside the Egyptian system.

Finally, something new is to be created. The departure from the corrupt and therefore impoverished world of Egypt would not have been a divine miracle, a new work of creation, if it had not at the same time marked the beginning of something new and greater. It is the departure from an old society to a new society. It marks the entrance into a "land flowing with milk and honey." Milk and honey are regarded in the ancient world as the Elysian food of the gods. This is an image of the plenitude of paradise.[5] At Mount Sinai Israel was made into a new society on its way through the desert. So changed, its people will now enter the promised land flowing with milk and honey to celebrate a feast for Yahweh. The aim of the Exodus is to create a new people that will forever celebrate its God in a new society.

The point of this is that the departure from the impoverished society was a genuine removal only if it led to the constitution of a new society that no longer knows poverty and in whose midst Yahweh its God is celebrated in an everlasting feast. Yahweh intends to create a society of brothers and sisters where there will be no poor any longer. The poor of Egypt are to become, through the Exodus, a kind of divinely willed contrast society.

This new society stands in contrast not only with the society it just left but with all other existing societies in its world. It is meant for the good of all humanity. Israel's laws and statutes aim to form the people into such a contrast society that others will marvel at what a wise and understanding people they are.

> You shall keep them and do them; for that will be your wisdom and understanding, which the nations seek. When anyone reads these laws to them, they will cry: "Surely this great nation is a wise and understanding

---

[5] Ibid., 43.

people!" For what great nation is there that has gods so near to it as Yahweh our God was to us, whenever we have called on him for help? And what great nation is there, that has statutes and ordinances so righteous as all this social order which I set before you this day? (Dt 4:6-8).

Walter Brueggemann shares this view with Lohfink in almost all aspects. He comments:

> The call of Israel can only be understood as a new call of God to create an alternative social reality. The break of Moses and Israel from imperial reality is a break from both the religion of static triumphalism and the politics of oppression and exploitation. What emerges is an alternative religion of the freedom of God, and the politics of oppression and exploitation is met with a politics of justice and compassion. What emerges is a new social community that matches the vision of God's freedom.[6]

The intervention of God into the history of humankind on behalf of Israel aims at creating an alternative social vision to the social vision that regarded oppression and dependence as part of human society. The Exodus opens up a new vision of what it means to be human in the eyes of God. The covenant with the people is God's view of how he envisions a society in which human beings will live as God's children in justice and peace with one another. They are to form a contrast society in opposition to the Pharaoh society in which they had experienced oppression and injustice. On this presupposition rested Israel's very reason of existence. In being such a society, the Covenant people revealed already what God had in store for all of humanity.

Israel was to witness to this plan, but its history showed clearly that the people failed to the degree that the Old Testament covenant has been looked upon as the history of a broken covenant. The leaders of the people always managed to return to the same Pharaoh society from which Yahweh had rescued them.

Jesus' main mission must be seen in this context of a broken covenant. He understood his mission as being sent to restore the Covenant to its original intention and meaning. But the social vision of society in his days had once again acquired all the features of a Pharaoh society, even though names and certain traits had changed.

The dominant social vision of Jesus' time was centered on *holiness* and *purity,* which in practice had ostracized almost half of the population. In protest and in opposition to this reality Jesus once again offered an alternative vision based on the ideal of the covenant that Yahweh had offered. Jesus' social vision focused on *justice* and *compassion,* as the prophets had already demanded from the people in their time. What should rule the life of a community was not holiness, which means separation and withdrawal leading to marginalization

---

[6] Walter Brueggemann, *Prophetic Imagination* (Minneapolis: Augsburg Fortress, 1978; London: SCM Press, 1992), 16.

and oppression, but compassion, which calls for creating a community that is inclusive and tears down that which separates and divides people. He understood his community to be a place where all people would be brothers and sisters, where justice and compassion would reign under the one Fatherhood of God.[7]

From this vision of God's covenant with his people as a contrast society and Jesus' ultimate intention of restoring this vision and leading it to completion, obviously a correct understanding of church cannot be attained without taking the whole of salvation history into account as it unfolded in the Old Testament.

Kingdom and Church in the Gospels

Since Jesus' central message was the kingdom, the first question to be dealt with is this: What exactly is the relationship between the kingdom that Jesus preached and the church he intended? The only biblical text where church and kingdom appear side by side in the teaching of Jesus is Matthew 16:18-19: "You are Peter and on this rock I will build my church. . . . I will give you the keys of the kingdom of Heaven: whatever you bind on earth will be bound in heaven; whatever you loose on earth will be loosed in heaven." Traditional apologetics look at this text as a church-founding logion of the earthly and historical Jesus. In this view Jesus declares, clearly and without any doubt, Peter as the head and foundation stone of his coming church community, and to him he entrusts the keys to God's kingdom. However, a fundamentalist interpretation of this text will not do. The relationship of Jesus and the church cannot be explained from this text alone. Today most exegetes hold that this wording points back to a post-Easter evaluation of Peter's role in the church at that time. The text as found in Matthew 16:18 is considered a later enlargement, in contrast to Mark's story of Peter's confession of Jesus as the Christ (Mk 8:27-30). Matthew added the so-called Petrine text to Mark's basic text to portray the head of the apostolic college as the prototype and example of faith in Christ. Peter, who was the first witness of Jesus' resurrection, became the basis of the resurrection faith and was accordingly regarded as the leader of the first community in Jerusalem. Matthew's version is regarded as *Gemeindebildung*, that is, the text was formulated by the evangelist and put into the mouth of the earthly and historical Jesus.[8] It is, therefore, not wise to put too much weight on this text, though at first sight it may appear clear and convincing.

The word *church* itself is found only twice on the lips of Jesus (Mt 16:18 and 18:17), while the phrase *kingdom of God* can be found 92 times in Jesus' own words. (In comparison, the phrase *kingdom of God* appears only 75 times in all the documents of Vatican II, while the word *church* appears approximately 2,000 times. If we limit our search to the two main Vatican II documents on the church,

---

[7] John Fuellenbach, *Throw Fire* (Manila: Logos Publication, 1998), 193-218.

[8] Robrecht Michiels, "Church of Jesus Christ, An Exegetical-Ecclesiological Consideration," *Louvain Studies* 18 (1993), 314-315.

Lumen Gentium and *Gaudium et Spes*, we find the word *kingdom* 48 times and the word church around 400 times.)

All together the term *ekklesia* appears 110 times in the New Testament: 65 times in Paul, 23 times in Acts, 20 times in Revelation, and twice in Matthew (it is not used in Mark, Luke, or John). It can signify the whole church (Eph 1:22f.; Col 1:18; Gal 1:13; 1 Cor 15:9), as well as local churches (the beginnings of epistles, 1 Cor 1:2; Rv 2:1; 8:12, etc.) and particular house churches (Phlm 1:2). The word did not have this meaning in its original Greek form, where it simply means "public gathering." It was borrowed from the Septuagint, where it is used approximately 100 times and most often signifies the cultic community, the *qahal Jahweh* (this is also the meaning of *synagogue*).[9] The *qahal Jahweh* designated the people of God gathered for worship and praise. Israel was called *qahal* only in those moments. Once the sacred assembly was dismissed, the people were people on their journey.

The early Christian community perceived the term *ekklesia* from this original meaning: God had called or convoked them and established them into a "sacred assembly," as God had done in the Old Testament (Ex 12:16; Lv 23:3). But the Christian community saw itself as the people of God, the *qahal Jahweh*, convoked in a new manner, that is, by the death and resurrection of Christ.[10]

The early Christians called themselves different names: followers of the way or the koinonia or even Christians. But as Joseph Ratzinger points out, the most important and lasting name the Christian community, universal as well as local, gave itself from the moment of its birth was *ekklesia*. It had an identity-instilling effect and was in no way just one name among others. Ratzinger regards this as "fundamentally normative for all the later developments of its being."[11]

Considering the rare use of the word *church* on the lips of Jesus (twice in only one gospel), can we conclude that the central teaching of Jesus was the kingdom while the church occupied no significant place in Jesus' thought? Did the early church substitute the church for the kingdom because the *parousia* did not come? It would be dangerous for theology to measure everything by the range of the names applied to it. The word church may not appear often in Jesus' teaching. Nevertheless, the concept of the messianic community, intrinsically bound up with the kingdom, implies what is meant by the concept church. It is therefore correct to say that "the kingdom of God and the Church are two key New Testament concepts, [and] both are crucial for the understanding of God's plan for humanity. They are central to the fulfillment of his redemptive

---

[9] Johann Auer and Joseph Ratzinger, *The Church: The Universal Sacrament of Salvation,* vol. 8 of *Dogmatic Theology* (Washington, D.C.: The Catholic University of America Press, 1993), 25; see also, Gerhard Lohfink, *Jesus and Community* (London: SPCK Press, 1985), 77.

[10] Pedro Rodriguez, "Theological Method for Ecclesiology," in *The Gift of the Church: A Textbook on Ecclesiology in Honor of Patrick Granfield, OSB,* ed. Peter Phan (Collegeville, Minnesota: The Liturgical Press, 2000), 152-155.

[11] Josef Ratzinger, "Kirche," *Lexikon für Theologie und Kirche,* 2d ed., vol. 6 (Freiburg: Herder, 1961), col. 174.

purpose. While the Church cannot be identified with the kingdom, for the latter is a larger and more comprehensive term, the two are nevertheless in such close correlation that they cannot be separated either."[12]

Most moderate theologians agree that the kingdom of God and the church as the messianic community are intrinsically connected and cannot be separated from each other. This holds true not only for the final fulfillment of the kingdom but already for the "kingdom now." The kingdom present in history and the church here on earth are two closely interrelated realities. The difficulty we encounter is how to explain their relatedness without doing violence to either one. Is it the kingdom that explains the church? Or is it the church that explains the kingdom? Does the kingdom need a church to remain present in the world? Does the church need the kingdom to be understood at all? These questions will be taken up later.

The other issue related to the question of Jesus and the church is the relationship between Jesus and Israel. For some exegetes, like Gerhard Lohfink, the question whether or not Jesus founded a church is superfluous. Jesus did not have to found a church; it existed already for many centuries as the people of Israel. For this reason Jesus addressed himself exclusively to the Jewish nation. Israel would constitute the definite people of God that was to come to power soon. Jesus' intention was to reassemble his people in the light of the imminent kingdom by making them into the true people of God, faithful to the real intentions of their covenant with God.

The question of the origin of the church is therefore intimately linked with Jesus' preaching and practice of the kingdom and with Israel's response or failure to respond to Jesus' message. The early Christian community understood itself in the context of Israel and had no intention of separating itself from the Covenant people. Only the resistance and rejection of the Jewish people forced the followers of Jesus to go to the pagans in the power of the Risen One's Spirit.[13]

The Kingdom Vision Mediated through the Church

We described the kingdom as the vision of reality, creation, God, and humankind that Jesus came to communicate. Jesus entrusted this vision to the community of his disciples. Those of us in subsequent generations received the kingdom vision of Jesus not like a sudden bolt of lightning but through the faith community into which we were born, the church. This community, in turn, has given to the vision of the kingdom its own framework and shape and communicated all this to us. In short, the vision came to us in the understanding and form it has taken in the long tradition of the church community. As members, we

---

[12] Peter Kuzmic, "The Church and the Kingdom of God: A Theological Reflection," in *The Church: God's Agent for Change*, ed. Bruce J. Nicholls (Flemington Markets, Australia: Paternoster Press, 1986), 49.

[13] Lohfink, *Jesus and Community*, 75-81.

have to ask how this community, called church, understands itself now vis-à-vis Jesus and his kingdom.

Jesus' vision is always communicated in some concrete shape, in this case through the preaching and teaching of the church. Thus the basic questions are: What image do we have of the church as the true bearer of Jesus' own vision? And must we confine the church's vision of reality to Jesus' own vision of the kingdom? One may object and insist that there is no other vision of Jesus' kingdom accessible to us than the one the church offers us. This might be true, but it is equally true that the church, while containing Jesus' kingdom vision, might have focused on secondary concerns and in so doing might have notably obscured the center. Because of this, many find it difficult to discover in the church easily and spontaneously the vision Jesus came to throw like fire into this world (Lk 12:49). For them the fire seems to have gone out, or at least it seems to have dimmed considerably.

The question is ultimately one concerning the *image* of the church. The crisis of faith today is largely a crisis of image. Images are powerful since they speak to us existentially and find an echo in the depth of our being. They have an evocative power. They convey a meaning that is apprehended in a non-conceptual way. Avery Dulles remarks: "Symbols transform the horizons of man's life, integrate his perception of reality, alter his scale of values, reorient his loyalties, attachments, and aspirations in a manner far exceeding the powers of abstract conceptual thoughts."[14]

Do we have an image of the church today that can inspire people and supply an ideal they can identify with and commit themselves to with enthusiasm and lasting zeal? For this we need a vision that does several things:

- explains the raison d'être of the church;
- clearly indicates the goal toward which the church is moving;
- corresponds to the faith experience of the individual member as well as the community;
- presents a set of values and priorities;
- clarifies the relationship between the church to which we belong and the world in which we live today; and
- acts as a guiding star, and yet not out of our reach, so that it can give us a clear mandate for action.

Do we have such a vision, and if not, can we develop one? Some scholars claim that the ineffectiveness of the church in many sectors of its apostolate today is due to the fact that we have no adequate image of the church "into which people can plausibly fit what they think they ought to be doing." They claim that "if we could fashion an inspiring and realistic image of the church, we might be able to

---

[14] Avery Dulles, *Models of the Church*, exp. ed. (Garden City, New York: Image Books, 1987), 20.

act confidently, and in such a way that our self-understanding would be reinforced by feedback from others."[15]

The prevailing image of the church in many parts of the world today is still that of organized religion with laws, rules, and structures. The church is seen as an institution in society that fulfills expected functions side by side with other entities like business, government, labor, and entertainment. Society has allotted a role to religion and expects it to fill that role without interfering in the functions of other agencies. In letting itself be integrated totally into society, the church loses its world-transforming power. Jesus gave the keys to the kingdom to his church, but to many today it appears that the church has lost the keys. The result is the frequently heard refrain, "Jesus yes, church no." The need for a prophetic ministry that can rekindle the fire that Jesus came to throw into the world is obvious.

The time may be ripe in the church for serious consideration of prophecy as a crucial element in ministry.[16] What Walter Brueggemann is asking for is the exercise of a prophetic ministry that can create a new consciousness in the church. Its task is to evoke an alternative to the consciousness and perception of the dominant culture around us with its overpowering ethos of consumerism. This alternative would engage in dismantling the way the present order of things is legitimized by the dominant mentality. But criticism alone is not enough. The new alternative must at the same time energize the faithful and the communities through its promise that there are ways of living Christian community different from the ones contemporary society offers. It must lead the church to form or reform itself into another kind of community in order "to live (once again) in fervent anticipation of the newness that God has promised and will surely give."[17]

It has become a commonplace truth to declare that the church of today is sick and needs serious attention. The cure, of course, depends largely on the right diagnosis. Many experts diagnose its sickness precisely as the lack of a comprehensive vision. Could a return to the fundamental vision of Jesus, the kingdom of God, be the best starting point for the necessary cure? There is no better way to start than to go back and to reclaim for ourselves the memory of that vision that Jesus came to throw like fire into this world (Lk 12:49). "The church will not have power to act or believe until it recovers its tradition of faith and permits that tradition to be the primal way out of enculturation. This is not a cry for traditionalism but rather a judgement that the church has no business more pressing than the re-appropriation of its memory in its full power and authenticity."[18]

According to the gospel of Matthew, Christ entrusted the keys of the kingdom to his church (16:18). In doing so, he gave it not only the medicine for the whole world but also the medicine for its own sicknesses. The cure for the

---

[15] Dulles, *A Church to Believe In*, 1-18.

[16] Brueggemann, *Prophetic Imagination*, 9.

[17] Ibid., 11-14.

[18] Ibid., 12. Brueggemann understands inculturation as the way the church has wrongly succumbed to the ethos of consumerism.

church is the return to the kingdom vision of Jesus. People looking at the church today might say: Physician heal yourself first before you offer your medicine to us. The kingdom of God symbol offers the church a horizon of transcendence that will save it from repeatedly closing itself up in stifling structures. Only this has the dynamic power to create new images and visions of what the church is to be and has to do in the concrete situations of human history on its way toward its final goal.

Summary

We have seen that the word *church* appears only twice on the lips of Jesus. Since Matthew 18:17 clearly refers to the local community, only once is Jesus remembered to have spoken about the church in the wider sense: "Upon this rock I will build my church" (Mt 16:18). Both texts, however, are generally regarded as formulated by the evangelist and put into the mouth of the earthly and historical Jesus. These words nevertheless remain important, for by means of these ecclesial Jesus-words the early church expressed its self-understanding and structured its ministries and offices.[19] Avery Dulles insists that this text, from a theological point of view, not only binds the church to the kingdom but also the kingdom to the church. He writes:

> So far as I am aware, there is only one text in which Church and kingdom are mentioned together: "And so I say to you, you are Peter, and upon this rock I will build my Church, and the gates of the netherworld shall not prevail against it. I will give you the keys of the kingdom of heaven. Whatever you bind on earth shall be bound in heaven; and whatever you loose on earth shall be loosed in heaven" (Mt 16:18-19). Peter, by the same act, is made the foundation of the church of Christ and the keeper of the keys of the kingdom of heaven. The metaphor of binding and loosing reappears in Matthew 18:18: "Whatever you bind on earth shall be bound in heaven, and whatever you loose on earth shall be loosed in heaven." "Heaven" in the second quotation may be equivalent to the "kingdom of Heaven" in the first. In both texts the correct interpretation may well be that decisions made in the church on earth have validity for a person's definitive participation in the ultimate kingdom.[20]

Although Jesus may have seldom if ever used the word *church*, it is amazing to see with how much ease the early Christian communities linked Jesus to the church and the church to the kingdom and Israel of Old. Referring to the minimal use of the word *church* by Jesus, Raymond Brown writes:

---

[19] Michiels, "Church of Jesus Christ," 313-317.
[20] Avery Dulles, "The Church and Kingdom," in *A Church for All People*, ed. Eugene LaVerdiere (Collegeville, Minnesota: The Liturgical Press, 1993), 15.

In spite of this slender terminological basis in Jesus' recorded ministry, within a half century Ephesians 5:25 claims: "Christ loved the Church and gave himself up for her." It is remarkable how quickly the Christians became community-minded even though Jesus showed little interest in a formally distinct society. The ritual of baptism—absent from Jesus' own ministry—seems to have become very soon the standard feature of Christian life as Matthew, Acts, Paul, and John indicate. The baptized were designated as those who "belonged" to the *KOINONIA*, the community, a name that seems to have been one of the first names the "followers of the way" assumed for themselves.[21]

JESUS AND THE FOUNDATION OF THE CHURCH

If we start with Jesus' own message in order to recapture his vision and furnish the church with a viable image, our first question will be: Did Jesus intend a church? What connection, if any, can we establish between the church's evaluation of itself and Jesus' evaluation of the church? The relationship between the historical Jesus and the church has remained one of the greatest problems in Christian theology. So far, no universally accepted solution has been found,[22] although many answers have been proposed. One extreme posits a direct, explicit, and deliberate act by which Jesus established a new religious organization with all its structures, seven sacraments, and hierarchy firmly in place and outlined in detail. The other extreme claims that Jesus came to proclaim the kingdom of God and had no intention whatsoever of founding a church. He came to teach us a way of life centered on love and based on freedom from any institutional oppression. He showed little interest in structural and foundational issues. His interest was the renewal of Israel, which already had established forms of worship, priests, sacrifices—Jesus did not need to plan such structures.

The Most Common Positions Today

The most commonly held views in Catholic theology today are expressed by authors like Hans Küng, Karl Rahner, and Gerhard Lohfink. Those who follow Küng maintain that Jesus neither founded nor instituted a church, that the church's origins are to be traced to the faith confession—the Easter faith—of the post-paschal community of Jesus Christ. According to this view the actual foundation and institution of the church are to be situated in the resurrection faith of the first church. Hans Küng expressed this view in *The Church* (1967) and, more markedly still, in *On Being a Christian* (1976). For Küng, the church represents the continuation of Jesus' mission and his activity, but it nevertheless is a post-paschal phenomenon.

---

[21] R. Brown, "Early Church," 1-2.

[22] Francis Schüssler Fiorenza, *Foundational Theology: Jesus and the Church* (New York: Crossroad, 1984), 59.

Robrecht Michiels holds that the best starting point for answering the question of the connection between Jesus and the church is Küng's position. He writes:

> Our point of departure will be the position of Hans Küng, which one can formulate either positively or negatively.
>
> Formulated negatively, one can only admit that the life of the earthly-historical Jesus contains neither a specific moment or instance, nor a word or deed which, strictly speaking, can claim to represent the distinct institution of the church. Such an admission does justice to the first position, i.e., that position which maintains that the historical Jesus did not found a church, and that Jesus' institution of the church has its foundations in the resurrection faith of the first church.
>
> Formulated positively, this first position consists in the affirmation that the church has only existed since the disciples believed in the resurrection of Jesus, that, therefore, it only exists by the grace of the risen and glorified Christ or in the power of his Spirit. Accordingly, the church was born or came to be on Pentecost, "instituted" as the harvest of Easter. Almost no one would now maintain that the concrete development or organization of the church, including its liturgies and offices (excepting, of course, the apostolic office, understood as "being sent by Jesus"), derives from Jesus himself. This organization and its accompanying structures are the result of a complex historical process, necessitated by the fact that God has placed his church firmly in history with all that attends on such a placement. One can give the ideological-ecclesiological expression to the fact that the earthly-historical Jesus did not found or institute the church by saying (first negatively, then positively) that the church is not so much the continuation of Jesus' humanity or the perpetuation of the incarnation of the Word, but rather the continuing mission of Jesus' Spirit, the perpetuation of his action in God's Spirit. The underlying truth in Küng's vision of the non-institution of the church by Jesus consists then in the ecclesiological perception that it is the Spirit which effects the actual and complete foundation and institution of the church from Pentecost onwards.[23]

Hans Küng insists that we should not speak of church unless we start from the resurrection of Christ and from the event called Pentecost. Surely before Easter there was a community of disciples gathered around Jesus. Jesus himself must have seen a connection between this group and the coming about of the eschatological community to which all of Israel was called. But for Küng it is not possible to give the title church to the group of those who responded to Jesus' proclamation of the kingdom. Whatever connection there may have been between those who followed the Lord when he walked this earth and the community that emerged after Easter, we should not call it church. Küng correctly makes the point that without the Easter faith and Pentecost we could hardly talk about church in the proper sense of the word.

---

[23] Michiels, "Church of Jesus Christ," 300-302.

Others, like Karl Rahner, insist that the earthly and historical Jesus did indeed lay the foundation for a church. In this view the foundation of the church is to be situated in the life of Jesus himself. Rahner uses the word *foundation,* which does not mean the same as saying that Jesus "instituted" the church. *Institution* would express a juridical act on Jesus' part, one which had the establishment of a new religious organization as its goal.

A third approach to the question of Jesus' relationship to the church was developed by Gerhard Lohfink in "Did Jesus Found a Church" (1982) and *Jesus and Community: Did Jesus Found a Church?* (1985). Lohfink insists that Jesus never intended to institute a new religion or a new religious grouping or a church, and certainly not a personal or distinct community within Israel itself. The church that Jesus wanted had long existed—Israel, the people of God. Accordingly, the beginning or coming of the church should not be situated in a special institutive act or plan of the historical Jesus or in some last will and testament of the crucified but divinely Risen Lord. On the contrary, the origin of the church is a process, intimately connected with Jesus' preaching and praxis of the kingdom of God and with Israel's response to it. This entire process is the work of God, God's way with God's people.

This view of the church begins with the Old Testament. It includes Jesus, who sought to reassemble his people but, having met with resistance, was obliged to concentrate on his own followers and the Twelve in particular. The latter represented the whole of Israel, to whom in turn they were sent. This perspective continues in the post-paschal community of Jesus' followers, who themselves met Jewish resistance and, therefore, in the power of the Risen One's Spirit, chose to go the way that brought them to the pagans. In short, Lohfink sees the foundation of the church in the existence of Israel as such.

Four Representatives of the Common Positions

Since none of the views can substantiate its claims from the sources themselves, we will briefly introduce four Catholic scholars from different theological backgrounds who represent variations of the common positions generally held in the Catholic church today.

Richard McBrien[24]

McBrien, following Rahner's lead, distinguishes between the church having its origin in Jesus and having been founded by Jesus. To the first he says yes, to the second no. Jesus never addressed his message to a selected group but intended it for Israel as a whole. The election of the Twelve has to be seen in this light. They were meant to represent Israel as a whole. Salvation of the individual was not conditioned by a specific rule of life nor was membership in the company of his disciples required. However, Jesus did lay the foundations for a church.

---

[24] Richard P. McBrien, *Catholicism* (London: Geoffrey Chapman, 1981), 571-577.

First, he gathered disciples around himself. They are the ones who accepted his message and to whom he gave a share in his ministry by sending them out to preach (Mt 10:1-16).

Second, Jesus anticipated an *interim period* between his death and the *parousia*. He could foresee that Israel as a whole would reject him and that the Gentiles would take the place of the Jewish people and thus become the new eschatological people.

Third, the group of the disciples stayed together after the rejection of Jesus. From this perspective, the Last Supper becomes decisive with its injunction to "Do this in remembrance of me." Likewise, the word to Peter suggests that Jesus intended his disciples to stay together: "I have prayed for you, Simon, . . . and once you have recovered, you in turn must strengthen your brothers" (Lk 22:31-32. See Mt 16:13-19: "You are Peter and on this rock I will build my church"). In that sense there was never a churchless period in the New Testament.

Gerhard Lohfink[25]

Lohfink summarizes his view in seven points: (1) Jesus never wanted to found a new religious body distinct from Israel. He saw and understood his mission in the confines of Israel. (2) Jesus did not intend to found a distinct community, a holy remnant *within* Israel, like the Essenes. (3) Jesus' concern was for *all* Israel; he wanted to gather and renew the whole people for the in-breaking of the final kingdom. The election of the Twelve is a clear sign of this intention. There were only two-and-one-half tribes left: Judah, Benjamin, and half of Levi. The complete restoration of the twelve tribes was expected for the eschatological time of salvation (see Ezek 37; 39:23-29; 40—48). (4) The early community saw itself as God's eschatological people, who, by faith in the risen Christ and his message, were to gather all Israel. (5) The fact that the majority of Israel rejected Jesus had a decisive influence on the phenomenon we call church. (6) It is hard to fix a point for the church's origin. It was rather a process that gradually brought forth what we now mean by church. (7) The establishment of the church is the work of God who, through Christ and the Spirit, created his end-time people.

Walter Kirchschläger[26]

Kirchschläger's position can be capsulized in five points. First, the most fundamental basis for the emergence of the church is *Jesus' proclamation of the kingdom of God*. This proclamation is directed to all, namely, to the community of those who are ready to convert and to accept God's offer of salvation present

---

[25] Gerhard Lohfink, "Did Jesus Found a Church?" *Theology Digest* 30 (1982), 231-235.

[26] Walter Kirchschläger, *Die Anfänge der Kirche: Eine Biblische Rückbesinnung* (Graz: Styria Verlag, 1990), 23-24.

now in Jesus. The presence of God's kingdom now is intrinsically connected with the person of Jesus. Fellowship with Jesus becomes, therefore, a fundamental concept regarding any definition or concept of church. The final revelation of God's message of salvation is only accessible through an orientation toward Jesus.

Second, Jesus *called* disciples, men and women (Lk 8:1-3), and *binds them to his person*. Two aspects are clearly distinct in the vocation stories of the gospel (Mk 3:13-15): those who are called enter into a deep communion with Jesus and are then sent out to spread the message of Jesus. This clearly indicates that Jesus intended to multiply his activity and to ensure the permanence of his proclamation of the kingdom through those whom he called. Through the election of the Twelve Jesus made it clear that he wanted to create a new people of God that would, of course, include Israel, but a restored and renewed Israel.

Third, the community that followed Jesus is *structured from the start and shows an initial ordering*. There were the Twelve, who formed a core group around Jesus. There were those who formed a wider circle of disciples, including men and women who followed him permanently on the road. Finally, there were others who followed him only occasionally. Yet what is common to them all is that they followed Jesus, although this following might have taken different forms and the life shared with him might have known different degrees of intimacy and intensity. In this connection it is important to point out the special role Peter seems to have played. The name Jesus gave him, Cephas (Jn 1:42), indicated that Jesus had in mind a permanent group among which Peter would have a special mission to perform.

Fourth, Jesus gathered disciples, both men and women, into a personal communion with him. The *purpose of such a gathering is missionary*. His message should not be limited to those gathered around him, but it must be spread through all the earth (Mk 6:7-13). The final revelation of God's saving love for all, now made irrevocably present through Jesus of Nazareth, is the most fundamental fact on which the church is founded.

Fifth, the *institution of the Last Supper* makes it clear that Jesus reckoned with the certainty that his disciples would continue to proclaim his message of salvation now sealed through his immediate death for the many. Jesus' death becomes the ultimate *yes* of God for the salvation of the world irrevocably sealed on the cross. Here Jesus laid the foundation for the *new covenant in his blood,* which created the new community of salvation. This covenant will be made present always anew wherever his disciples celebrate this Last Supper, doing it "in memory of me."

Leonardo Boff [27]

Jesus' concern was the kingdom of God, not the church as such. For him, the kingdom contained the global transformation of the old world. It would become

---

[27] Leonardo Boff, *Church, Charism, and Power: Liberation Theology and the Institutional Church* (London: SCM Press, 1985).

the new world without sin, sickness, hatred, and all alienating forces that affect both human life and the entire cosmos.

In his preaching Jesus introduced elements, such as the gathering of the twelve apostles and the institution of the Last Supper, which later would form the basis of the church. But these elements do not constitute the entire reality of the church. The church exists only because the kingdom was not accepted by the Jewish people and Jesus was rejected by them. Therefore, the church substitutes for the kingdom and must be seen as an instrument for the full realization of the kingdom and as a sign of a true yet still imperfect realization of this kingdom in the world. We could also say that the church is the presence of the kingdom in history insofar as the Risen Christ is present in this community of believers. But the church is not the kingdom insofar as the kingdom is still to be realized eschatologically in its universal dimension. The church must see itself totally in the service of the kingdom. It is the sacrament of the kingdom in the sense that it is a sign and instrument of the kingdom's appearance and realization in history.[28]

The apostles went out to preach the kingdom to Israel as Jesus had done and awaited the imminent eruption of the kingdom with the glorious and definite coming of the Risen Lord. Since Israel refused their message, as it had refused to listen to Jesus himself, they were prompted by the Holy Spirit to turn to the pagans. This turning to the pagans became the decisive step toward the foundation of a church. By taking the elements introduced by the historical Jesus—his message, his summoning of the Twelve, baptism, and the eucharist—the apostles founded the church. In its concrete historical form the church is based on the essential elements given by Christ and the decision of the apostles inspired by the Holy Spirit. The church as an institution in space and time arose from a historical decision by the apostles, enlightened by the Holy Spirit. For Leonardo Boff, then, the church will continue to exist only if people of faith in the Risen Christ and his Spirit continually renew this decision and incarnate the church in ever new situations.

Concluding Reflections

We have looked at a wide spectrum of what Catholic theologians hold today. McBrien sums up a whole generation of theologians like Rahner, Vögtle, Semmelroth, Ratzinger, and so forth. For them, the church is a post-Easter reality brought about through the outpouring of the Holy Spirit but having its origin in the historical Jesus. Lohfink as an exegete is more critical. For him, the church is based on a whole string of elements out of which it gradually emerged. It is not possible to fix one particular event and regard it as the decisive act that created the church. In his concern for flexible structures, Boff, while not denying it divine origin, sees the *concrete historical form* of the church first and

---

[28] Leonardo Boff, *Ecclesiogenesis: The Base Communities Reinvent the Church* (Maryknoll, New York: Orbis Books, 1986), 55.

foremost as resulting from the decisions made by the apostles and their successors after them. While the church is based on Jesus and his Spirit, the existence of the church as a historical reality also depends on the willingness of the faithful to go on "reinventing" the church in ever new situations. Boff's ecclesiology is very much concerned with showing that the Basic Ecclesial Communities are the ones that, so to speak, reinvent the church today in new situations, which demand new forms of structures under the guidance of the same Spirit whom Jesus had promised to his apostles and their successors.

In conclusion we could say with Michiels: "As far as the institution of the Church by Jesus Himself is concerned, what are involved are not so much Church-foundational movements or words but the continuation of Jesus' mission in and through the mission of the first Church."[29]

Vatican II had this to say about Jesus and the church:

> The mystery of the holy Church is manifested in its very foundation, for the Lord Jesus inaugurated it by preaching the good news, that is, the coming of God's kingdom. . . . When Jesus rose up again . . . he poured out on His disciples the Spirit promised by the Father. The Church, consequently, equipped with the gifts of its founder . . . received the mission to proclaim and to establish among all peoples the kingdom of Christ and of God. It becomes on earth the initial budding forth of that kingdom *(Lumen Gentium,* no. 5).

The council agrees that the empowerment to continue the mission of Christ by bringing God's kingdom to the ends of the earth is the most essential aspect of the foundation of the church by Jesus himself. It is the decision to carry on the mission of Jesus' kingdom that remains the basis of the church. This decision flows from the desire to follow the Lord, who had called the disciples precisely for that purpose and promised them his continuing presence in the Holy Spirit. Thus the church is, first of all, not a matter of holding on to particular structural elements. It involves, rather, obedience in order to fulfill faithfully the mission entrusted to her, that is, carrying on the message of the kingdom as Jesus brought it.[30]

While the different authors may stress particular aspects, the common points that emerge from these different views can be summarized as follows:

- Jesus preached the kingdom as God's final coming to save his people. To this proclamation of the end-time belongs the *eschatological community* to which the kingdom will belong. This community was expected to be Israel, gathered and restored. Only then would the nations be taken into God's saving activity.

---

[29] Michiels, "Church of Jesus Christ," 300 n.8.

[30] Jürgen Werbick, *Kirche: Ein Ekklesiologischer Entwurf für Studium und Praxis* (Freiburg: Herder, 1994), 76-80.

- The gathering of Israel began in Jesus' ministry to the disciples, whom he invited to follow him and participate in his mission (see Mt 10:5-6). They were the first fruits to which all of Israel would soon be joined.
- Jesus' death for his people and his resurrection changed the whole situation. His death is now preached as the basis of the possibility of new repentance on Israel's part. Salvation is again offered first to Israel, but now it includes the demand to accept it as accomplished through the death and resurrection of Jesus. An individual can enter the new eschatological community only through baptism in the name of Jesus.
- Israel's refusal to accept the kingdom of God, originating in Jesus' death and resurrection, leads the disciples to go to the Gentiles. The no to Jesus creates a new situation. The insight emerges that God is now calling into existence a new people made up of believing Israel and of many nations. This new perception comes through the concrete events in which the Spirit of Jesus reveals the direction the community has to take.
- While remaining rooted in the old people of God ("grafted into the olive tree of Israel," Rom 11:17), this new people of God will be the new agent and carrier of God's universal will of salvation for all. It will continue the mission of Jesus by being sent by the crucified and Risen Lord. The content of its mission will remain the kingdom of God realized through Jesus' death and resurrection.

We conclude with the words of Joachim Gnilka: "The Church originated from the death and resurrection of Jesus, through the work of the Holy Spirit. It remains a provisional entity. What is ultimate is the kingdom of God. The better the Church understands its interim status and is determined by the ultimate [the kingdom], the more it will be able to correspond with Jesus' ministry."[31]

---

[31] Gnilka, *Jesus of Nazareth*, 198.

2

The Church in the Teaching of Vatican II

THE COUNCIL'S THEOLOGICAL VISION OF THE CHURCH

We have seen an enormous interest in the church, particularly in the years prior to Vatican II. The climax of this ecclesial interest was the council itself with two important documents: *Lumen Gentium* and *Gaudium et Spes*. We should also include the encyclical of Pope Paul VI, *Ecclesiam Suam*. The council was very much concerned with presenting an image of the church as a reference point to grasp its identity and its mission in the world today. It wanted to express a vision of the church that would generate new enthusiasm among the faithful and offer an alternative to the way the world perceived reality. What was this vision? And did the council succeed?

The council did not define the church in clear concepts. The council fathers, however, were very concerned with correcting a church-image that was generally considered as being too rigid and in many ways out of touch with contemporary reality. Their first concern was to go beyond any purely apologetical approach to a self-understanding of the church, so common in the time after the Reformation and in the wake of the Enlightenment.

As a result, we find in the documents on the church a refreshing return to the biblical understanding of church and the rich heritage of the fathers, particularly St. Augustine. In addition, the theological and spiritual insights of contemporary theologians were seriously considered when the council elaborated a new self-understanding of the church. The liturgical and biblical movements prior to Vatican II deserve special mention as do the return to a more universal view of salvation as found in the Greek fathers and the awakening awareness of the mission churches. All these aspects were employed to develop an image of church that would be more credible for our age and time.[1]

Being fully aware of the mystery of the church, the council shunned definitions and fixed concepts. Biblical images and symbols from Patristic literature

---

[1] Medard Kehl, *Die Kirche: Eine katholische Ekklesiologie* (Würzburg: Echter Verlag, 1992), 48-49.

were used to portray the mystery and the mission of the church. Although the council fathers recognized the many images offered in scriptures[2] that could be applied to the church, they chose three of them as a kind of reference point to indicate the perspective from which we should look at the church in order to recognize its identity and mission once again more clearly.

Knowing how ecclesial documents want to express their main concern and thrust in their first words, we can already sense how the council wanted to define and see the church for today by reading the opening phrases of the two main council documents on the church. *Lumen Gentium* (Light for the nations) defines the church as being light to all nations (although the term *light* refers first and foremost to Christ). Here the church may be compared to a ship equipped with powerful lights, moving through the ocean of centuries and indicating to other ships the way they should move to reach the shores of salvation. If we compare this picture with the older one, there is indeed a change of how the church is perceived. The older ecclesiology took the scriptural image of the dragnet, which Jesus used in his kingdom parables, and applied it to the mission of the church. The church was seen as a ship moving through the centuries, dragging behind it an enormous net and trying to catch as many fish as possible—all in the firm belief that only those actually caught in this net will be saved. Today we would say there are as many ships as there are religions that can carry people to salvation. The church's mission is viewed here not as taking the people from their ship into the "bark of Peter" but rather as indicating to them which way to steer their boats. A research seminar in India uses another image to present the church's mission today in this statement: "Today we realize that the welfare of the whole creation is the object of the Christian mission. It is not a project for the construction of Noah's ark to rescue the 'Christian remnant' from the irredeemable rest. Instead, the Church is like the leaven that is meant to facilitate the transformation of the word."[3]

The document *Gaudium et Spes* (Joy and hope) seeks to spell out the church's relationship to the world. It basically describes the church as a community whose mission is to give joy and hope to a world that often looks so gloomy and desperate, without real joy and knowledge of the way to move and the direction to take.

The council looked at the church not as a place where people are getting prepared for eternal life and where the faithful are instructed and remolded in a way that final salvation in the future will assuredly be theirs. Instead it started describing the church more positively by envisioning it as the community of the end-time in the "here and now," as the fulfillment of the eschatological kingdom anticipated in space and history. It is the historical anticipation or the historical concretization of God's ultimate plan for humankind and creation as a whole. It is the "already" of the "not yet" meant to be the concrete realization of

---

[2] *Lumen Gentium,* no. 6 n.12, lists a whole range of images found in scripture.

[3] Ishvani-Kendra Research Seminar 2000, "A Vision of Mission for the New Millennium," *Sedos Bulletin* 32 (2000), 100.

God's kingdom now and sent to witness to the kingdom's presence and to proclaim it to the whole world. Wherever a Christian community emerges, its ultimate mission is to be a "light for the people" and to give "joy and hope" in the midst of an often hopeless situation. It can do this only because right in its midst the community experiences *already* the vision that God intended to come true for all the world at the proper time.

In these two images the council provided us with a vision of the church for our age and time, something that can instill enthusiasm and renewed commitment, something we can live for, work for, suffer for and, if necessary, die for.

In the encyclical *Ecclesiam Suam* (His church), Paul VI emphasizes the true origin of the church, its Trinitarian dimension. It is not merely a human reality but a divine mystery that ultimately escapes definition. Unless we realize this we would despair because of its all-too-human appearance and sinfulness down through the ages. With his Trinitarian stress Paul VI brought out the view commonly held today that the basic understanding of church presented in the council was the church as an "icon" of the Trinity.

RETRIEVING BIBLICAL IMAGES OF THE CHURCH

In making concrete its vision of the church, the council chose the following images from the ninety-five images and symbols that the scriptures use in referring to the entity called church[4] and presented them as basic for our time:

> Church as the *new people of God*
> Church as *body of Christ*
> Church as *temple of the Holy Spirit*

These three images seem to have been chosen because of their central importance in the New Testament and because of their significance for the Trinitarian dimension of the church. Theologically, these images adequately describe the essence and function of the church and, as such, will always remain important points of reference when we are looking for an image of the church.

The New People of God

The favorite image the council employed was St. Paul's vision of the church as the new people of God. In taking the Jewish idea of Israel as the people of God, Paul sees the Christian community as the "new People of God" but profoundly linked with the Old Testament. For him, the history of salvation is one (Rom 9—11). The *berit* (covenant formula) "You are my people and I am your God" (Dt 6:6) finds its eschatological fulfillment in the new *berit*, in Christ's

---

[4] Paul S. Minar, *Images of the Church in the New Testament* (Philadelphia: Westminster Press, 1977).

blood. The church is grafted into the tree of Israel and lives from the power of the ancient olive tree (Rom 11:17). God has not rejected God's people, for they remain the beloved of Yahweh. The privileges of Israel have been granted now to all who believe in Christ. Israel of old may have rejected Christ for the time being; nevertheless, the history of the new community in Christ remains inseparably bound to the history of nonbelieving Israel. It is precisely because of the failure of Israel that salvation has come to the Gentiles.[5]

Paul opposed any Gentile Christian claim that (a) regarded Judaism as a relic of the past and an interim (though long) step on the way to the Gentile church or (b) assumed that God had repudiated Israel and that in its stead the church was the true people of God; that is, Paul repudiated any effort to develop a unique Christian identity without Israel.

> According to Paul, Israel remains chosen, and Christians from the nations are incorporated into God's covenant with Israel. Without this incorporation of Gentile Christians into Israel's faith history, which began with Abraham, we are, says Paul, nothing but wild shoots that wither. The church of God in Jesus Christ can exist only as a "sharer in the rich root" (Rom 11:17). The church represents not the new people of God but the expanded people, who, together with Israel, form the one people of God. The image is that of an ellipse with two foci. For Paul, this salvation history model means that Yahweh is not only Israel's God but also the God of all nations (Rom 3:29f.).[6]

The New Covenant, therefore, can be understood and explained only in terms of its origin: the Old Covenant.

> Although the church, as a community founded by Jesus Christ, appears only in the New Testament, it can be understood only in connection with the history of the people of God in the Old Testament. . . . There are at least two basic notions of the cultic community of the Old Testament which have become important for the church: the idea of the covenant with God, and the idea of the people of God.[7]

However, the new people of God formed by Christians are the community of the true descendants of Abraham, built upon the twelve forefathers of the new

---

[5] Gerhard Lohfink, *Jesus and Community: Did Jesus Found a Church?* (London: SPCK Press, 1985), 80; see also, Jürgen Werbick, *Kirche: Ein Ekklesiologischer Entwurf für Studium und Praxis* (Freiburg: Herder, 1994), 80-83. Werbick follows Lohfink but sees this view particularly expressed already in the gospel of Matthew.

[6] Hubert Frankemoelle, "The Root Supports You (Rom 11:17-18)," *Theology Digest* 47 (2000), 227.

[7] J. Auer and Joseph Ratzinger, *The Church: The Universal Sacrament of Salvation,* vol. 8 of *Dogmatic Theology* (Washington, D.C.: The Catholic University of America Press, 1993), 26.

people of God in the Holy Spirit, the apostles. Christ is the new primogenitor of these new people of God. He is the head of his people and the ever-living mediator of the new covenant. For this reason Paul frequently replaces the notion of the people of God with the term "church of God."[8]

We have to realize that from a historical perspective the metaphor *people of God* did not play a dominant role in the tradition of the church. This was basically due to a negative view of the Old Testament people who had failed to keep their part of the covenant. Only in the twentieth century was the metaphor newly discovered in connection with the theology known as salvation history. As Auer and Ratzinger observe: "Especially since the 40s, exegetical research has led to a new understanding of this historical people of God. Through a clearer grasp of the term 'eschatological,' among Catholics as well, the bases were created for a concept of the people of God based upon the history of salvation. It was this concept which became the basis of Vatican II's Constitution on the church."[9]

However, the change that had come through Jesus Christ gave a fuller meaning to the ancient term *qahal.*

The word "church," in fact, bears witness to the consciousness that the apostles had, and with them the primitive Christian communities, of being the new and true People of God which is now permanently convoked by its Lord and gathered in a continuous and mysterious manner into a holy assembly, even though its members remain scattered throughout the city. Note that it is the permanent being of the church that receives the name *qahal-ekklesia*, and not only the concrete assemblies and the liturgical meetings. This is already clear in the first word of the first writing of the New Testament, that is, the first letter to the Thessalonians. St. Paul addresses himself to the Christians living in Thessalonica and calls them "the *ekklesia* . . . in God the Father and the Lord Jesus Christ" (1 Thess 1:1). The *ekklesia* is the people of God ransomed by Jesus Christ, scattered throughout the earth, but living, already now and always, in a mysterious and holy congregation. The plural *ekklesiai* (1 Thess 2:14; Gal 1:22) indicates that this people, wherever they are located, are always the one church of God, the Holy People gathered together for praise in this or that location: "the church of God which is in Corinth," according to the greetings in the letters to the Corinthians.

The mystery of this new people, in our perspective, consists in the fact that no new convocations are expected: it is always the ekklesia, the eschatological communion already present on earth, because they—the People whom Christ has convoked on the part of the Father—are for always the body of Christ and the Temple of the Holy Spirit. The believers have from the first moment understood the new People of God as the people whom the Father convoked through Christ and who gather around

---

[8] Ibid., 30.
[9] Ibid., 70.

Christ "to go to the Father." Hence, the denominations "church of God" and "church of Christ" are interchangeable.[10]

By stating that the church is the people of God, the council affirmed some other important aspects, discussed below.

A Gratuitous Election by God

The New Testament church is seen as the people of God created and constituted through the revelation of God in Jesus Christ. This view stresses the *gratuitous election and mission of the new people of God* in line with God's election of individual persons in the Old Testament. In the plan for salvation God "elects" people not on the basis of any merits but only out of a preferential love with the sole purpose of drawing them closer into the accomplishment of God's salvific plan for all.

The idea of "election" or of "chosen" people for the church is often offensive and has been the subject of much theological controversy. Most biblical references to election by God have to do with the choice of a group. It means a corporate election. God chose Abraham and all who are in him, that is, his descendants. God chose David in a similar way. But election of one does not mean rejection of the other. The words "I have loved Jacob but I have hated Esau" can only be understood from the Hebrew usage. "To love" is to choose; "to hate" is not to choose. These words are not about emotions but are acts of the will. Love in biblical language involves choice.[11]

But the choice of a group in the Old Testament did not guarantee the inclusion of all individuals in that group in the blessings for which they were chosen. There was often a progressive narrowing of God's choice. This narrowing has been described as an hourglass. Christ is seen as the center of this hourglass through which the sand flows. God's saving action starts with creation. From there it narrows down to humanity, Israel, the remnant, and then to the center: Christ. Then it broadens out again, from Christ to the Twelve, the church, humanity, and the new creation.[12]

God's choice within Israel finally focused on the *one person*, Christ, the "Chosen One." This title was given to him on the Mount of Transfiguration (Lk 9:35). Therefore, we can say: "All who are in Christ are included in this election. God chose Abraham (and all in him); God chose Jacob (and all in him); God chose David (and his descendants); God chose Christ (and all in him). Just as all who are 'in' Abraham, Israel, or David were included in their

---

[10] Pedro Rodriguez, "Theological Method for Ecclesiology," in *The Gift of the Church: A Textbook on Ecclesiology in Honor of Patrick Granfield, OSB,* ed. Peter Phan (Collegeville, Minnesota: The Liturgical Press, 2000), 153-154.

[11] Everett Ferguson, *The Church of Christ: A Biblical Ecclesiology for Today* (Grand Rapids, Michigan: Eerdmans, 1996), 77-88.

[12] Oscar Cullmann, *Christ and Time* (Philadelphia: Westminster, 1950), 115-116.

election, so it is with Christ. The election in Christ entails the election of those in Christ."[13]

The new election of the community called church is, therefore, related to Christ. The elected people are those chosen in Christ. The corporate nature of the election emphasizes the importance of the church. This also makes it clear that election by God does not mean that the people involved are better than others nor should it give them a sense of superiority (Dt 7:7). Christians are the elect because they have been called by God through an act of infinite love and mercy: "You are a chosen race, a royal priesthood, a consecrated nation, a people set apart to sing the praises of God who called you out of darkness into his wonderful light" (1 Pt 2:9).

Yet we cannot emphasize enough that the idea of service and biblical election are inextricably intertwined. Whoever is called is chosen not for personal gain but to participate more actively in God's plan of salvation meant for the salvation of all human beings; it means to do something for one's brothers and sisters; it means that one is to be their representative by engaging actively with God in God's desire to save them all.[14] Of course, this carries with it a special closeness to God, joy in God's friendship, and love in a conscious and intensive way.

This view clarifies the historicity of the church and its place in the realm of earthly history. The future and the mission of the church are seen together with those of Israel of old: chosen for a purpose and not for personal gain. The saving function of the people of God for the whole of humanity is enjoined now on both, Israel and the church. Auer and Ratzinger write:

> The most important element in this model of the church is historicity in the variety of its relations: back to the past of the Old Testament people of God with which the New Testament people of God will be judged and fulfilled in the coming end times; as a transformation in the present, in the conversion of the individual and the church in the spirit of the call, through immersion in historical revelation and sanctification by the ever-active Spirit of God in the church. The invisible in the visible, the past and future in the present, salvation in sinfulness, eternal election in the course of history, the individual and the community, all of these polarities in their dialogical unity in earthly history are expressed in the image of the people of God.[15]

The Communitarian Aspect

Prior to all individuality and every individual calling, the church is seen as a *people* founded by divine calling into which the individual is incorporated. *The*

---

[13] Ferguson, *The Church of Christ*, 82.

[14] John Fuellenbach, *Throw Fire* (Manila: Logos Publication, 1998), 69-84.

[15] Auer and Ratzinger, *The Church,* 70.

communitarian aspect of salvation takes priority over the individual-personal dimension. The individual's relationship to God is not private, independent of all socialization; rather, the divine calling is aimed at constituting humanity as a people by reason of its common eschatological destiny, the kingdom.[16] The background of this communitarian view is an ecclesiology as it transpired during Vatican II, namely, that of *community* taking its image from being an icon of the Trinitarian community. The church should echo the interrelation between the three Persons who together constitute the Deity. The church is called to be the kind of reality at a finite level that God is in eternity.

The nature of that community, therefore, cannot be measured by the standard of any purely human community. Gennadios Limouris, mentioning the basic scriptural images for the church found in the New Testament—that of body of Christ and temple of the Holy Spirit—adds a third one (which he calls the first one) defining the church negatively, saying what it is not. He writes:

The first image [for the church] is found in an incident during our Lord's last journey to Jerusalem. There had been an argument among the twelve apostles about precedence, about who should be the first in the kingdom, and Christ put an end to it by saying: "You know that the rulers of the Gentiles lord it over them, and their great men exercise authority over them. It shall not be so among you" (Matt. 20:25-26). Here, then, is a negative picture, indicating what the church is not. "It shall not be so among you." The statement means that the community which Jesus came to establish is radically different from any other type of community. The church is not to be understood in terms of human worldly power of earthly authority and jurisdiction. In ecclesiology, then, we must be exceedingly careful not to take as a "model" some political or cultural forms existing in the secular pluralistic society around us. We must not assimilate the church to monarchist structures like those of the Roman Empire, or hierarchies like those of medieval feudalism, or even to the patterns like those of modern democracy. The bishop (the leader of the historic church), for example, is to be thought of neither as a feudal overlord nor as a democratically appointed "representative." The chief bishop or primate is neither an absolute monarch nor a constitutional president nor the chairman of a board of directors. To interpret the church's leadership, and by implication the church, by such analogies as these is to overlook its uniqueness. It is to forget Christ's warning: "It shall not be so among you."[17]

---

[16] Christian Duquoc, *Provisional Churches: An Essay in Ecumenical Ecclesiology* (London: SCM Press, 1986), 39.

[17] Gennadios Limouris, "The Church as Mystery and Sign in Relation to the Holy Trinity—In Ecclesiological Perspectives," in *Church—Kingdom—World: The Church as Mystery and Prophetic Sign*, Faith and Order paper no. 130, ed. Gennadios Limouris (Geneva: World Council of Churches, 1986), 23.

The example of Jesus' own lifestyle must remain the pattern of how any church community sees its own life and practice. "I did not come to be served but to serve and to lay down my life for the many" (Mk 10:45). If we use the doctrine of the Trinity to suggest ways of allowing the eternal becoming of God—the eternally inter-animating energies of the three—to provide the basis for the personal dynamics of the community, it is obvious that the internal structures of the church community will have to follow similar patterns.[18] All community structures have to be modeled on the image of the Trinitarian God and not on any purely human model of community.

A number of theologians have observed the tendency of Catholic theology toward *modalism,* which seems to surface most clearly in an understanding of church as a community that is first and foremost hierarchical in structure.[19] Orthodox theologians have repeatedly pointed out this tendency. Marie-Dominique Chenu, for example, referenced a talk that was given during the council by the Patriarch of the East, Msgr. Hakim, who said: "Western theologians have always the tendency to *modalism* (and today, alas, to "deism" . . .): an *abstract* God, subjected to analysis by reason; not the living God, in whom the inaccessible mystery of the Father *(theologia)* is revealed by and in the Son, and communicated to men in history *(oikonomia)* through the presence of the Spirit."[20] Only a Trinitarian approach to the church could help us to overcome such tendency and to rethink and reformulate our understanding of church structures.

An Egalitarian People

By choosing the image people of God for the church, the council wanted consciously to *counterbalance a too hierarchically perceived image of the church.* It wanted to restore to the people of God their legitimate right to participate in the governing power of the church, since all are equal before God. The image was thought to break with a non-egalitarian and antidemocratic ideology of the earlier ecclesiology. Prior to dealing with structure and order and deciding who exercises particular ministries and functions in the church, we must give precedence to the basic reality of the ecclesial community: all are first and foremost brothers and sisters united in Jesus Christ. All ordering into higher or lower offices and functions in the community are of secondary importance and can never be overruled by any position or rank one may occupy in the assembly.

---

[18] Colin Gunton, "Church on Earth: The Roots of Community," in *On Being the Church: Essays on the Christian Community,* ed. Colin E. Gunton and Daniel W. Hardy (Edinburgh: T&T Clark, 1989), 78.

[19] Werner G. Jeanrond, "Community and Authority: The Nature and Implication of the Authority of Christian Community," in *On Being the Church: Essays on the Christian Community,* ed. Colin E. Gunton and Daniel W. Hardy (Edinburgh: T&T Clark, 1989), 81-109.

[20] M.-D. Chenu, "The New Awareness of the Trinitarian Basis of the Church," *Concilium* 146 (1981), 15.

The council precisely aimed at undoing the wrongly chosen way of defining the church from its officeholders down, by assigning rank and honors to particular members in the church according to their position in the community and so allocating the people of God to the bottom of the barrel. The most appropriate image of the church in this configuration was the *pyramid*, where one starts with the "top pick" (the pope) and moves down to the base of the pyramid (the ordinary faithful). We can rightly say that the council replaced the pyramid metaphor with that of the *circle,* within whose embrace all are deemed equal and no one can claim to have special rights to lord it over others. In the words of Jesus, the council wanted to say, "Among you it should be different. Whoever wants to be first should be last" (Mk 9:35-36; 10:41-45).

A Pilgrim People

This metaphor people of God sees the church as a *pilgrim people,* a people on the road toward its final goal, the fullness of the kingdom to come. The church is only the sacrament of the kingdom, which accounts for its preliminary character because a sacrament is never the full reality to which it points and which it wants to open up to people in the here and now.

By using this image for the church, the council further wanted to stress that the church has to be seen as a growing community involved in history, one affected by the weaknesses and infidelities of its members, who constantly stand in need of God's mercy and forgiveness. This notion serves as a corrective and a warning against all triumphalism. It reveals the humanness of the church, a community composed of people who, like the Old Testament people, are imperfect and unfaithful, a murmuring people who feel the heat of the sun on their march through the desert of this world. They cry out to God for help and relief and want to see an end to their journey. So they fervently pray and wait for the Lord to return. This brings out the eschatological and provisional character of the church. As such, it should never settle in this world or live in well-established structures and houses but rather in tents and booths. It knows its home lies in the world to come and not here in this world. This view could serve as a critique for a church that has too comfortably settled into a culture and lost the sense of constant longing for the day of the Lord, as the early church constantly cried, "Lord Jesus come." J. B. Metz might be right when he observes that the Second Coming of the Lord does not seem to occur since no one in the church seriously longs for his Second Coming.

For some time after the council, this image of people of God was in vogue. It is still used, but its popularity is limited. Seemingly the faithful in many parts of the world cannot see themselves so easily as a "people" in an Old Testament sense. This is because religious affiliation today is not congruent with one's ethnic and political identity, as in the case of Israel. However, the image continues to appeal to marginalized groups in the church who experience situations comparable to those of Israel: oppressed and dependent, struggling for identity and freedom. This is also the case where church communities see themselves as tiny minorities whose views and values contrast to commonly held views. These minorities find in this image the vision that could lead and guide them in their struggle and search.

However, in the church as a large-scale institution, the people of God image did not become *the* image of the church that could provide an inspiring vision to lead to the desired reform of the church. The image was highly praised and regarded as a major breakthrough in the church's self-understanding, since it demonstrated the effort to move away from clericalism and to assess the rightful place of the laity in the church anew. The other churches present as observers during the council, however, cautioned against any euphoria because in their opinion the chapter following the treatise on the people of God in *Lumen Gentium* stressed the hierarchical aspect so heavily that they found it impossible to reconcile it with the chosen image of people of God. The result is that, in spite of the effort made by the council, many theologians do not see much change in the church's way of exercising its authority by trying to share it with the laity.

> The Roman Catholic Church continues to defend the "status" of its male clergy as willed by Christ. Thus, the organization of authority in this church is seen to come directly from God and to demand absolute obedience from the members of the community. The model of vicarious representation of authority operative in the Roman church has survived the changes of the Second Vatican Council. Although this council's Constitution on the Church *(Lumen Gentium)* describes the church as the people of God and emphasizes the equal importance of all its membership, the equality of the faithful breaks down when in the same document we do not meet the view of one priestly character and diversity of function but two ontological qualities, resulting in two essentially different lines of functions, whereof the one is representative and the other is not. The tragedy of the Second Vatican Council lies in its failure to agree wholeheartedly on the redefinition of the church as communio and to abandon the concept of the church as *societas*. As long as the final power over the community remains only in the hands of one section of the community, the essence of communio authorized by God is destroyed in favor of an ecclesial society authorized only by itself.[21]

In spite of the ambiguity of *Lumen Gentium* and *Gaudium et Spes,* the invitation to work for a more authentic communal faith-praxis with appropriate structures did find an echo in the church. The basic ecclesial communities that emerged all over the world after the council are an important example of this renewal in spite of the continuing authoritarian government still found in the Roman Catholic Church.

---

[21] Jeanrond, "Community and Authority," 91-93.

The immense potential of the image carries an explosive power. It contains a "dangerous memory" for any church that envisages itself too easily in terms of hierarchy and order and forgets that the root metaphor for the church will always have to remain the community that God chose in the beginning, a community in which there are no rulers or ruled but only equals who serve each other as brothers and sisters, a community in which compassion and justice are lenses for seeing and the core values of an alternative way of thinking about society. Ultimately, the church is constituted to be an icon of the Trinity already here on earth.

The Church as Body of Christ

The Image as Used in the Council

To complement the people of God image the council felt obliged to use another biblical image for the church: the body of Christ. This metaphor has been applied to the church through the centuries and is most probably the one most theologians would agree upon.[22] Pius XII gave it magisterial approval in his famous encyclical *Mystici Corporis* (1943). With this document he wanted to provide a balance to the heavily one-sided ecclesiology of Vatican I, which so emphasized the institutional element of the church that its inner, divine dimension was hardly recognizable. Thus this metaphor became *the* image of the church in most textbooks on ecclesiology. Strangely enough, although it was meant to balance the hierarchical aspect in the church, in fact it made the hierarchical structure even more untouchable. Supporters of this view argue that, because the structures of the church belong to the body of Christ, they are therefore divine and immutable. A further drawback was that the encyclical identified the church with the *Roman* Catholic Church by stating that the body of Christ exists *only* in the Roman Catholic Church. This view gave little opening for ecumenical dialogue.

The Second Vatican Council did choose to use the metaphor again, but it applied it to the church in a more nuanced way than did *Mystici Corporis.*[23] The council felt that the people of God image could not adequately express the overwhelming change brought about by Christ. Body of Christ, on the other hand, expresses the intimate union of the church with the risen and glorified Lord as his continuing presence in the world. It reveals the innermost heart of the church, namely, dependence on and union with Christ. Some hold this understanding of the church as the most mature result of the New Testament thinking of the church. It certainly is the most important New Testament image for the church employed by Paul. Vatican II summarizes the wealth of this image in *Lumen Gentium,* no. 7.

---

[22] Werbick, *Kirche*, 277.

[23] Ibid., 277-281. Werbick shows how the council reformulated the intent of the encyclical and how carefully it softened its anti-ecumenical interpretation.

The Origin of the Body of Christ Symbol in St. Paul

The idea of the body of Christ is definitely linked to the idea of corporate personality or extended personality. The content fits well into the Jewish way of thinking, in which a group derived its identity from the identity of one person. Israel was both the forefather of the people and the whole people itself. Adam was both a person and humanity. In the same way Jesus includes all believers in himself. Paul lived in this pattern of Old Testament thinking and developed his understanding of the body of Christ image along these lines. He unfolded this concept in connection with the words used in the eucharist: "My Body given for you."[24] Paul's concept of body was based on the Hebrew idea of *basar,* which sees the body first and foremost as the means of rendering service to others. The understanding of body as the means of communication, even of service to others, became predominant in the New Testament church.

From this understanding Paul develops the three most important aspects regarding the body concept: first, the total dependence of the church on Christ based on the *corporate personality* metaphor of the Old Testament; second, also taken from the Hebrew background, the idea of bodily service for one's fellow human beings in the footsteps and in union with the Lord; and third, the idea of unity and harmony of the whole body based on the Greek understanding of the term *soma.*

First, the church is totally dependent on the crucified and risen body of Christ, that is, on the saving event that took place at a specific time in a specific place within our human history. This dependence on God's act is underlined by the fact that it is primarily in the eucharist that this character of the body of Christ is given to the church.

> The church is the body of Christ, because it lives by all that has been done by Jesus Christ for its sake. It is united with him by the fact that his history, namely his life and death and resurrection, is the foundation of the church's life, without which it would not exist at all. The church exists in the body of Christ through the body of Christ crucified and risen for the sake of the world, still present in its blessing and challenge, for instance when the Eucharist is celebrated. Outside this body of Christ, for its sake, the church does not exist. The saying in 1 Cor 12:27: "You are the body of Christ," and the surprising end of verse 12 in the same chapter: ". . . just as the body is one and has many members . . . so it is with Christ," are possible because the idea that a whole tribe is included in its ancestor is familiar to Paul. Hence these sayings describe the total dependence of the church on its founder, on Jesus Christ, in a most impressive way.[25]

---

[24] Edward Schweizer, *The Church as the Body of Christ* (Atlanta: John Knox Press, 1976), 41-47.

[25] Ibid., 55.

For Paul, the body of Christ means the crucified body in its *for-our-sake-ness*. The crucified body of Jesus is the place in which the human person finds meaning for life, because the crucified Jesus becomes the sign of God's incredible love and the challenge to service that makes his life meaningful. The body of Christ is something like a sphere, a reality into which a person has to go or to be put in order to find life. Or, to say it in another way, it is the church, understood as the place, the realm, the sphere, in which Jesus, crucified but raised two thousand years ago, is still telling us of God's love and is still challenging us and calling us under his Lordship.[26]

Second, being the body of Christ is not a mysterious experience but is lived daily in bodily manifestations of the church's faith, namely, in the concrete brotherhood and sisterhood in which obedience to the Lord is manifested in love for the brothers and sisters. The church as body of Christ is to be understood in such a way that it could be seen primarily in its openness for others and for the world, in its mission to the nations and its self-sacrifice for those who are outside of it. Schweizer concludes his investigation by saying:

> This means that the last result of this investigation is the insight that the church can be body of Christ only if it is willing to suffer and thereby to be the body of its Lord who, in his body, goes into the world, serving all humankind. If the church is willing to live in this way as Christ's body, often suffering and dying, it will experience time and again that he himself creates in it that obedience and that readiness for self-sacrifice, in which he as its Lord encounters the world and converts Gentiles into members of his body.[27]

The community that unites itself with the Lord in the eucharist by eating his body and drinking his blood becomes so united with the Lord that it takes on Christ's eucharistic existence, which is totally determined by the symbolism of the eucharist: bread to be broken and wine to be poured. The community's whole being is now determined by the existence of the Lord. It becomes the body of Christ and takes over the mission of the Lord: to give oneself away in order to carry on this mission of Christ by being the means through which others are brought into unity with Christ and with each other. The members of the church are to the world what the body of Christ is for them. The eucharist should determine the life of Christians worthy of the name.

It is through the community's body that Christ remains present. He continues to "lay down his life" in his chosen body, the church, in order to fulfill his mission on earth until he comes again. Christ, who is gone, needs human bodies in order to make himself present in this world and to carry on his world-redeeming mission.

---

[26] Ibid., 46.
[27] Ibid., 78.

The participation in the body of Christ in the eucharistic celebration not only leads the Christian into deep union with Christ, but it is at the same time a mission. After having been united with the Lord in the eucharist, having been remolded into the shape of the master, the disciple is now sent out to continue the Lord's mission by serving in the way the Lord served when he walked this earth. Of course, no one can take on such a mission solely of his or her own volition. It is precisely because we are in the "new ancestor," are his descendants, that we have to reproduce the pattern of his life in our own lives (an idea richly unfolded in 2 Corinthians). Seen from such a perspective, the eucharist could be regarded as a sacrament of mission for Christians.

St. Paul had to clarify over and over again that being the body of Christ meant to carry on the mission of Christ here on earth, which means to participate in his suffering rather than in his glory now. He had to convince his opponents in Corinth that being body of Christ as community meant not primarily to participate in the glory of the Risen Christ now but to be chosen to carry on Christ's mission here on earth. Equipped with Christ's Spirit they could continue his mission, which existed in doing what Jesus had done when he walked this earth. The pattern for action of the Christian community was the Jesus who had brought God's salvation by living a life in a body *as physically as anybody* and in that body had redeemed the whole world (Rom 3:8). This Jesus would be the one they were to follow in continuation of his mission for all. As James D. G. Dunn sees it, the reasoning of Paul's opponents in Corinth seems to have gone like this:

We believe in Christ as risen and exalted Lord; we believe that through the Spirit we are brought into union with Christ in his exaltation; therefore the hallmark of the experience of the Spirit should be experiences of exaltation, of being taken out of our lowly, narrowing human condition and being united with Christ in heaven, enjoying experiences of heavenly glory. . . . Against this over-concentration on the exaltedness of Christ, Paul insists again and again: the model for our present experience of Christ is not the glorified Christ, but the suffering, crucified Christ. While believers are yet firmly rooted on earth, it is the earthly Jesus who provides the pattern for their pilgrimage on earth. The point is not simply that if Jesus suffered and was rejected, his followers should expect no better. It is rather that the way of Christ in suffering and death is the only way for believers to follow Christ to glory. . . .

In many ways the most striking example of Paul's forcefulness here comes in Philippians 3, where he speaks of "the surpassing worth of knowing Christ Jesus my Lord," and he goes on to say what that means for him: "All I want is to know him [then note the order of the phrases], and the power of his resurrection, and the sharing of his sufferings, becoming like him in his death, that if possible I may attain to the resurrection from the dead" (Phil 3:8-11). Notice that what he envisages is not a kind of spiritual escalator, where sharing in Christ's sufferings comes first, to be left behind as he moves on to the experience of Christ's resurrection. On the contrary, experience of the power of Christ's resurrection and sharing in his sufferings are for Paul two parts of the same process, a process which must continue through to the end, when and only when he will enjoy the resurrection from the dead.[28]

Those who are the body of Christ on earth will show this first in their behavior toward each other. Participation in the body of Christ means to participate in the Spirit of Christ. The Faith and Order Commission has this to say:

> The Eucharistic celebration demands reconciliation and sharing among all those regarded as brothers and sisters in the one family of God and is a constant challenge in the search for appropriate relationship in social, economic and political life (Mt 5:23ff.; 1 Cor 10:14; 1 Cor 11:20-22). Because Holy Communion is the sacrament which builds up community, all kinds of injustice, racism, estrangement, and lack of freedom are radically challenged when we share in the body and blood of Christ. . . . As participants in the Eucharist, therefore, we prove inconsistent if we are not actively participating in the ongoing restoration of the world's situation and the human condition. Holy Communion shows us that our behavior is inconsistent in the face of the reconciling presence of God in human history: we are placed under continued judgement by the persistence of unjust relationships of all kinds in our society, manifold divisions on account of human pride, material interest and power politics and, above all, the obstinacy of unjustifiable confessional oppositions within the body of Christ.[29]

Thirdly, one of the main concerns for Paul was the unity of the church. He unfolds this idea against the background of those in the Corinthian community who had a rather anti-body view of things. Here the concept *body* is understood as in Greek philosophy, namely, as a unifying whole consisting of many parts and organs but making up one whole being. Unity can be served only if all parts play their role and function in harmony with the whole body. The oneness of the body derives ultimately from the oneness of the Spirit. The unity of the body comes from the common experience of the same Spirit. The experience of the Spirit is not something merely personal, something individual. It was a community-creating experience, a body of Christ experience, an experience of being knit into a community.

Above all we should remember the full implications of the imagery of the body of Christ. For one thing, as the parallel between Rom. 6:3 and 1 Cor.

---

[28] James D. G. Dunn, *The Christ and the Spirit,* vol. 2, *Pneumatology* (Edinburgh: T&T Clark, 1998), 350-351.

[29] *The Nature and Purpose of the Church,* Faith and Order paper no. 181 (Bialystock, Poland: Ortdruck Orthodox Printing House, 1998), 80.

12:13 makes clear, membership in Christ is not separable from membership in the body of Christ. The body of Christ rules out the concept of the
individual Christian in his or her aloneness. For Paul certainly, the grace
of Christ, the Spirit of Christ, and the body of Christ are coterminous. The
Christian presence in the world is irreducibly corporate.[30]

The concern for unity Paul develops even further when he looks at the church as
a charismatic entity, a community that is held together by the different charisms
given by the Spirit to the individual to be lived totally for the benefit of the
whole.

The Body of the Risen Christ

One difficulty felt by Vatican II was that the physical body of Christ had
been the point of comparison for the model for the church. The physical human
body is limited and well defined. The church, as the body of Christ, is also
limited and well defined. Thus members are clearly defined and so are the institutions that must maintain the church's unity and strength in the world. It is
argued that just as the body has various members and different functions, so
also does the church have many members with various functions. The point of
comparison is always the physical body of Christ. The metaphor is taken literally, and therein lies the problem. In the view of Werbick:

> The conflictual character of metaphor "the Body of Christ" rests in its
> tendency towards identification: the church which identifies herself with
> the "Body of Christ" identifies herself rather quickly with the head that
> unites the Body of Christ. And those in the church who represent the "head"
> too readily identify with the head itself and act as well as decide on behalf
> of the head which they represent. This tendency towards identification
> implies—more or less explicitly—a monopoly or a set of boundaries: it
> lays claim to the "head" for *this* visible Catholic Church and denies the
> being "Body of Christ" to other churches, because there can be only *one*
> body. It focuses very much on the close relationship between head and
> body, sees in it the only meaning for being church and tends so easily to
> overlook that the church is called to live its "being the Body of Christ" for
> others, for the world—as a living witness. In this way the "Body of Christ"
> metaphor can favor an ecclesial introversion.[31]

Thus arises the danger of defining the church too narrowly, because the church
is not the physical body of Christ. Through the resurrection, the body of Jesus
Christ was not simply brought back to life. It was completely liberated from
every temporal and spatial limitation. Christ was no longer simply a carnal body,

---

[30] Dunn, *The Christ and the Spirit,* 2:346.
[31] Werbick, *Kirche*, 300.

that is, a body subject to an earthly condition, a prisoner to the conditions of space and time, in need of food and drink, and subject to limitations and ambiguous communication through word and gesture. The resurrection transformed Jesus' carnal body into a spiritual body (see 1 Cor 14:44f.). A spiritual body is the new reality of the Risen Jesus, now free from limitations of earthly existence, enthroned in eternity and in the limitless arena of divine life, liberated from space and time. Through the resurrection the limits of the carnal Jesus fell away and were replaced by his global relationship with all of reality. The risen Jesus became the Cosmic Christ of Paul's letters to the Ephesians and Colossians, the Prologue to the Fourth Gospel, and the Letter to the Hebrews. The body of the risen and pneumatic Christ can no longer be considered a physically definable entity from which we can deduce the limits of the church as the body of Christ.[32]

However, we can also overstress this point, because the church as institution and corporate body is not a merely human establishment. The image of the body of Christ clearly does express the divine dimension of the church in spite of its limitations. The church is not a club of like-minded people who pursue a common interest. Without the divine dimension one would have to despair of the church. Body of Christ best expresses theologically why the Risen Lord will stay with his church. It is his chosen partner or, as scripture has it, his bride, in spite of all its faults and infidelities. Therefore we are assured that the church can never really "lose the Spirit"; it has been promised that it will never completely lose the right path. Concerning the sacraments, it has been assured that the Risen Christ can be encountered in these wherever they are performed in his name. It is the universal sacrament of salvation through which Christ continues to be present to carry on his mission through the community. The church as a whole should make Christ visible in all its lived expressions and forms as well as in its institutional shape.

Still, the church cannot presume that it is the authentic incarnation of this Spirit in the way it concretely appears. On the contrary, in all its lived expressions it is constantly challenged by God's Word and Christ's Spirit to witness to this Word and this Spirit, to become an instrument of God's actions, and so make it possible for people to experience God's grace. Where it is not sufficiently open to the Spirit of Christ, there the Spirit is reduced to insignificance and it loses sight of following in the footsteps of Jesus Christ (1 Pt 2:21).

A mere "residual presence" of the Spirit would be at the same time the judgment of an ecclesial organization which has become "spiritless" and fossilized in the routine of its religious cults and should not be surprised that it is being shunned by people. The ecclesial body is not always nor automatically filled with the Spirit of Christ and alert to the presence of Christ witnessed by its members. Unfortunately, she can even be resistant

---

[32] Leonardo Boff, *Church, Charism, and Power: Liberation Theology and the Institutional Church* (London: SCM Press, 1985), 145.

to the Spirit's breath; she may atrophy by assertively and stubbornly focusing on the institution and the individual. The metaphor "Body of Christ" is not simply a state but expresses a tension: the essence of being church is to incarnate the Spirit of Jesus Christ, to witness to it. However, there is no guarantee that she will always and everywhere live up to this essential calling. She is constantly in danger of betraying her very self and of becoming insignificant.[33]

The visibility of the ecclesial body of Christ is very important. It is not sufficient to appeal to God's (Christ's) Spirit. The Spirit of Christ wants to be made present in those and through those who allow their lives and the life of their communion to be determined by the Spirit. Perhaps it is this experience of the Spirit, wanting to be made visible, which became for Paul the deepest motivation repeatedly to use the metaphor of the body. The exegete Hermann-Josef Venetz describes it in this way:

This is what Paul experienced: Jesus and his mission were present and tangible in the early Christian community. Here he saw how the poor are included and true solidarity is being practiced. Here he discovered new and alternative ways to live. Here God's entering into the world became a tangible reality. Paul experienced the early church as the place where faith in Jesus, the Christ, was incarnate. In the early congregations of the faithful the apostle encountered the living Christ. . . . Here he was visible, tangible and could be experienced. How? Because in its words and actions the community put its faith into practice. Jesus Christ was the motive for all its activities and the source of its life.[34]

Paul probably had this experience in mind, but he also had noticed how the body of Christ was endangered by selfishness and claims to power. This negative experience explains his warning words to the community of Corinth. This experience of tension within the body of Christ is probably still having its effect on our present experience of the church. The community, the church, can be a visible experience of Christ, the community of authentic disciples, and thus it is all the more painful if this is either not the case or hardly so. The community of the faithful can be a place where I can begin anew again and again, because the community accepts me just as I am: a sinner, a failure, someone who did not "make it." The community provides this visible experience of Christ in that moment when this acceptance is not merely a theory but a true experience: a helping hand is offered, someone sees to it that I have a roof over my head and work to do, I am trusted. Again, it the kingdom already present that is experienced in such instances mediated through the community that makes up the church.

---

[33] Werbick, *Kirche*, 296-297.

[34] Hermann-Josef Venetz, "So fing es mit der Kirche an," *Ein Blick in das Neue Testament* (Zürich: Benzinger Verlag, 1981), 131.

This is the most serious challenge to the church today: Will people be able to experience community or church as the tangible Christ? Do they see and feel in our communities today the Spirit of Christ? Or is it rather the spirit of "territorial rights and power," of dogmatism and fear of life?

> We are not talking about a way-out community romanticism, but we are asking whether communities consider it their essential vocation, not just to talk about the Spirit of Jesus, but to go beyond such words and witness to it with their lives. This witness means that they allow themselves to become servants of Christ in his body the church. The central issue is the question whether believers consider it their task to share in the servant spirit of Christ so that they become "his instruments" and that he can hardly be thought of as separate from them.[35]

It was the experience made during the celebration of the eucharist, the celebration of the body and blood of Christ, in which the early church reflected on being the body of Christ, in which it renewed itself as it allowed the Spirit of Christ to flow through it as a power of renewal and aspired to be what it received (Augustine). In the celebration of the eucharist the church becomes the body of Christ through the Spirit of Christ and the sacramental reality of the body and blood of Christ, a bodily communion with Christ. And it is called to manifest this sacramental essence and meaning of its communion of body and life with Christ in its own bodily form. When Jesus offers himself in the eucharist as "body given for others," the church likewise has to become body given for others.

It is the bodily saving presence of Jesus among the people in which he can be touched and experienced through our senses; it is the act of communication through which the Lord wants to come to his people. The church becomes the body of Christ through the *corpus Christi* of the eucharist by way of representing the healing and saving body of Christ among the people. There is a prayer from the late Middle Ages that has been part of our oral tradition and expresses in a beautiful way this theological intention:

> Christ has no hands but our hands to do his work
>   today.
> He has no feet but our feet to guide others to him.
> Christ has no lips, only our lips to speak about him.
> He has no help but our help to call people to his side.

It is our fundamental vocation to build community, that is, to make the concern of Christ our own and to continue his mission by bringing all people to union with God and with one another.[36] It is the church's mission to continue

---

[35] Werbick, *Kirche*, 298.
[36] Ibid., 299.

the proclamation of the kingdom of God, which found in the paschal mystery its high point. It is the eucharist that gives the church its final definition and demand for mission. The kingdom has to remain the reference point if we are not to distort the central message of Jesus. As William V. Dych points out:

> When the church is taken out of the larger context of God's reign and is understood as something that Jesus explicitly set out to establish, what is called "the mystery of the church" becomes a theoretical doctrine made up of various beliefs about such things as structures, offices, and authority in the church supposedly intended by Jesus. But when the church is seen in its original functional relationship of service to the coming of the reign of God, the mystery of the church is none other than the paschal mystery of Jesus' own dying and rising now shared in by the community of his disciples. Belief in the church becomes a practical imperative, a principle of action on behalf of the kingdom of God. It means living and dying with Jesus for the sake of this kingdom in the hope of sharing with him in the new and risen life of God's universal reign. The Christian identity of the individual disciple, and of the church as the community of disciples, is derived from association with this paschal mystery, and there is no mystery of the church apart from this.[37]

Accordingly, the metaphor of the body of Christ is unsuitable to justify claims that would imply that the hierarchy is in any way identical with the head of the body of Christ. Already from the christological point of view, it is not possible either that a human being identifies with God or that a human person claims to be God's representative. On the contrary, according to the faith of the church it is God who identifies himself in and through Christ with a human being and his life lived in and through the Spirit of God. And Jesus identifies himself to the point of "mistaken identity" with the "little ones," the exploited and the sinners; he ultimately suffers their lot. If this is the case, would we not have to accept the theological premise that the risen and glorified Christ does not identify with those who would like to use such identification as a legitimation of their high office? Rather, he identifies with those who try to continue the way of the Jesus who walked this earth and sided with those who had no rights and were marginalized.

The Broken Mirror Model

Christian Duquoc, the French Dominican theologian, recently proposed another metaphor, one which offers itself rather forcefully as a corrective to the body-of-Christ ecclesiology, especially to those who prefer correct and clear metaphors. He speaks about the church and its witness character as a broken mirror:

---

[37] William V. Dych, *Thy Kingdom Come: Jesus and the Reign of God* (New York: Crossroad, 1999), 86-87.

The church is a broken mirror; she reflects only in fragments that for which she is called to bear witness: Jesus Christ. The ecumenical movement was born from the desire to overcome this brokenness. Because the break is still present and manifests itself in the pluralism of the church, in a poly-centric way.[38]

The pieces of the mirror are a "broken witness." Where the churches of the different denominations are aware of it, they will admit that their witness remains selective and that they choose each time what manifests the coherence of their faith and their praxis when they try to speak of the presence of Christ among his people; they admit that they need to restore again and again the central position of Christ; and they accept more readily that they do not have any claim to privileges that have been derived from a too direct identification of the church with the head of the body of Christ. Such privileges lose their theological and christological foundation when it is made clear that the church cannot be identified with the kingdom of God. They lose their political foundation because of the lack of unity among the churches, which Duquoc can value positively:

> Her division is somehow a means of self-protection: none of the churches can insist that she replaces Christ in the world. . . . The guidance and leadership of the Risen Christ through the mediation of the Holy Spirit cannot be identified with the politics of the churches. It is outside of our realm. The mediation role of the churches is biased and partial at the same time.[39]

The Risen Christ cannot be claimed by anyone. He does not allow the visible churches to simply identify with him. Duquoc repeatedly points to the lived witness of the incarnate Logos, the way of Jesus Christ, which is reflected in various ways in the New Testament and finds a polyphonic and hard to harmonize echo in the witness of the hagiographers. The New Testament itself is a mirror in many small mirrors that cannot form a unified and closed picture of the historical Jesus, but makes him a challenge for the visible churches, who cannot monopolize him.

Vatican II tried to balance this tendency to identify the body of Christ with one church, the Catholic Church, and we can see this in the *subsistit* formula (*Lumen Gentium*, no. 8). Similarly, *Gaudium et Spes* confirms this when it speaks about the church in today's world and further develops the understanding of the church as sacramental reality of God's salvific action toward and in the world, as it is expressed in *Lumen Gentium*. The council tried to balance the rather one-sided metaphor of the body of Christ with that of the people of God. However,

---

[38] Christian Duquoc, "Jesus Christus, Mittelpunkt des Europa von Morgen," in *Das Neue Europa, Herausforderung für Kirche und Theologie* (QD 144), ed. P. Huenermann (Freiburg i. Br., 1993), 105f.

[39] Ibid., 108.

the tension between the two metaphors was not resolved in the council's ecclesiology. It seems that these two metaphors, together with others, remain distinct though side by side.[40]

Yet the body of Christ metaphor does express the divine dimension of the church, without which the church would remain a purely human institution. It is not we who create the church, it is not we who have chosen to be the church; the choice is God's and Christ's. Despite all the criticism of the church, it does remain God's chosen community. In this community Christ will always be present and continue his mission on earth, no matter how unfaithful and distorted the church might be in representing his Spirit and proclaiming his mission.

The Church as Temple of the Holy Spirit

The Spirit Who Constitutes the Church

With this image the council wanted to stress the third major aspect of the church: its being a creation of the Holy Spirit. This view was never denied in Catholic theology, but most often the christological aspect was so highly stressed that the pneumatological played only a subordinate role. By contrast, the Orthodox churches always maintained a deeper appreciation of the Holy Spirit's church-creating activity and developed this view accordingly. The council realized this neglect and wanted to correct it. The Orthodox theologian Gennadios Limouris writes:

> While thinking of the church Christologically as the body of Christ, we need also to keep in mind another "icon" to complete and balance our ecclesiology—a pneumatological "icon" of the church as the kingdom of the Holy Spirit. St. Irenaeus spoke of the Son and the Spirit as the "two hands of God" which always work together. If the church is eucharistic, it is at the same time Pentecostal: it is an extension of the incarnation and of Pentecost. After the upper room of Maundy Thursday there comes the upper room of Whitsunday, and both upper rooms are normative for a just appreciation of the nature of the church.[41]

Jean Zizioula, another Orthodox theologian, in his book *Les Eglises* devised the phrase "Christ *institutes* and the Holy Spirit *constitutes* the church." With this distinction he brings the Spirit into play concerning the creation of the church. Zizioula writes:

> Ecclesiologically, the difference between . . . *in* and *con* can be very great. "Institution" is . . . presented more or less as a "fait accompli." As such, it

---

[40] Werbick, *Kirche*, 300.

[41] Limouris, "The Church as Mystery and Sign in Relation to the Holy Trinity—In Ecclesiological Perspectives," 29.

is a challenge to our freedom. "Constitution" is something that involves us in its very being, something we freely accept because we are involved in its very coming to be. The notion of communion must be . . . applied to the very ontology of ecclesial institutions, and not simply to their dynamism and effectiveness.[42]

In other words, communion in the Spirit goes beyond institutionalism. It is constitutive of the church in its source and historical unfolding.

Zizioula's formulation was used in the Catholic-Orthodox document "The Primacy of Rome in the Communion of Churches" (1991): "The Father brings about the church through the joint mission of the Son, who institutes it, and the Spirit, who constitutes it." The phrase "the Spirit constitutes" expresses better than any other the relationship of Christ and the Spirit in their post-Easter work. During Christ's earthly mission, we could say, the relationship of human beings to the Holy Spirit was brought about only by and in Christ, because he alone was the "bearer of the Spirit" from whom it flowed. By contrast, after Pentecost the relationship to Christ is brought about only by and in the Holy Spirit.[43]

This constitutive relationship between the church and the Holy Spirit is expressed by the Faith and Order Commission in this way:

Reference to the constitutive relation between church and Holy Spirit runs through the whole New Testament. Nevertheless there is no explicit image for the relation. The imagery that comes particularly close to the figurative description of this relation entailed in the New Testament, and renders it in a particularly appropriate way, is the imagery of "temple" and "house." This is so because the relation of the Spirit to the church is one of indwelling, of giving life from within.[44]

The Christian community at its earliest stage considered itself as the fulfillment of the eschatological expectation promised through the prophets and brought about by Christ. The realization and understanding of who they were came to the early community through the outpouring of the Holy Spirit, *the* gift of the Risen Lord. The experience of the Holy Spirit was so powerful that Christians regarded their new existence as a creation of the Holy Spirit.

In John, this outpouring of the Spirit happened on Easter Sunday, when the Risen Lord "breathed over" the apostles. For Luke, it is the day of Pentecost, when the eschatological Spirit came down on the community of the disciples in *tongues of fire*. The Spirit, who was at work at the beginning of the world, who "hovered over the chaos" to bring forth the world of creation (Gn 1:1), now hovers over the small group of Jesus' disciples (Acts 2:1-4) and brings forth the

---

[42] As quoted in Jean Rigal, "Towards an Ecclesiology of Communion," *Theology Digest* 47 (2000), 120.

[43] Ibid.

[44] *The Nature and Purpose of the Church,* 23.

new creation, the eschatological community. The church is created by this event. It is the sphere in which Christ makes himself constantly present through the power of his Spirit. To have received the Holy Spirit means to be in contact with the Risen Lord, and to be in contact with him means to be living *already* in the sphere of the new creation: "Anyone who is in Christ Jesus is a new creation" (2 Cor 5:17).

Limouris makes an interesting distinction between the Pentecost event as recorded in John and that in Acts. He indicates how both hierarchy and laity received the gifts of the Spirit but distinctly:

> The Spirit is not conferred solely upon a particular hierarchical order, but is a gift to the whole people of God: "They were all filled with the Holy Spirit" (Acts 2:4). It is helpful to recall the distinction, emphasized by Vladimir Lossky, between the two givings of the Spirit. The first occurs on Easter Sunday, when Jesus—risen but not yet ascended—breathes upon the disciples and says to them: "Receive the Holy Spirit. If you forgive the sins of any, they are forgiven; if you retain the sins of any, they are retained" (John 20:22-23). At this moment the apostles represent the hierarchy of the church: the gift of the Spirit is specifically linked with the authority to bind and loose, and this particular power is not conferred upon the whole body of Christ, but is transmitted through the apostolic college to the episcopate. In the second giving of the Spirit, recorded in Acts 2ff., on the other hand, the apostles no longer represent the hierarchy, but rather they constitute the entire body of the church as it then existed. The Spirit descends at Pentecost upon each and every member of the redeemed community, and this universality of the Pentecostal gift continues in the church throughout all the ages. Therefore we are all of us Spirit-bearers: "You have been anointed by the Holy One, and you all know" (1 John 2:20).[45]

From here he explains the diversity and the unity in the church. It is the Spirit who give both the gift of binding and loosing to the apostles and their successors but makes all one in the possession of the one great Easter gift of the Risen Lord. There is no distinction in the new life in the Trinity brought about through the Holy Spirit.

> The church is a mystery of unity in diversity and of diversity in unity. In the church a multitude of persons are united in one, and yet each of them preserves his/her personal integrity unimpaired. In any association on the purely human level there will always exist a tension between individual liberty and the demands of corporate solidarity. Only within the church, and through the gift of the Spirit, is the conflict between these two things

---

[45] Limouris, "The Church as Mystery and Sign in Relation to the Holy Trinity—In Ecclesiological Perspectives," 29.

resolved. In the kingdom of the Holy Spirit there is neither totalitarianism nor individualism, neither dictatorship nor anarchy, but harmony and unanimity.[46]

The community knows that part of the future hope is already realized in its midst. But it knows equally well that another part still remains in the future. It does experience, at least dimly or as a foretaste, the justice, peace, and joy of the kingdom in the power of the Holy Spirit (Rom 14:17).

The experience of those who allow the power of the Risen Christ into their lives has been described in many ways. The Spirit of Jesus, the Risen One, has given them a new way of life: "We were all as good as slaves . . . but freedom is what we have, for Christ has set us free" (Gal 4:3; 5:1). Now they are called to a new life in community where there is no longer a "difference between men and women, Gentile and Jew, rich and poor" (Gal 3:28). "We have moved from death to life because we love our brothers and sisters" (1 Jn 3:14). Christ has already drawn his community through the Spirit into this new union with the Father and one another. An absolutely new intimacy is now offered that we cannot verbalize but to which the Spirit gives expression: "We do not know how to pray, but the Spirit witnesses with our spirit that we are God's children since he cries in us 'Abba! Father!'" (Gal 4:6; see Rom 8:15).

Call to Mission

The possession of the eschatological Spirit forbids withdrawal from the world. Those who have the first fruits of the Spirit did not receive them for their own selfish needs. Like Jesus filled with the power of the Holy Spirit after his baptism, so the disciples after their baptism with the Holy Spirit at Pentecost are to go out to proclaim and witness to the kingdom. Their task is to continue Jesus' own mission in the power of the Spirit, whom they received from him. The Spirit empowered them for mission after Easter. In the words of Edward Schweizer: "The new creation of man and woman by the Spirit is not a flight of faith into heaven or an abandonment of this imperfect world. On the contrary, the new creation means beginning to see the world as it is, suffering with it and taking its suffering to heart. The work of the Spirit is to make us aware of our solidarity with the world."[47]

The true sign of whether the church is open to the Spirit of the Risen Lord present in its midst is its willingness to engage in creating that ultimate community where there will be no more division. Here the ultimate goal of God's intentionality with creation will come to completion, union and communion with the Triune God and with one another in the eternal banquet: "I will be their God and they shall be my people for ever and ever" (Rv 21:3). The true mission of the church is now clearly revealed. The power of the Spirit that was operative

---

[46] Ibid.

[47] Edward Schweizer, *The Holy Spirit* (Philadelphia: Fortress Press, 1980), 109-110.

in Jesus when he walked this earth and through whom he made the kingdom present in word and action is now bestowed on the church. It must now continue to do what Jesus did: bring all people into contact with the kingdom.

In the light of the Spirit the church comes to see that creation is one. It is the possession of the Holy Spirit that leads it into solidarity with the whole of creation in its destiny and its hope. This is well expressed by Dietrich Bonhoeffer: "The hour when the church today prays for the coming of God's kingdom drives it for better or for worse into the company of the earthlings and worldlings, into a contract to be faithful to the earth, to its distress, its hunger, and its dying."[48] The notion of the church as a creation of the Holy Spirit was further developed in the theology after the council due particularly to the Charismatic Renewal movement. Some theologians, in search of a deeper appreciation of the Holy Spirit in relation to the church, advanced this thesis: The church *is a sacrament of the Holy Spirit*. That would mean that as the "already" of the "not yet," the church signifies the new creation, the world to come, which is the work of the Holy Spirit.[49]

Its mission is to release the end-time Spirit, who is operative in it as the future of the world, with the intention of leading creation into its final destiny. This aspect brings out the universality of its mission: to lead the world into the *new* creation, to discover where the Spirit is at work in the world, and to be open to the signs of the times. Boff has put very heavy stress on this aspect. By delineating the way in which the church came into existence after the Easter event, Boff relies on the Pauline view that the Risen Lord is now represented through the Spirit (2 Cor 3:17), who creates the church and makes Christ constantly present. This view opens us to the fact that the Spirit, and that means ultimately the Risen Lord, is not bound to the church alone; the Spirit moves where it wills.[50]

Church as "Charismatic Entity"

The church, perceived as a creation of the Holy Spirit, opens a new way of conceiving itself as a charismatic community in which every member has a function to fulfill. Each member has received a charism for building up the whole community (Rom 12; 1 Cor 12). Not only is there a hierarchical structure in the church, but equally basic is the charismatic structure that calls every member to participate actively in the mission of the church. The well-being of the eschatological community depends on the exercise of these charisms. These gifts are given directly to the individual by the Spirit. Office and charisma are the two sides of the church's structure. The pneumatological image of the church brings into focus the charismatic element while a too strongly stressed

[48] Dietrich Bonhoeffer, *Gesammelte Schriften*, vol. 3 (München: Kaiser Verlag, 1958), 274.

[49] Walter Kasper and Gerhard Sauter, *Kirche Ort des Geistes* (Freiburg: Herder, 1976), particularly Part One, "Kirche als Sakrament des Geistes," by Walter Kasper, 13-55.

[50] Boff, *Church, Charism, and Power*, 144-153.

christological understanding will put the stress on the office at the expense of the charisms. To neglect one of these two distinct but essential aspects of the church will only lead to distortions. This can be seen in scripture, where we find different concepts of church organization. The church in Corinth is often seen as a pattern of a purely conceived charismatic church and then exalted as a model to be followed. However, we should not overlook that this model of church as it is presented in the letters of St. Paul had its difficulties and did not survive because it was basically conceived against the background of an imminent coming of the Lord. As James D. G. Dunn sees it:

> The Pauline concept of church differs from the discipleship of Jesus' ministry in that it was a concept of charismatic community, characterized by mutual interdependence, where each member, though experiencing the Spirit for himself, must depend on his fellow members for a whole range of ministries. So too it differs from the pattern which evolved at Jerusalem in that it was essentially a concept of charismatic community, of free fellowship, developing through the living interplay of spiritual gifts and ministries, without benefit of official authority or responsible elders. . . . Secondly, within Paul's eschatological perspective—looking for the imminent coming again of Christ (1 Thess. 4:13-18; 1 Cor. 7:29-31), and seeing the apostles as the last act on stage before the final curtain (1 Cor. 4:9)—his churches did not require a structure that would endure. Charismatic community was a one-generation ideal—nor is it finally clear whether his vision actually worked for any length of time in any particular church.[51]

Neglect of the charismatic aspect in the church, however, in favor of the hierarchical has also shown its negative effect in the history of the church in all kinds of clericalism resulting in a static, lifeless conception of dogmatic truth, a reliance on power mechanisms, and a depreciation of the laity. Dunn's comment on the importance of the charism community for today may suffice:

> On the other hand, Paul's concentration on the building up of the church was fully appropriate in that evangelistic situation, and underlines the importance of a spiritually sensitive, supportive community for new converts. Perhaps we need to revive the one-generation perspective lest we bestow on our successors the sort of entrenched structures and traditions which have proved so inhibiting for the present generation.[52]

Church—Icon of the Trinity

If we look back at the council after thirty-five years, the leitmotif for its idea of the church seems best described with the word *communio*, although this might

---

[51] Dunn, *The Christ and the Spirit,* 2:252.
[52] Ibid.

not have been recognized immediately. Medard Kehl defines the self-understanding of the Catholic Church as it emerged in Vatican II as "sacrament of communion with God." It is the communion of the faithful united by the Holy Spirit, joined to Christ, and called together with the whole of creation into the kingdom of God the Father. The church is viewed as sacramentally expressing here and now the mystery of the communion of the Trinity.[53] As Walter Kasper says:

> The mystery of the church consists in the access we have to the Father in the Holy Spirit through Jesus Christ, so that we may share in God's divine nature. This communion of the church is made possible and sustained through the Trinitarian communion of Father, Son and Holy Spirit. Finally, the church as communion, as Vatican II said following up what the martyr bishop Cyprian said, is participation in the Trinitarian communio itself. The church is in the same way the icon of the community of Father, Son and Holy Spirit.[54]

This view of the church as an icon or image of the Trinitarian Community—although not new—could only be appreciated once again because of the development of the pneumatical dimension of the church.

Hans Küng calls these three images—people of God, body of Christ, and temple of the Holy Spirit—"the fundamental structure" of the church.[55] As such, they will remain forever a reference point for any accurate and correct understanding of that entity we call the church. Theologically they express the essence of the church and its true nature. We cannot dispense with them. They reveal the real mystery of the church: the Holy Trinity. This Trinitarian and pneumatic view of the church runs, thanks to the Eastern churches, through all sixteen documents of the council.

In choosing as the fundamental structure of the church the biblical images people of God, body of Christ, and temple of the Holy Spirit, the communion ecclesiology of the council emerged almost as a logical consequence. Particularly by taking the image people of God as the central metaphor for the church, the Second Vatican Council gave Catholic Christians a new root metaphor. This meant a change from a self-understanding as an institution to an understanding of being the people of God. This shift in metaphor has significant consequences in how the church sees itself and understands its very essence and mission.[56] The church is first the people of God. That means an entity that exists prior to all structuring and prior also to the call of individual members. With this conception of church the council did away with any pyramidal system and restored

---

[53] Kehl, *Die Kirche*, 51-52.
[54] Walter Kasper, "The Church as Communio," *New Blackfriars* 74 (1993), 235.
[55] Hans Küng, *The Church* (New York: Sheed and Ward, 1967), 107-260.
[56] Bernard J. Lee and Michael A. Cowan, *Dangerous Memories: House Churches and Our American Story* (Kansas City, Missouri: Sheed and Ward, 1986), 4-9.

the fundamental equality of all members in the Christian community. "There is no longer Jew nor Greek, nor male nor female but all are one in Jesus Christ" (Gal 3:28). The differentiation that emerges in the structuring of this people is secondary and cannot touch the primary rights.

Among the scriptural images of the church, the images of the people of God and the body of Christ, accompanied by the imagery of temple or house of the Spirit, are particularly important since they refer most directly to the Trinitarian dimension of the church. We must note, however, that none of these images is exclusive; all of them implicitly or explicitly include the other Trinitarian dimensions as well.[57] These three images have been chosen because of their central importance in the New Testament and because of their significance for the Trinitarian dimension of the church. The council saw the fundamental structure of the church most adequately expressed in them. Each of them aims at community and presupposes it.

We should not forget, however, that there are other images of the church in the New Testament, most of them christological, such as vine, flock, wedding party, and bride. They all serve to highlight certain aspects of the church's being and life. The vine image stresses total dependence on Christ, the flock image stresses trust and obedience, the party image stresses the eschatological reality of the church, and the bride image stresses the intimate though subordinate relation of the church to Christ. At the same time these images have their limits. The vine image does not take into account the interpersonal relationship between Christ and the church; the flock image does not take into account the freedom of the believers; the party image does not take into account the not-yet-fulfilled dimension of the church's life *in via*; and the bride image presupposes the subordinate status of women in ancient times.[58]

Unfortunately, the three fundamental images the council employed did not find among the faithful the echo that had been hoped for. The main reason for this seems to be the diverse situations and surroundings in which people must live their faith today. Their faith experience does not correspond with the modes of faith expressions that the church offered in these images.[59] This is most likely due to the fact that the unreflected, unspoken interpretation these images received in the past continues to dominate their application in the current life of the church.

These images contain lofty language but, if correctly understood and explained from their original meaning, they reflect a church perfectly focused on the Spirit of Christ. Ironically, these images led often to the exact opposite of what they wanted to symbolize as a vision for the church, whether the image of people of God, body of Christ, or temple of the Holy Spirit. They frequently led to a triumphalistic and utterly clerical conception of church in contrast to what

---

[57] *The Nature and Purpose of the Church*, 16.

[58] Ibid., 25.

[59] Avery Dulles, *A Church to Believe In: Discipleship and the Dynamics of Freedom* (New York: Crossroad, 1982), 1-4.

they were meant to express, namely, service and equality of all, based on the life principle of Jesus summarized in the words of Mark 10:41-45, "I did not come to be served but to serve and to lay down my life for the many," or of John 10:10, "I came that they may have life and have it in abundance."

The vision that the council wanted to express through these biblical images for a renewal of the church remains valid and viable today. In spite of all the disappointments voiced and experienced concerning the church over the last thirty-five years, when looking back at the council and reflecting on the sixteen documents it produced one can still sense the grandiose vision it wanted to put forth concerning the church for our time. The *community ecclesiology* of the council, in particular, emerged ever more clearly as time passed. It contains a power that will not fade away very soon. The images expressed in *Lumen Gentium* as the fundamental structure of the church carry a dynamism that will keep on creating great hopes—helping the church not to forget its very essence as an icon of the Trinity or its mission to continue its founder's basic message to bring the kingdom, the great vision of God for all of creation, to the ends of the whole world until the final fulfillment occurs.

3

The Meaning of "Church"
in the Teaching of Vatican II

As indicated in the previous chapter, Vatican II did not give us a definition of church; in fact, the term *church* has a number of different meanings in the conciliar documents. Gregory Baum has pointed out at least six different descriptions of the church in the documents.[1]

CHURCH AS *CATHOLIC CHURCH*

The church is equated with the Catholic Church as defined in the traditional teaching of the church as possessing (1) the same faith, (2) sevenfold sacramental liturgy, and (3) legitimate pastors with the pope as supreme authority. The argumentation for the equation of church with the Catholic Church starts with the definition of the church in *Lumen Gentium (LG)* as the "universal sacrament of salvation" (*LG*, no. 48). The Church of Christ and the Catholic Church are not two realities but one. The analogy is made between the incarnation and the church: "Just as the eternal Son of God assumed only one individual body for the ransom of humanity, so the Spirit of Christ through 'the social structure' of the Catholic Church *(socialis compago)* is the organ of salvation for the world. Thus the Church develops a special pneumatic 'life of its own in all the forms which are proper to it as a social structure in the Spirit.'"[2] Those holding this view deduce from this that the ecclesial elements and the means of salvation which are present in the separated churches and communities are present to the extent of their union with the Catholic Church. Separated churches and

---

[1] Gregory Baum,"The Meaning of Church," in *The Credibility of the Church Today* (New York: Herder and Herder, 1968), 20-28.
[2] Alois Grillmeier, "Dogmatic Constitution on the Church, Chapter I, The Mystery of the Church," in *Commentary on the Documents Vatican II,* ed. Heribert Vorgrimler (New York: Herder and Herder, 1967), 1:149.

communities function as means of salvation because elements of the Catholic Church subsist in them. This means that they draw their efficacy from the fullness of grace and truth found in the Catholic Church.[3]

CHURCH AS *LOCAL CONGREGATION*

The council generally adopted a universal perspective when it was talking about the church. At the same time it asserted quite strongly that it is only in and out of the particular churches that the one and single catholic church exists (*LG*, no. 23). This has been called by some theologians "the most important ecclesiological formula of the council."

> It guarantees, or should guarantee, that the relationship between the whole church and the individual churches is seen as one of reciprocal or mutual inclusion, that individual churches are not considered administrative subdivisions of a pre-existent reality, and that the one church is not a federation of individual churches. The many churches are not churches except in the one Church; the one Church does not exist except in and out of the many churches. Since the council, these carefully nuanced and mutually conditioning statements have prompted what some called a *Copernican revolution* in ecclesiology and have engendered a renewed interest in the local churches, whose communion is the whole church.
>
> The council's teaching is finely balanced: The church is not *catholic* if it is not particular, that is, *local*; but the particular or local is not the church unless it is *catholic* at every level, that is, redemptively integrated.[4]

This has been called one of the great achievements of Vatican II. Through the celebration of the word and the eucharistic meal Christ is present in the worshiping community and the power of the Holy Spirit transforms it into his body (*LG*, no. 26). This idea of local congregation or church in action is of great importance, particularly for basic ecclesial communities. The Faith and Order Commission expresses it this way:

> The Communion of the Church is expressed in the communion between local churches in each of which the fullness of the Church resides. The communion of the Church embraces local churches in each place and all

---

[3] For an in-depth treatment and a critical evaluation of this aspect, see J. Francis Stafford, "The Inscrutable Riches of Christ: The Catholic Church's Mission of Salvation," in *A Church for All People*, ed. Eugene LaVerdiere (Collegeville, Minnesota: The Liturgical Press, 1993), 35-44.

[4] Joseph Komonchak, "Ecclesiology of Vatican II," *Origin* 28 (1999), 765.

places at all time. Local churches are held in the communion of the Church by the one Gospel, the one baptism and the Holy Communion, served by common ministry. The communion is expressed in service and witness to the world.[5]

CHURCH AS *COMMUNITY OF THE BAPTIZED*

The council stated that baptism, properly celebrated, incorporates believers into Christ (*Unitatis Redintegratio,* nos. 3, 22; *LG*, nos. 14, 15). There exists a Spirit-created sacramental communion between Catholics and other Christians, even if one dimension of communion is incomplete. The council acknowledged that other Christian churches are communities in which Christ is present and that they are instruments of the Spirit in saving and sanctifying people.

There are two basic reasons why the church cannot just be identified with the Roman Catholic Church alone. First, the reality of communion exceeds the boundaries of the Catholic Church. There are baptized non-Catholics who, by their faith, hope and love, live the life of communion with Christ and the Spirit; and there are Roman Catholics who do not live in the Spirit.

Second, if we consider the elements, spiritual, sacramental, and ministerial, that constitute and animate the church, we can discover these elements in various degrees also in other Christian churches and communities where they can mediate salvation as well.

Correspondingly, the council nuanced the claim that the Roman Catholic Church is the true church of Christ and asserted that the church of Christ *subsists in* (rather than simply *is*) the Roman Catholic Church. By accepting such elements as justifying grace, incorporation into Christ, communion with the Holy Spirit, holy scripture, sacraments, devotion to Mary, and so on, the council found the phrase the "true Church subsists" more appropriate, since these elements can also be found to some extent in the other churches.

The controversy concerning the phrase "the true Church of Christ . . . 'subsists in' the Catholic Church" (*LG*, no. 8) is widely known.[6] The issue has recently been raised once again in the Vatican document *Dominus Iesus* concerning the question whether Catholic communities can be called churches in the proper sense. The document, referring to Vatican II, objects to the phrase commonly used today when referring to the non-Catholic churches as "sister churches." In the view of the document such use would confuse the issue and make the Catholic Church just one among others.

---

[5] *The Nature and Purpose of the Church,* Faith and Order paper no. 181 (Bialystock, Poland: Ortdruck Orthodox Printing House, 1998), 66.

[6] Stafford, "The Inscrutable Riches of Christ," 38-39. Stafford deals in detail with the explanation given by Francis Sullivan, which he strongly opposes.

Those who maintain the equation between church of Christ and Catholic Church argue that those ecclesial elements found in these churches are elements of the Catholic Church that subsist in these non-Catholic churches and communities.[7] George H. Tavard seems to come closest to the real meaning of this phrase when he writes:

> "Subsistence in" implies that the Church, which is the body of Christ in mystery, now lives in a hidden state. It is invisible to the eyes of the flesh, and therefore its existence and nature as the Church are empirically unverifiable. Yet being constituted and organized as a society, it also is an organic body, the members of which relate to one another according to some effective norms. By confessing that this Church subsists in the Roman Catholic institution, the council indicates that it knows where the Church is. Yet it also teaches that the Church of Christ is invisible, lying where it is in a hidden state that may not be recognizable to all Christian believers. And the council says nothing for or against the possibility of its also invisibly subsisting in other ecclesial institutions and other visible churches. Logic would seem to make this contention acceptable in the problematic of Vatican II.[8]

CHURCH REFERS TO THE *PEOPLE OF ISRAEL*

The council realized that the roots of the church lie in the past. It is in continuity with the people of the old covenant. By tracing back the beginnings of God's calling of humankind to a covenant people, the council sees the entire "Abrahamic community" as church, which is the "community of the called," beginning with Abraham and stretching through history as a whole. This view sees the Jewish people once again as belonging to the church in a broader sense.[9]

THE CHURCH *FROM ABEL ON*

The council envisioned God's searching for humankind right from the beginning of history. The words "universal church" refer to the entire family of the human race inasmuch as it is touched and transformed by God's saving grace. Gregory Baum sees here the church as the community of all persons, extending as far as the human race extends.

---

[7] Ibid., 38-45.

[8] George H. Tavard, *The Church, Community of Salvation: An Ecumenical Ecclesiology* (Collegeville, Minnesota: The Liturgical Press, 1992), 86.

[9] Gerhard Lohfink, *Does God Need the Church?* (Collegeville, Minnesota: The Liturgical Press, 1999), 51-106.

However, he maintains that the grace of God, which is operative in the whole of humanity, is dependent on Jesus Christ, the one mediator between God and each human being and hence also related to the church, which is his body. In effect, by designating the entire family of the human race as church universal, he is saying, in scholastic terminology, that the whole of human history is supernatural.

Among the better known, though also more controversial, theological explanations of this line of thought is Karl Rahner's theory of "anonymous Christianity." Here, as elsewhere, the starting point for Rahner is his theology of grace. Convinced of the universality of God's salvific will, the necessity of grace for salvation, and the universal mediation of salvation by Jesus Christ, Rahner argued in numerous works that God's free self-gift in grace tends of its own nature toward visible manifestation in Christ and the church. As a kind of sacrament, the church is the visible sign and instrument of the grace that is offered to all human beings. In order to express simultaneously both the possibility of salvation outside the church and the objective Christian ecclesial character of salvation, Rahner proposed that those non-Christians whose lives (unknown to them) constitute a positive response to God's free self-gift in grace may appropriately be termed anonymous Christians. Ultimately identifiable only by God, they are *Christians* (in a certain sense of the word) because the grace they have received and accepted is in fact intrinsically linked to Christ; they are *anonymous* Christians because this dimension of their own real situation remains unrecognized (and perhaps unrecognizable) by them.[10]

The following question, however, has to be asked: Is it permissible to extend the concept church to such an extent that it actually includes everybody? For Baum, the axiom "outside the church, no salvation" does not cause any problem, because the church is to be identified with the whole of the human race.

Hans Küng, in various writings, has opposed this use of the word *church*. His basic thesis is that he stands against any extraordinary way of salvation. Rightly understood, the ordinary way of salvation for non-Christians exists in following their own religious traditions. The concept Church should be applied to the Christian churches only and not to non-Christian communities because (1) it is contrary to the evidence of the New Testament and the tradition based on it; (2) the extension of the notion of church is not necessary to account for the salvation of non-Christians; (3) the broad notion of the church renders missionary work unnecessarily difficult, for it presumes that people of goodwill really belong to the church; and (4) it offends nonbelievers to be told that they are Christians at least in implicit desire; they reject such theological speculations.

Rahner's theory of anonymous Christianity is intended neither as a comprehensive Christian interpretation of other religions nor as vocabulary that

---

[10] John P. Galvin, "Salvation outside the Church," in *The Gift of the Church: A Textbook on Ecclesiology in Honor of Patrick Granfield, OSB*, ed. Peter Phan (Collegeville, Minnesota: The Liturgical Press, 2000), 250.

non-Christians themselves should be encouraged to adopt. Its purpose is rather to express in a brief formulation some consequences of Christian understanding of the multidimensional divine offer of salvation. From a pastoral perspective, it seeks in part to prevent the church from succumbing to a sect-like mentality in assessing its position in the world.

The teaching of Vatican II, which is clearly influenced by the council's understanding of the church as the "universal sacrament of salvation" (*LG*, no. 48) or "instrumental sign of intimate union with God and of the unity of all humanity" (*LG*, no. 1), is thus marked by a high degree of optimism with regard to salvation. In view of earlier history it is not surprising that Karl Rahner, in a lecture first delivered in 1971, called this optimism regarding salvation "one of the most noteworthy results of the Second Vatican Council" and suggested that the council's assertions on this subject "marked a far more decisive phase in the development of the Church's conscious awareness of her faith" than other important doctrinal developments at the council.[11]

THE *HOUSE CHURCH*

The community of father, mother, and children is called church. In recent years in particular the theology of marriage has come to discover the ecclesial dimension of marriage (*LG*, no. 11). As Paul VI put it: "The family is a place where hospitality is experienced, the paschal mystery is fulfilled and evangelization occurs. The family is church by its mission and its special aptitude for transmitting the gospel."[12]

There are four elements that we might mention here which constitute a family as church:

- *Christ's presence:* The sacrament of marriage guarantees Christ's presence in the family, since this sacrament "contains and radiates" the mystery of Christ's union with the church. Where Christ is, there is the church.
- *Evangelization:* A healthy experience of family life is the best preparation for grasping and accepting God's message of salvation. God's self-disclosure to humankind is most intimately described in the Bible through images that are taken from family life: spouse, mother, father, bride, and so on.
- *Prayer:* Vatican II encourages the family to become a "sanctuary of the church by its common prayer." Family prayer, scriptural reading, and so forth should lead the whole family to a better participation in the church's liturgy.

---

[11] Karl Rahner, "Observations on the Problem of the 'Anonymous Christian,'" *Theological Investigations*, vol. 14 (New York: Seabury Press, 1976), 284.

[12] Paul VI, "Allocution aux 'Equipes Notre-Dame,'" in *Documentation catholique* (1970), no. 1564, 504; see also *Evangelii Nuntiandi*, nos. 70-71.

- *Experience of love:* The family is the place where children experience love in all its aspects: they see love as fidelity and affection; they come to know its freeing aspect and its power to grow and to open up to others; and finally, they are led to discover God's love as the ultimate source of all human love and freedom.[13]

---

[13] See N. Provencher, "The Family as Domestic Church," *Theology Digest* 30 (1982), 149-152.

4

The Church in the Context
of the Kingdom

THE CHURCH IN RELATION TO THE WORLD
AND TO GOD'S PLAN OF SALVATION

What is the relationship among church, world, and God's universal plan of salvation? Whenever the church in its history was closely identified with the kingdom now present in history, the church's relationship with the world was portrayed accordingly. The world was the object that the church had to act upon or influence. The church was the active subject. Such deliberations always focused on the internal reality of the church and affirmed its self-sufficiency in relation to the world. The question asked was simply: How can the world be used to build up the church?

Since Vatican II the question has been reversed. Now people ask: What can the church do to make the world a better place in which to live? Theologically this is based on the insight that the kingdom of God is meant for the world and that the church must see itself and its mission in the service of the kingdom. For the kingdom is not only the future of the church but also the future of the world as well. In God's plan of salvation we cannot separate the church from the world. As Yves Congar points out:

> In God's unitary design the Church and the world are both ordered to this Kingdom in the end, but by different ways and on different accounts. Church and world have the same end, but only the same ultimate end. That they should have the same end is due to God's unitary plan and the fact that the whole cosmos is united with man in a shared destiny. That they should have only the same ultimate end prevents a confusion that

---

I have presented the content of this chapter in almost identical terms in *The Kingdom of God* (Maryknoll, New York: Orbis Books, 1995), 248-272, and in *Throw Fire* (Manila: Logos Publication, 1998), 287-314.

would be bad for the Church, as raising a risk of dissolving her own proper mission in that of history, and bad for the world, as raising the risk of misunderstanding and hindering its own proper development.[1]

The *Pastoral Constitution on the Church in the Modern World (Gaudium et Spes)* presents this new understanding of the relationship between the church and the world in this way. After recognizing the world's legitimate autonomy, the council asserts that the church must consider itself part of the total human family, sharing the same concerns as the rest of humankind. Articles 3 and 92 state that just as Christ came into the world not to be served but to serve, so the church, carrying on the mission of Christ, seeks to serve the world by fostering unity among all people.

The advantage of such a view of the church in its relationship to the world lies in three points: First, it helps the church to turn away from an exaggerated concern about its own internal affairs and to look at the world for which the kingdom is meant. The important thing for the church is not to withdraw into itself and reduce itself to a small group that keeps its distance from the world. Rather, it must take part in constructive action and liberation. Second, viewed in this way, the church can give hope to a world stricken by war, injustice, and hatred by pointing constantly to the coming kingdom as meant for the whole world and as having appeared already in Jesus Christ. The church gives meaning to the small services everyone can do for a better world, a world of justice, peace, and unity. Every good work done in this world means building up the kingdom that is coming. Third, this view underlines the principle that *diakonia* (service), which includes the struggle for a new social order, is as essential to and even constitutive of the mission of the church as are proclamation and sacramental celebration.

The kingdom demands the transformation of all human reality, and the church must be an "agent" of this transformation. The council starts off by describing the church as the mystery of Christ. In it is realized the "eternal plan of the Father, manifested in Jesus Christ, to bring humanity to its eternal glory." Here the church is seen in connection with the "bringing about of the secret hidden for ages in God" (1 Col 1:16; see Eph 3:3-9; 1 Cor 2:6-10). Therefore, the church has to be seen in this broad perspective of God's plan of salvation, which includes all human beings and creation as a whole (see 1 Tm 2:4; Rom 8:22 ff.). The most comprehensive symbol for God's plan with creation is the biblical phrase *kingdom of God.*

The kingdom aims at the transformation of the whole of creation into its eternal glory, and the church must be seen and understood in the context of this divine intentionality. Its essence and mission make sense only in this setting. Her mission is to reveal through the ages the hidden plan of God to lead all humankind toward its final destiny. The church must see itself entirely in the

---

[1] Yves Congar, *Lay People in the Church* (London: Bloomsbury Publishing Co. Ltd., 1957), 88.

service of this divine plan meant for the salvation of all creation.[2] The church has no monopoly on the kingdom of God. Citizenship in the kingdom never means a privilege but rather an ongoing summons to solidarity with people, particularly with the excluded and discriminated against.[3] One of the chief temptations for the church in history is to claim the kingdom for itself, to take over the management of the kingdom, and even to go so far as to present itself as the realized kingdom of God vis-à-vis the world. The kingdom of God is not the kingdom of the Christians.

God has inaugurated the kingdom in the world and in history in two stages. First, the kingdom was initiated through the earthly life of Jesus, his words and works, and fully inaugurated through the Paschal Mystery of his death and resurrection. This kingdom, present in history, must now grow through history to reach its eschatological fullness at the end of time. The council clearly accepted this distinction between the kingdom present in history now and the eschatological fullness still to come in *Lumen Gentium* (see *LG*, nos. 5, 9). But the question not clearly answered is whether the council also made a clear distinction between the kingdom present in history now and the pilgrim church.

THE CHURCH AS NOT IDENTICAL WITH THE KINGDOM

There are, therefore, two questions to be answered. First, did the council identify the kingdom of God in history with the pilgrim church? Or did it consider the kingdom of God in history a reality that is broader than the church and extends beyond its boundaries? Second, is the kingdom of God in its final fulfillment identical with the church in its eschatological fullness? Or does the kingdom extend beyond the church while it simultaneously embraces it?

Arguments for an Identity of the Church with the Kingdom in History

A number of theologians still hold that a close analysis of the relevant texts of *Lumen Gentium* (nos. 3, 5, 9, 48) would show that in Vatican II the kingdom of God remained identical with the church, whether with the historical reality of the kingdom now or with the eschatological fulfillment where it will find its fulfillment as well.[4]

This view was taken up and restated in the final document of the International Theological Commission in 1985. Once again the distinction between the pilgrim church in history and the heavenly church in its eschatological fullness

---

[2] Wolfhart Pannenberg, *Theology and the Kingdom of God* (Philadelphia: Westminster Press, 1977), 72-75.

[3] Jan Milic Lochman, "Church and World in the Light of the Kingdom of God," in *Church—Kingdom—World: The Church as Mystery and Prophetic Sign*, Faith and Order paper no. 130, ed. Gennadios Limouris (Geneva: World Council of Churches, 1986).

[4] Jacques Dupuis, "Evangelization and Kingdom Values: The Church and the 'Others,'" *Indian Missiological Review* 14 (1992), 4-21.

is made, but the document continues to identify, on the one hand, the kingdom of God in history with the pilgrim church, and, on the other hand, the eschatological fullness of the kingdom with the heavenly church. Regarding the fullness of the kingdom to come the document says: "It is clear that in the Council's teaching there is no difference so far as the eschatological reality is concerned between the final realization of the Church (as *consummata*) and of the Kingdom (as *consummatum*)."[5]

The reasoning for an identification of the kingdom in history with the pilgrim church follows from this argument: If the glorious kingdom to come coincides with the church in fullness at the end, it is obvious that the kingdom here on earth in its preliminary state coincides with the pilgrim church as well. Since kingdom and church will be identical in the final state, one must presume that they are also now identical in their preliminary historical state. This means, positively expressed, that the kingdom in history now is identical with the pilgrim church. However, the commission does adopt the theological phrase "the church, sacrament of the kingdom," although the council did not use this expression. The phrase is seen as valid from the following perspective: (1) in its ecclesiological application, the term *sacrament* is used analogically, as the first paragraph of *Lumen Gentium* stresses: "Veluti sacramentum . . . "; (2) the expression's aim is to relate, on the one hand, the kingdom, understood in the plenary sense of its final realization, with, on the other hand, the church and its "wayfaring" aspect; (3) the term *sacrament* here is understood in its full sense of *iam praesens in mysterio* (cf. *LG*, no. 3) ("already present in mystery"), where the reality present in the sacrament (the pilgrim church) is the kingdom itself; (4) the church is not a mere sign *(sacramentum tantum)* but a sign in which the reality signified *(res et sacramentum)* is present as the reality of the kingdom; and (5) the notion of the church cannot be limited to its temporal and earthly aspect alone. Conversely, the notion of the kingdom includes a present "already" *in mysterio.*[6] While this language is very precise and does not claim an absolute identification of kingdom and church, it seems to imply it. Dupuis concludes his investigation by saying: "It would seem that one must conclude that in keeping to the teaching of *Lumen Gentium,* the theological commission, while distinguishing clearly between history and eschatology, affirms that at both levels kingdom and church coincide."[7]

The same identification between church and kingdom of God, both in history and eschatology, is maintained in the *Catechism of the Catholic Church* (nos. 865, 541, 670-71, 768-69): "The Church is ultimately *one, holy, and apostolic* in her deepest and ultimate identity, because it is in her that 'the kingdom of Heaven,' the 'Reign of God,' already exists and will be fulfilled at the end of time" (no. 865).

---

[5] International Theological Commission: Text and Document 1969-85, ed. M. Sharky (San Francisco: Ignatius Press, 1989), 302.

[6] Ibid., 303-304.

[7] Jacques Dupuis, *Toward a Christian Theology of Religious Pluralism* (Maryknoll, New York: Orbis Books, 1997), 338.

Arguments against an Identity of the Church with the Kingdom in History

A number of theologians, contrary to the commission's view, see the documents of Vatican II as making a clear distinction between the church and the historical reality of the kingdom of God now. They even regard this distinction as one of the major achievements of Vatican II. The theological basis for doing so is seen in the council's definition of the church as a "sign *(sacrament)* of the kingdom" *(LG*, no. 9). Since God's saving grace can never be bound exclusively to a sacrament, one has to accept that the kingdom is still broader than the church. Richard P. McBrien comments:

> The nature and mission of the Church are always to be understood in relationship and in subordination to the kingdom of God. This principle is expressed in article 5 of *Lumen Gentium* and again in article 45 of *Gaudium and Spes*. It replaces what was perhaps the most serious pre–Vatican II ecclesiological misunderstanding, namely, that the Church is identical with the kingdom of God here on earth. If it is, then it is beyond all need for institutional reform, and its mission is to bring everyone inside lest salvation elude them.[8]

Rudolf Schnackenburg affirms McBrien's view regarding the ecclesiological misunderstanding that resulted from the identification of the kingdom now present in history with the church when he writes:

> Let us ask ourselves here immediately about the relationship between the church and the kingdom or the Lordship of Christ. Is the church the kingdom of God on the earth, admittedly in a provisional form, until the kingdom is fulfilled eschatologically? This view, long held within Catholic theology even though with various nuances, leads to a dangerous image of the church, to a triumphalistic understanding of the earthly Church, and is definitely to be rejected. True, in the New Testament the church is seen in strict relation with the Lordship of Christ, for example in Colossians 1:12f.: "God has delivered us from the dominion of darkness and transferred us to the kingdom of the Son." We are only received into his kingdom. Christ exercises his Lordship of grace in the church by means of the Holy Spirit, but the church remains a community of human beings who are at the same time sinful and weak.[9]

Karl Rahner says something similar:

> The Church is not identified with the Kingdom of God. It is the sacrament of the Kingdom of God in the eschatological phase of sacred history which

---

[8] Richard P. McBrien, *Catholicism* (London: Geoffrey Chapman, 1981), 686.

[9] Rudolf Schnackenburg, "Signoria e regno di Dio nell'annuncio di Gesu e della Chiesa delle Origini," *Communio* 86 (1986), 41-42.

began with Christ, the phase which brings about the Kingdom of God. As long as history lasts, the Church will not be identical with the Kingdom of God, for the latter is only definitely present when history ends with the coming of Christ and the last judgment. Yet the Kingdom of God is not simply something due to come later, which later will replace the world, its history and the outcome of history. The Kingdom of God itself is coming to be in the history of the world (not only in that of the Church) whenever obedience to God occurs in grace as the acceptance of God's self-communication. . . . For [of] this Kingdom of God in the world, which of course can never simply be identified with any particular objective secular phenomenon, the Church is a part, because of course the Church itself is in the world and in its members makes world history. Above all, however, the Church is precisely its special fundamental sacrament, i.e., the eschatological and efficacious manifestation (sign) in redemptive history that in the unity, activity, fraternity, etc., of the world, the Kingdom of God is at hand. Even here, therefore, as in the various individual sacraments, sign and thing signified can never be separated or identified (cf. *LG* 9).[10]

Avery Dulles, however, who also seems to favor a distinction between the glorious kingdom of God and the church admits that

if one looks on both the kingdom and the Church as existing proleptically within history and definitively at the close of history, it becomes more difficult to see how they differ. With regard to the final phase it must be asked—is the consummation of the Church something different from the definitive arrival of the kingdom of God? *The Pastoral Constitution on the Church in the Modern World* makes the point in article 39 that "all the good fruits of our nature and enterprise produced on earth in the Spirit of the Lord and in accord with his command" will be found again, in a purified and transfigured form, in the final kingdom. This text seems to imply that the world itself, in all its secularity will be transformed in Christ. It then becomes very difficult to distinguish between the glorified Church and the transformed cosmos. Perhaps one should say that the heavenly Church, as the place where Christ rules in the assembly of the saints, will be at the heart of the center of the ultimate kingdom. The new heavens and the new earth, while they may include more than the transfigured Church, will serve to mediate and express the blessed life of the redeemed.[11]

While it is arguable whether Vatican II really made this distinction, some theologians hold that this distinction is clearly made only in *Redemptoris Missio*

---

[10] Karl Rahner, "World and Church," *Sacramentum Mundi*, 8 vols., ed. Karl Rahner et al. (New York: Seabury Press, 1975), 1:348.

[11] Avery Dulles, "The Church and the Kingdom," in *A Church for All People,* ed. Eugene LaVerdiere (Collegeville, Minnesota: The Liturgical Press, 1993), 17-18.

(RM) and in the Document *Dialogue and Proclamation (DP)*, a joint statement of the Council for Interreligious Dialogue and the Congregation for the Evangelization of People. Both documents acknowledge rather than confess that the kingdom of God is a broader reality than the church.

> *RM* and *DP* appear to be the first two documents of the recent central doctrinal authority to distinguish the pilgrim Church from the reality of the reign of God in history; both documents profess that the reign of God is a broader reality than the Church which is present and operative beyond her boundaries among the members of other religious traditions.[12]

The encyclical *Redemptoris Missio* as well as the document *Dialogue and Proclamation* acknowledge the working of the kingdom outside the church by seeing there the values of the kingdom of God concretely lived. "It is true that the inchoative reality of the kingdom can also be found beyond the confines of the church among people everywhere, to the extent that they live 'gospel values' and are open to the working of the Spirit who breathes when and where he will" *(RM,* no. 20). These values of the kingdom are spelled out as "peace, justice, freedom, brotherhood, etc." They are clearly seen as manifestations of the kingdom present right there where they occur in whatever religious tradition or secular situation *(RM,* no. 17).

The description of the kingdom given in *Redemptoris Missio* emphasizes the all-pervasive and all-embracing presence of God's saving grace brought through Jesus Christ. Such a description would not be possible if an identification between church and kingdom were presupposed.

> The kingdom is the concern of everyone: individual, society, and the world. Working for the kingdom means acknowledging and promoting God's activity, which is present in human history and transforms it. Building the kingdom means working for liberation from evil in all its forms. In a word, the kingdom of God is the manifestation and the realization of God's plan of salvation in all its fullness *(RM,* no. 15).

The most recent document of the magisterium, *Dominus Iesus (DI),* aligning itself with *Redemptoris Missio* and *Dialogue and Proclamation,* accepts the non-identification of the kingdom and the church in history quite clearly:

> To state the inseparable relationship between Christ and the kingdom is not to overlook the fact that the kingdom of God—even if considered in its historical phase—is not identified with the church in her visible and social reality. In fact, "the action of Christ and the Spirit outside the church's

---

[12] Jacques Dupuis, "A Theological Commentary: Dialogue and Proclamation," in *Redemption and Dialogue: Reading* Redemptoris Missio *and* Dialogue and Proclamation, ed. William R. Burrows (Maryknoll, New York: Orbis Books, 1994), 150.

visible boundaries" must not be excluded. Therefore, one must also bear in mind that "the kingdom is the concern of everyone: individuals, society and the world. Working for the kingdom means acknowledging and promoting God's activity, which is present in human history and transforms it. Building the kingdom means working for liberation from evil in all its forms. In a word, the kingdom of God is the manifestation and the realization of God's plan of salvation in all its fullness" (*DI*, no. 19).

There are similar documents produced by various bishops' conferences and theological congresses in Latin America, Asia, and Africa that have expressed the broader outreach of the kingdom explicitly and drawn from there far-reaching conclusions for their understanding of the church and its mission today. A more recent theological consultation organized by the Federation of Asian Bishops' Conference's Office for Evangelization was held at Hua Hin (Thailand) in November 1991. In its conclusions, entitled "Evangelization in Asia," it wrote:

> The Kingdom of God is therefore universally present and at work. Wherever men and women open themselves to the transcendent Divine Mystery which impinges upon them, and go out of themselves in love and service of fellow humans, there the Reign of God is at work. . . . "Where God is accepted, where the Gospel values are lived, where the human being is respected . . . there is the Kingdom." In all such cases people respond to God's offer of grace through Christ in the Spirit and enter into the Kingdom through an act of faith. . . . This goes to show that the Reign of God is a universal reality, extending far beyond the boundaries of the Church. It is the reality of salvation in Jesus Christ, in which Christians and others share together; it is the fundamental "mystery of unity" which unites us more deeply than differences in religious allegiance are able to keep us apart. Seen in this manner, a "Regnocentric" (Kingdom-centered) approach to mission theology does not in any way threaten the Christocentric perspective of our faith; on the contrary, "Regnocentrism" calls for Christocentrism, and vice versa, for it is in Jesus Christ and through the Christ-event that God has established his Kingdom upon the earth and in human history (cf. *RM*, nos. 17-18, 29, 30).[13]

Biblical Foundation for a Non-Identity

Dupuis sees the foundation for a non-identity of kingdom and church already present in Jesus' own behavior and actions during his public ministry. Jesus seems not to have identified the kingdom with the group of disciples but envisioned the

---

[13] Text in Federation of Asian Bishops' Conferences (FABC) papers, no. 64 (Hong Kong, 1992), 31; see also, *For All the People of Asia: Federation of Asian Bishops' Conferences Documents from 1970-1991*, ed. Gaudencio B. Rosales and C. G. Arevalo (Maryknoll, New York: Orbis Books, 1992), 341-42.

kingdom as being broader than the group that became the church after his resurrection. Jesus saw his mission limited to the "house of Israel." Yet there are instances in the gospel where Jesus overstepped the boundaries of Israel. Jesus made the kingdom present through his healings and exorcisms (see Mt 12:25-28; Lk 4:16-22). The gospel tells us that he healed those who did not belong to the people of Israel (see Mk 7:24-30; Mt 15:21-28). These miracles signify, therefore, that the kingdom is operative and present among the pagans as well. Thus Jesus did not identify the kingdom with the movement created by him and destined to become the church.[14]

In the letters of St. Paul the kingdom of God is seen present under a new form, that of the kingship of the Risen Christ in which it is realized. In Colossians 2:10 and Ephesians 1:10 the kingship of Christ extends not only to the church but to the entire world: Christ is the head of the world and of the church, but only the church is his body (Col 1:18; Eph 1:22; 4:15; 5:23). Church and world should be seen as concentric circles whose common center is Christ. The kingship of Christ as the presence of the kingdom in history extends to the whole world, visible and invisible.

> "Kingdom of Christ" is . . . a more comprehensive term than "Church." In the Christian's present existence on earth his share in Christ's Kingdom and his claim to the eschatological Kingdom . . . find their fulfillment in the Church, the domain in which grace of the heavenly Christ are operative. . . . But Christ's rule extends beyond the Church . . . and one day the Church will have completed her earthly task and will be absorbed in the eschatological Kingdom of Christ or of God.[15]

The Theological Fruits of Non-Identity

The acceptance of a clear distinction between church and kingdom has far-reaching consequences for theology, particularly for the church's relationship with the world and the other religious traditions. The symbol kingdom of God, being broader than the church, provides the horizon for a solution of two theological problems.

First, in the context of the church and her relationship to the world, it shows how the work for justice and liberation inside and outside the church is intrinsically linked with the kingdom present now, since the ultimate goal of the kingdom of God is the transformation of all reality.

Second, in interreligious dialogue the kingdom symbol furnishes the theologian with a broader perspective to enter into dialogue with other religious traditions. If the kingdom is the ultimate goal of God's intentionality with all of humanity, then the question is no longer how these other religious traditions are

---

[14] Dupuis, "Evangelization and Kingdom Values," 10.

[15] Rudolf Schnackenburg, *God's Rule and Kingdom* (New York: Herder and Herder, 1968), 301.

linked to the church but rather how the kingdom of God was and is concretely present in these religions. In the words of Jacques Dupuis:

> There follow important consequences for interreligious dialogue. Dialogue takes place between persons who already belong together to the Reign of God, inaugurated in history in Jesus Christ. In spite of their different religious allegiance, such persons are already in communion in the reality of the mystery of salvation, even if there remains between them a distinction at the level of the "sacrament," that is, the order of mediation of the mystery. Communion in the reality is, however, more fundamental and is of more consequence than the differences at the level of the sign. This explains the deep communion in the Spirit which interreligious dialogue, if it is sincere and authentic, can establish between Christians and other believers. . . . This shows also why interreligious dialogue is a form of sharing, both receiving and giving, in a word, that it is not a one-way process, not a monologue but a dialogue. The reason for this is that the reality of the Reign of God is already shared together in mutual exchange. Dialogue makes explicit this already existing communion in the reality of salvation, which is the Reign of God that has come for all in Jesus.[16]

Voiced Reservations to a Kingdom-Centered Church

While accepting the distinction between the church and the kingdom in principle, the authorities in the church have been very eager lately to assure that the two concepts are not to be pulled apart, whether in liberation theology or in interreligious dialogue. Having admitted the distinction, both *Redemptoris Missio* and *Dialogue and Proclamation* express concern that this view easily leads to two pitfalls. The kingdom-centered approach seems to stress the kingdom to such a degree that it leaves out the church almost entirely. Additionally, in so doing it forgets to bind the kingdom to Jesus Christ. These are clearly the worries the pope voices in *Redemptoris Missio*: "One may not separate the Kingdom from the Church. It is true that the Church is not an end unto herself, since she is ordered towards the Kingdom of God of which she is the seed, sign and instrument. Yet while remaining distinct from Christ and the Kingdom, the Church is indissolubly united with both" (*RM*, no. 18). The same concern is echoed in *Dialogue and Proclamation*: "The Kingdom is inseparable from the Church because both are inseparable from the person and work of Jesus himself. . . . It is therefore not possible to separate the Church from the Kingdom as if the first belonged exclusively to the imperfect reality of history, while the second would be the perfect eschatological fulfillment of the divine plan of salvation" (*DP*, no. 34).

Some theologians, particularly in India, fear that we are once again heading toward a crypto-identification of church and kingdom. By stating strongly that

---

[16] Dupuis, *Toward a Christian Theology of Religious Pluralism*, 346.

the kingdom is intrinsically bound up with Christ, and that the church is his chosen instrument for the kingdom, the whole argument seems to go so far as to say that we cannot promote the kingdom unless we are promoting the church. If the kingdom can be found only in Jesus, and if the church is the continuation of Jesus' presence through the ages, then, so the argument goes, the kingdom can be found only in the church. (In such an argumentation one wonders if the church is not being compared once again with the physical body of Jesus instead of being compared with the body of the Risen Christ.) Concerned theologians see here a subtle return to an ecclesiocentric approach to the kingdom, which makes it impossible to develop a kingdom-centered understanding of the church. The danger is that the universality of the kingdom is reduced to the particularity of the church once again. In the words of Felix Wilfred:

> Since certain trends in liberation theology and in the theology of religions seemed to highlight the reality of the kingdom at the expense of the Church and to distance themselves from the Church, the reaction (of the official Church) has taken the form of barring any access to the kingdom except through the Church. Or to put it in another way, instead of understanding the Church in relation to the mystery of the kingdom, this trend wants to understand the kingdom of God in terms of the Church, and indeed turn the Church itself into the kingdom.[17]

In the view of these theologians, if such a trend toward identification were to gain the upper hand in Catholic theology today, one of the most powerful sources for the renewal of the church and its theology could be seriously stifled. Only if we maintain the distinction between church and kingdom clearly and uncompromisingly can such a symbol once again become *the* religious symbol of our time. It provides us, on the one hand, with a way to relate to this world and its destiny productively and, on the other hand, with a way to enter into a more open and creative dialogue with other religious traditions and ideologies.

Therefore, we have to be on our guard not to allow again such an identification, subtle as it may be. The church is not the kingdom now since the kingdom makes itself felt outside the church as well. The church's mission is to serve the kingdom, not to take its place.

The many qualifications made by *Redemptoris Missio* and *Dialogue and Proclamation* to the statement that kingdom and church are not identical are true to the firmly held position of the magisterium that whatever "traces of the kingdom" may be found outside the church must be seen and related to the kingdom that Christ proclaimed and brought. There cannot exist any "kingdom revelation" in the world that is not related to or independent of Christ. Referring to the reality of the kingdom outside the church *Dialogue and Proclamation* adds the following caution, which once again makes clear the strong stand of the official teaching authority:

---

[17] Felix Wilfred, "Once Again . . . Church and Kingdom," *Vidyajyoti* 57 (1993), 10.

Part of the Church's role consists in recognizing that the inchoative reality of his kingdom can be found also beyond the confines of the Church, for example in the heart of the followers of other religious traditions, insofar as they live evangelical values and are open to the action of the Spirit. It must be remembered nevertheless that this is indeed an inchoate reality, which needs to find completion through being related to the kingdom of Christ already present in the Church yet realized fully only in the world to come (*DP*, no. 35).

For those theologians who hold on to a non-identity there remains an unsolved theological problem: how to relate a kingdom outside the church to the kingdom that Christ proclaimed and gave to the church. Should one assume that there are other revelations of the kingdom not related to Christ? While such views are voiced today by a number of theologians, the official church has so far steadfastly refused to allow any such propositions to be even considered.

One way of responding to the question of how the kingdom of God, which Jesus brought irrevocably into this world through his life, death, and resurrection, is now also to be found outside the church is this: God's kingdom entered this world finally and definitely with the incarnation of Jesus but took on a more comprehensive presence in the resurrection of Jesus, the Christ. In the resurrection the limitations of Jesus' earthly existence are gone. The kingdom was definitely present in the Jesus who walked this earth, but its presence was, so to speak, restricted to the physical body of Jesus. This is to be concluded from the fact that John could speak about the Spirit who "was not yet because Jesus was not yet glorified" (Jn 7:39). But in his death and resurrection the kingdom he had proclaimed as having arrived with him took on a new dimension: it now embraced the whole of creation. In the Risen Christ matter has been transformed into the state of the new creation. He, therefore, assumes a new global relationship with reality as a whole; he is present in creation in a new way.[18]

As the future of the present world, Christ relates to creation in a new way. The whole world belongs to him not only on the basis of creation (Col 1:1-15; Jn 1:1-14) but now also on the basis of its transformation in the resurrection of his body into the new creation. We cannot limit the presence of the new creation to the church alone. This all-pervasive presence of the kingdom of Christ in the world makes itself visible not only in the church but also in historical movements outside the church and in the other religious traditions found anywhere in the world. This was expressed by the International Ecumenical Congress of Theology in São Paulo (Brazil 1980) in these words:

The coming Kingdom as God's final design for his creation is experienced in the historical processes of human liberation. On the one hand, the Kingdom has a utopian character, for it can never be completely

---

[18] Leonardo Boff, *Church, Charism, and Power: Liberation Theology and the Institutional Church* (London: SCM Press, 1985), 145-146.

achieved in history; on the other hand, it is foreshadowed and given con-crete expression in historical liberations. The kingdom pervades human liberations; it manifests itself *in* them, but it is not identical *with* them. Historical liberations, by the very fact that they are historical, are limited, but are open to something greater. The Kingdom transcends them. There-fore it is the object of our hope and thus we can pray to the Father: "Thy kingdom come." Historical liberations incarnate the Kingdom to the de-gree that they humanize life and generate social relationships of greater fraternity, participation, and justice.[19]

There are three dangers of which we have to be mindful: First, church and kingdom are seen to be so closely connected that an identification takes place. The result is then an abstract and idealistic image of the church cut off from real history and its traumas. Second, church and world are identified with the result that the image of the church is secular and mundane, and a constant conflict with the powers of the world cannot be avoided. This has been called "the secu-larist temptation," when the kingdom of God is consciously or unconsciously identified with some earthly goal or other, and the goal of the kingdom of God entrusted to the care of the church.[20] Third, a church totally centered on itself, out of touch with the world and the kingdom, becomes a self-sufficient, trium-phal, and perfect society not recognizing the relative autonomy of the secular sphere. According to Boff, "These dangers are theological 'pathologies' that cry out for treatment; ecclesiological health depends on the right relationship between Kingdom—World—Church, in such a way that the Church is always seen as a concrete and historical sign (of the Kingdom and salvation), and as its instrument (mediation) in a salvific service to the world."[21]

Whatever doubts there may have been as to whether Vatican II made a clear distinction between the kingdom in history and the church in its present pilgrim state, the church's magisterium in more recent documents seems to have clari-fied the matter in favor of a non-identification.

These documents not only clearly distinguish church and kingdom, recog-nizing that the larger reality of the kingdom cannot be encompassed by and contained within the church, but they also unambiguously subordinate the church to the kingdom by affirming that the church is meant to be a servant of the broader and more important kingdom of God. Thus:

- It is true that the church is not an end unto itself, since it is ordered toward the kingdom of God of which it is the seed, sign, and instrument (*RM*, no. 18).

---

[19] *Challenge of Basic Christian Communities,* Papers from the International Ecumenical Congress of Theology, February 20-March 2, 1980, São Paulo, Brazil, ed. Sergio Torres and John Eagleson (Maryknoll, New York: Orbis Books, 1981), 236-237.

[20] Lochman, "Church and World in the Light of the Kingdom of God," 59.

[21] Boff, *Church, Charism, and Power,* 1-2.

- The church is effectively and concretely at the service of the kingdom (*RM*, no 20).
- The church's mission is to foster the "kingdom of the Lord and his Christ" (Rv 11:15), at whose service it is placed (*DP*, no. 35; see also no. 59).

With these statements the official church has passed another milestone. In Vatican II the Christian church was no longer totally identifiable with the Catholic Church alone. The church was seen as embracing other churches as well. Now it is stated that the kingdom of God is not to be identified with the Christian church.

THE KINGDOM OF GOD AS PRESENT IN THE CHURCH

Although the kingdom may not be identified with the church, that does not mean that the kingdom is not present in the church. The word *church* may not appear often in Jesus' teaching, but the very concept of the messianic community, intrinsically bound up with the kingdom, implies the same thing as the concept of church. It is, therefore, correct to say that "the kingdom of God and the church are two key New Testament concepts, both . . . crucial for the understanding of God's plan for humanity. They are central to the fulfillment of his redemptive purpose. While the Church cannot be identified with the kingdom, for the latter is a larger and more comprehensive term, the two are nevertheless in such close correlation that they cannot be separated either."[22]

The Kingdom in Spatial and Dynamic Terms

The following observations should clarify what we mean by saying the church is not the kingdom, and yet it is a community chosen by God in which the kingdom is made present in a special way. In the New Testament we find two sets of ideas connected with the kingdom of God. These might be helpful to better understand the tension that exists between the kingdom and the church. They are the following.

First, in the Old as well as in the New Testament, the kingdom is mostly understood as God's sovereignty or kingly rule. Perceived as a dynamic concept, kingdom means God's active rule over all reality but particularly at the end of time. It is all-embracing but still provisional, still to come in all its fullness. This strand is the most dominant one and can be found in all the writings of the Bible. It expresses clearly God's intention to save all human beings and the whole of creation.

Second, there is also a strand in the message of Jesus that understands and portrays the kingdom in spatial terms, as a territorial reality. This is expressed

---

[22] Peter Kuzmic, "The Church and Kingdom of God: A Theological Reflection," in *The Church: God's Agent for Change*, ed. Bruce J. Nicholls (Flemington Markets, Australia: Paternoster Press, 1986), 49.

in sayings like these: One can enter the kingdom (Mt 5:20; 7:21; 18:3); and one can be thrown out of it (Mt 8:31). There are the keys of the kingdom (Mt 16:18-19). The kingdom is compared with a house into which people are invited. This strand of the message of Jesus is largely new but pervasively present in his kingdom message.

These two strands create a tension that is fundamental in the New Testament.[23] While they help us to better understand the world in relation to the kingdom, they certainly could help us also to clarify the tension between church and kingdom. They indicate that while the kingdom is a reality that embraces all of creation, God still has bound it in a particular way to a particular group in space and time now. Dulles makes a similar observation, that the symbol kingdom in the New Testament refers to reign and realm:

> The term basileia in the Greek New Testament frequently means kingship (reign) but it sometimes must be translated as kingdom (realm). The two concepts are inseparable. Christ's kingship or lordship implies a community over which he reigns—in other words, a kingdom. Conversely, the concept of the kingdom always implies a king. Several different expressions such as "kingdom of God," "kingdom of heaven," "kingdom of the Son," and "kingdom of Christ" are used almost interchangeably in the New Testament, and the differences of nuance among them need not concern us here.[24]

It is the kingdom present now that creates the church and keeps it constantly in existence. The church is therefore the result of the Spirit, who makes God's final saving intentionality effectively present as the true source of the community called church.

Although the kingdom cannot be identified with the church, that does not mean the kingdom is not present in the church. While acknowledging the difference between the kingdom and the church, *Redemptoris Missio* is very much concerned that the church should not be seen and treated as separated from the kingdom: "One may not separate the kingdom from the Church. It is true that the Church is not an end unto herself, since she is ordered towards the kingdom of God of which she is the seed, sign and instrument. Yet while remaining distinct from Christ and the kingdom, the Church is indissolubly united with both" (*RM*, no. 18). The kingdom makes itself present in the church in a particular way. We can say that the church is an "initial realization" or a "proleptic anticipation" of the plan of God for humankind, or, in words of Vatican II, "becomes on earth the initial budding forth of the kingdom" (*LG*, no. 5). The definition of the church as "sacrament of the kingdom of God" given by the theological commission (1985) expresses perhaps most deeply the connection of the church with the kingdom. The church contains what it signifies: a community in which

---

[23] Lochman, "Church and World in the Light of the Kingdom of God," 61-63.
[24] Dulles, "The Church and the Kingdom," 14.

the kingdom of God is already present and mediated to all who come in contact with this community. The church as an icon of the Trinity brings forth that unity with the Triune God and with one another for which the kingdom of God is the perfect expression. But the concept *sacrament* indicates also that a strict identification is not possible because, as Karl Rahner points out, a sacramental reality cannot totally be identified with the reality it effectively signifies and mediates.

The church is a *means or sacrament* through which God's plan for the world realizes itself in history (*LG*, nos. 8, 48). As George Ladd puts it, "The kingdom creates the Church, works through the Church, and is proclaimed in the world by the Church. There can be no kingdom without the Church—those who have acknowledged God's rule—and there can be no Church without the kingdom; but they remain two distinguishable concepts: the Rule of God and the fellowship of men."[25] We should never separate the kingdom from the church because the church is God's chosen instrument for God's kingdom here on earth.

Difficulties with This View

This view of the kingdom (as present in the church in a preeminent way) and of the church (as an anticipation of the final destiny of humankind) creates a series of difficulties and problems that need to be addressed. First, how can the absolute and final reconciliation of the whole of history "already"—although initially—be realized in a particular phenomenon of history? Second, how can the already realized reconciliation of history be mediated through the church in the face of human freedom and in view of a constantly open future of history? And third, in what sense does the church, as a social entity of salvation, occupy a middle position concerning the question of individual fulfillment and the final universal fulfillment of humanity's social destiny in the universal resurrection of the dead? Only the kingdom in its ultimate fullness will be the final reconciliation of the two seemingly dialectically opposed dimensions of human personality: the *individual* (every human being is unique and unrepeatable) and the *social* (communitarian and belonging to the species). Only the coming kingdom can and will solve this apparent dichotomy between the individual and the social since it will fully reveal the image according to which we are created: the *Triune God* whose very essence is *One in Three*. The apparent conflict between both exists only in this present condition of humankind. Only in a sinful and untransformed world does the constant conflict between the rights of individuals and the structures of society arise. They will never really be reconciled as long as the kingdom has not come in its fullness. This conflict keeps arising to the extent that modern society is becoming increasingly complex and in need of more sophisticated structuring. The instinctive aversion of many people to all institutionalization will not make it easier for the church to present itself as a model of human society.

---

[25] George Eldon Ladd, *The Present of the Future: A Revised and Updated Version of Jesus and the Kingdom* (Grand Rapids, Michigan: Eerdmans, 1974), 277.

One more difficulty is the growing awareness that the church itself, as a reality in history, easily falls prey to class-consciousness and yet pretends to be neutral, that is, not to be affected by such prejudices, though, in reality, the church always serves some class interests. There is a refusal to submit to ideological critique, which alone can unmask such class biases.[26] In the light of such difficulties it is all the more important for the church to present itself as an "honest institution"[27] or as "God's counter society"[28] to witness to the whole of society what it is really destined for. Its essence and mission are to offer itself as a "test case,"[29] showing that the rights of individual persons and a society of justice, peace, and joy are reconcilable and livable in the present world with the understanding, of course, that they are only a sign of what is to come. A perfect society is not possible in this world. But the church can offer, in an "initial and anticipatory way," the fulfillment of humanity's social destiny because the kingdom of God has already broken into this world and indicates the direction toward which all history has to move and to be transformed. "It is therefore the Church's duty to display in an evil age of self-seeking, pride, and animosity, the life and fellowship of the kingdom of God and of the age to come. This display is an essential element in the witness of the Church to the kingdom of God."[30]

We know that God's kingdom is present. Even if the hoped-for future drags on and seems not to come, the choice of living from it is not wrong. The kingdom releases energies that affect the course of history deeply and in often unintended ways. To live from the future means to have a vision of a world and to stop trying to succeed and to establish our security in the present socioeconomic order.[31] It is this vision that created the church; it is this vision from which the church lives; it is this vision that is the mission of the church. Looking at the all-too-human face of the church, we can easily identify with Pedro Casaldáliga's dream:

> I dream of a Church wearing only the gospel and
>   sandals;
> I believe in the Church despite the Church,
> sometimes, in any case I believe in the Kingdom,
> journeying in the Church.
>
> The Kingdom unites.
> The Church divides
> when it does not coincide with the Kingdom.

---

[26] Boff, *Church, Charism, and Power*, 108-110.

[27] Wolfhart Pannenberg, "The Kingdom of God and the Church," in *Theology and the Kingdom of God* (Philadelphia: Westminster Press, 1977), 82-84.

[28] Gerhard Lohfink, *Jesus and Community: Did Jesus Found a Church?* (London: SPCK Press, 1985), 122-132.

[29] McBrien, *Catholicism*, 716.

[30] Ladd, *The Present of the Future*, 269.

[31] John B. Cobb, *Sustainability: Economics, Ecology, and Justice* (Maryknoll, New York: Orbis Books, 1992), 13-14.

Part 2

MODELS OF THE CHURCH

5

Emergence of a World Church

Jesus' vision of the kingdom has been transmitted to us through the faith community into which we were born: the Roman Catholic Church. Over many centuries this community grasped and framed the message of Jesus according to the culture that received it. The Catholic faith tradition was formulated over the centuries by saints and great theologians who shared a common culture that rested on Greek and Roman foundations as well as on the diverse cultures of people who had joined these empires and had made their own contributions. The theology that gradually arose became the official teaching of the church. Culture and gospel became almost identical as the following often-heard phrase might indicate: Europe is the faith, and the faith is Europe. We exported this theology to the Third World in good faith and we established churches *in* many countries. But are they churches *of* these countries?

The philosophical and theological synthesis achieved over the centuries is undoubtedly one of the most impressive ever created. But what we have come to realize today is that this grandiose synthesis of theology is built on a particular culture with its values and customs. The message of the gospel might be so well presented and interpreted through the values and customs of one culture that the people of that culture cannot perceive that the same message could be expressed equally well or even better in other cultures with different value systems and customs. If we accept that the Christian message can be expressed differently in diverse cultures, then we have to accept at the same time that the Bible will be read differently in these cultures. But have we really taken inculturation seriously?

There's no doubt that the future of the Christian faith lies with the emerging churches of the developing world. A few simple statistics support this statement. The Catholic Church is growing by around fifteen to twenty million members a year. This number includes three million adult baptisms; 90 percent of these new members are in the Third World. Today 70 percent of all Catholics live in the Third World; 50 percent of these are found in Latin America. These Christians demand the right to express themselves in their own cultures.

If the future of Christianity belongs to these countries, we have to expect that they will express their faith experience in a different way and develop a theology rooted in their experience. There will be a "back-flow" of theology from the Third World to the First World. How will we meet this challenge? Something is happening that hardly anyone could have imagined fifty years ago.

A THEOLOGICAL INTERPRETATION OF VATICAN II AS "WORLD CHURCH"

I would like to review a theory which Karl Rahner presented fifteen years after Vatican II in an article entitled "Towards a Fundamental Theological Interpretation of Vatican II."[1] If Rahner's thesis is true—and I basically agree with it—we can at least see what is coming and what will shape theology in the near and distant future. For Rahner, Vatican II was *the event* of the last century for the history of the Catholic Church. Whatever future synods may have to add or to comment upon, there is no way back. There might well be different opinions, but the council provided official guidelines outlining the directions in which the church will have to move. Most significant, for Rahner, was the nature of the Council itself: Vatican II was for the first time a Council of the world church.

The Council for the first time in a formal way was a Council of the world Church as such. We need only compare it with Vatican I to see its uniqueness in the formal juridical sense. It is true that there were representatives of the episcopal sees in Asia or Africa present at Vatican I. But these were missionary bishops of European or American origin. At that time there was not yet a native episcopate anywhere in the Church. But one appeared in Vatican II. Perhaps this was far from proportionate to the representation from European episcopates. But it was there. These bishops did not come simply as individuals, *ad limina,* to give an account of their dioceses and to take home missionary alms; Vatican II really was the first assembly of the world-episcopate, not acting as an advisory body to the Pope, but with him and under him as itself the supreme teaching and decision making authority in the Church. There really was a World-council with a World-episcopate such as had not hitherto existed and with its own autonomy. The actual significance of the non-European part of this total episcopate may have been comparatively slight; the consequences of this conciliar event for the post-conciliar life of the Church may still be very limited, as the Roman synods of bishops have shown since then; none of this alters the essential fact that the council made manifest and brought into activity a Church which was no longer the European Church with its American areas of dissemination and its exports to Asia and Africa.[2]

---

[1] Karl Rahner, "Towards a Fundamental Theological Interpretation of Vatican II," *Theological Studies* 40 (1979), 716-27.

[2] Ibid., 718-19.

This thesis sounds innocent, but it has enormous potential consequences. For Rahner there are, theologically speaking, three great epochs in church history, of which the third has only just begun and made itself observable officially at Vatican II.

The First Epoch: Jewish Christianity

The disciples of Jesus did not move away from Israel after Easter. They saw themselves wholly as Jews and not yet as a "group alongside others." They continued to take part in the temple cult: "Day after day they met as a group in the Temple" (Acts 2:46). They kept the Old Testament Law and its tradition (Temple cult, Law, and circumcision). To be a disciple of Jesus meant to be a Jew first; only in this way could a non-Jew enter the circle of Jesus' disciples. The apostles remained in Jerusalem and did not take up mission work to the Gentiles.[3] Peter, in fact, had to defend himself for eating with an uncircumcised pagan: "You were a guest in the house of uncircumcised Gentiles, and you even ate with them!" (Acts 11:3). In short, circumcision (a sign of the covenant), keeping of the Law, and attendance at the cultic services were regarded as normative for anyone who joined the new movement.

Although remaining in the Jewish tradition, the community did have its own rules and celebrations from the very beginning: (1) *baptism* as an initiation rite of the new fellowship; (2) *communal prayer services* in private houses, which were directed to Jesus the Lord and not to Yahweh (Acts 2:46); (3) the *breaking of bread* as their interpretation of the Passover and the Exodus; (4) their *own leaders*, Peter and the other apostles; and (5) the *fellowship of love,* which was linked with the breaking of bread that bound them together as brothers and sisters who put their possessions at one another's disposal (Acts 4:32-35). What led ultimately to a separation from "Israel of Old" was the "yes" or "no" to Christ. The disciples did not seek this separation; it was forced on them.[4]

Jesus' own ministry was geared to "gathering together Israel of Old," and he understood his mission in the setting of Israel.[5] Jesus did not take up any mission to the Gentiles. Granted that Jesus foresaw the coming of a Gentile church after his death (Mt 8:11), but there was no word from him about how his message should be carried to the Gentiles. Only new situations and new circumstances imposed on the disciples made them gradually see that the message was for the pagans as well. And this not by them becoming Jews first but by entering directly into the new community.

We have a beautiful illustration of how difficult it was for Peter and what kind of conversion it demanded for him to accept that God had chosen the Gentiles as well as the Jews without any distinction whatsoever:

---

[3] Raymond Brown, *Priest and Bishop: Biblical Reflections* (New York: Paulist Press, 1970), 51-52.

[4] Edward Schweizer, *Church Order in the New Testament* (London: SCM Press, 1961), 41.

[5] Gerhard Lohfink, *Jesus and Community* (London: SPCK Press, 1985), 7-29.

About noon the following day as they were on their journey and approaching the city, Peter went up on the roof to pray. He became hungry and wanted something to eat, and while the meal was being prepared, he fell into a trance. He saw heaven opened and something like a large sheet being let down to earth by its four corners. It contained all kinds of four-footed animals, as well as reptiles of the earth and birds of the air. Then a voice told him, "Get up, Peter. Kill and eat." "Surely not, Lord!" Peter replied. "I have never eaten anything impure or unclean." The voice spoke to him a second time, "Do not call anything impure that God has made clean." This happened three times, and immediately the sheet was taken back to heaven (Acts 10:9-16).

As Gentiles were admitted into the community, however, the requirements made of them were not always the same. Raymond Brown distinguishes four types of Jewish/Gentile Christianity. *Type one* consisted of Jewish Christians and their Gentile converts who kept the Law, circumcision, and cult and regarded these as necessary for receiving the fullness of the salvation brought by Christ. *Type two* consisted of those Jewish Christians and their Gentile converts who observed only some Jewish purity laws without insisting on circumcision as salvific for Gentile Christians. Peter and James seem to have been of this kind. *Type three* consisted of Jewish Christians and their Gentile converts who did not insist on circumcision or demand the observance of Jewish purity laws with regard to food. However, they did not ask for a break with the Jewish feasts and Temple or impel Jewish Christians to abandon circumcision and the Law. *Type four* consisted of Jewish Christians and their Gentile converts who did not insist on circumcision and Jewish food laws and did not ascribe any significance to the Jerusalem Temple.[6] Rahner seems to address himself only to two of these types, the two most opposed, that is, one and four.

The Second Epoch:
The Gentile Christian Community Freed from Jewish Law

As more and more Gentiles joined the community, the question had to be faced: Did the Gentiles who wanted to join the Christian community have to become Jews first through circumcision and the keeping of the Law? Or could they become members of the community through baptism administered without requiring the observance of the Law and the practice of circumcision?

The problem was felt quite early and some ad hoc solutions were arrived at, since Jesus had not left clear instructions on what to do. This can be seen in the way Peter justified to the assembly of the Jerusalem church his baptizing

---

[6] Raymond Brown, *Biblical Exegesis and Church Doctrine* (New York/Mahwah, New Jersey: Paulist Press, 1985), 133-34; see also, idem, "Not Jewish Christianity and Gentile Christianity but Types of Jewish/Gentile Christianity," *The Catholic Biblical Quarterly* 45 (1983), 74-79.

Cornelius and his household without first making them Jews. Peter reported to the assembly: "'When I began to speak, the Holy Spirit came down on them just as on us at the beginning, . . . Who was I, then, to try to stop God!' When they heard this they stopped their criticism and praised God" (Acts 10:15-18).

But it was Paul who thought out and formulated theologically what took shape in the history of the primitive church. The First Apostolic Council in Jerusalem settled the issue: To become a Christian does not require circumcision and keeping of the Law. The theological reasoning was purely christological. But the resolution was based on the inspiration of the Holy Spirit and not on the word of the Lord: "The Holy Spirit and we have agreed not to put any burden on you" (Acts 15: 28). One has to concede that something like a mission to the Gentiles would have been possible in the setting of Jewish Christianity, and the solution of Paul and the council in Jerusalem was theologically not so self-evident as it looks to us today. The Paschal meal, circumcision, and most of the Law could have been retained just to indicate the connection with the Old Testament.

It is regrettable that Jewish Christianity vanished from the scene. There are many scholars who argue that it was Jewish Christianity that "wrote" our gospels and that this "formidable minority" had an enormous influence on the church. In terms of ecumenism, it would be excellent if we still had a Jewish Christianity that could really carry on the dialogue between Jews and Christians once again on a common basis. Some even think it would be easy to re-create such a Christianity for the good of the whole church.[7] But the fact is that the First Apostolic Council in Jerusalem, with its decision concerning Law and circumcision, introduced a radically new period in church history, "a Christianity that was not the export of Jewish Christianity to the Diaspora but instead a Christianity which, for all its relationship to the historical Jesus, still grew on the soil of paganism."[8]

What happened here was the transition of Christianity from one historical and theological situation to an essentially new one. Rahner sees this transition extending into the Greek-Roman era, as well as into the medieval and modern European era. He regards the Roman-Hellenistic Mediterranean culture and its transmission to the Germanic peoples as one unity.

However, Rahner is not so much concerned with the historical character of such a transition as with its theological significance. The abolition of circumcision can certainly not be derived from Jesus' own explicit preaching or from the preaching about the salvific meaning of his death and resurrection. But Paul regarded this principle as belonging to the gospel. This principle represents a break with salvation history that Paul could not undertake on his own. The fact is that we rarely realize what such a break meant: the church became a Gentile

---

[7] F. Rossi de Gasperi, "Continuity and Newness in the Faith of the Mother Church of Jerusalem," in *Bible and Inculturation,* Inculturation working papers on living faith, Rome (1983), 63.

[8] Rahner, "Towards a Fundamental Theological Interpretation of Vatican II," 721.

church. (In our own times this break should be worked out in dialogue with the synagogue of today in order to discover what is still valid from the Old Testament and what is not.)

The Third Epoch:
Transition from a Western Church to a World Church

Rahner proposes that today we are experiencing a break such as occurred only *once* before, that is, in the transition from Jewish to Gentile Christianity. He then highlights the significance of Vatican II, namely, at the Council the church, even if only initially and unclearly, proclaimed the transition from the Western church to a world church. For Rahner, "the difference between the historical situation of Jewish Christianity and the situation into which Paul transplanted Christianity as a radically new creation is not greater than the differences between Western cultures and the contemporary cultures of all Asia and Africa into which Christianity must inculturate itself if it is now to be, as it has begun to be, a genuinely world Church."[9]

The challenge is the following: Either the church recognizes the essential differences of other cultures and by boldly embracing the consequences of this recognition becomes a world church, or it remains a Western church and thereby betrays the true meaning of Vatican II.

Here it is useful to recall the distinction made by many scholars today: The church has to move from being, for example, the local church *in* India to being the local church *of* India. The big question, however, is this: Does the present church still have the creative power and authority that it had initially as the apostolic church? The decision taken then was an irreversible basic decision that affected the church's very essence. And the authority to do this came to it over and above that which came to it directly from Jesus or now from the Risen Lord. More precisely, Rahner asks, "Can the church legitimately perceive possibilities of which she never made use during her second major epoch because those possibilities would have been meaningless in that epoch and consequently illegitimate?"[10]

Vatican II regarded itself as the active subject of the highest plenary power in the church. While the direction this council gave lacks conceptual clarity, what it did can justly be compared with the transition from Jewish to Gentile Christianity. There are many statements in the council documents that indicate this break clearly. I will summarize them in three points: First, for the first time and formally the council was a world church council: a gathering of the world episcopate. In comparison, Vatican I had no native-born bishop from the Third World present during its deliberations. Second, the leap to a world church becomes clear by looking at the decrees of the council, which shifted from Latin

---

[9] Ibid., 723.
[10] Ibid., 724.

(as the language of a small and particular cultural region) to the vernacular. This meant moving away from the official interpretation of the gospel message in terms of the classical culture of the West to an interpretation that respects the categories, values, and attitudes proper to other cultures. And finally, concerning doctrinal matters, the council did two things that are of fundamental significance for a worldwide missionary effort. For the first time in the history, the church offered a positive evaluation of the great religions of the world. In so doing, the council proclaimed that the salvific will of God is limited only by the evil decisions of the human conscience. This opens the way to accepting the view that other religions may be revelatory and salvific, and "dialogue" becomes the key word when the church's mission is explored and discussed in relation to other religious traditions.

Rahner's thesis that Vatican II was the great event in which the church for the first time came to the reality of being world church[11] calls for a new understanding of the relationship between the church and cultures. Now that the church is a world church, it must incorporate a world perspective into its modus operandi. It cannot be exclusively married to the Roman or European way of life. In Rahner's view, now that the Roman Catholic Church is a world church, it is time to act like a world church. Each culture has contributions it can and must offer the church. Conversely, the church must accept and incorporate these gifts into itself.

In *Church, Charism, and Power,* Leonardo Boff underscored how the church assimilated secular organizational structures from the Roman Empire and from feudal society. It would be very difficult to defend the theological position that all these structures are in themselves *ius divinum* and constitute the very nature of the church. As history shows, the church has always been influenced by the society in which it has lived. Now that the church is no longer strictly a European creation, it ought to incorporate the variety and diversity brought to it by the cultures and societies of its worldwide membership. Joseph Ratzinger defines this tension in a very impressive manner: "After decades of concentration on 'Roman,' which followed the (First) Vatican Council, the church has again directed more attention to the other side of the scale, to 'Catholic.'"[12]

It is far easier to focus on the "Roman" aspect of the church than on the "Catholic" aspect. "Roman" implies unity in and allegiance to the church of Rome. "Catholic" implies the diversity of the church throughout the world. It seems to me that the struggles over authority occurring in the church today are partly the price the church is paying for being "Catholic." Certainly before Vatican II, the church prided itself on being "Roman," the same thing always and everywhere. With the advent of Vatican II and the world church we come to realize once again what being Catholic really means. Universality includes an

---

[11] Karl Rahner, *Concern for the Church, Theological Investigations,* vol. 20 (New York: Crossroad, 1981), 78.

[12] Karl Rahner and Joseph Ratzinger, *The Episcopacy and the Primacy* (New York: Herder and Herder, 1963), 38.

ambiguity that is at times not easy to live with. If the church is at the same time Roman and Catholic, then there is no way to avoid this struggle. With the advent of Vatican II the church set itself on an irreversible course, which will be marked by the attempt to balance Roman and Catholic in the church. As Rahner succinctly says: "The Church at the Council surrendered a good deal of power that it formerly assumed. At this point a frontier has been crossed behind which it will never again be possible to return, even to a slight degree."[13]

Rahner goes on to argue that the emphasis in the past has been placed too heavily on the Roman side of the scale to the detriment of the Catholic side. One can sense his frustration as he writes:

Have not the Roman Congregations always had the mentality of a centralized bureaucracy, claiming to know what is best everywhere in the world for the service of the Kingdom of God and the salvation of souls and do not their decisions appear to be shockingly naive, based as they are on the assumption that the Roman or Italian mentality is the obvious standard of judgement?[14]

MEGATRENDS AFFECTING THE CHURCH TODAY

There are two simultaneously evolving realities the church must reckon with: first, the ever more felt importance of the local cultures concerning the church's mission; second, and contrasting with the emphasis on the local, the emergence of a global culture that affects almost all cultures. This shows itself in particular trends that are pervasively present everywhere. These trends have to be evaluated critically, but they cannot be ignored.

From now on the context into which the gospel has to be translated will be global. The world with its different cultures and perceptions of reality will become the arena in which God's kingdom has to be discovered as already present and has to be articulated in the words of these cultures. Looking at the new situation we have to realize that, as John Paul II wrote in *Redemptoris Missio*, "profound transformations are taking place at the moment which characterize today's world especially in the southern hemisphere" (*RM*, no. 37). No one can attempt to do any serious theological reflection on the church and its mission in the world today and the near future without taking these facts into account. Different names have been given to these "profound transformations," and different aspects have been stressed depending on what part of the world and out of what kind of situation one sees and evaluates these trends. European theologians will come up with a different list from Asians or Latin Americans, but the differences are not that great. Since they affect all cultures and peoples in the whole world, they are often called *megatrends*. Some of the most important of

---

[13] Rahner, *Concern for the Church*, 94.
[14] Ibid., 79.

these for our topic concerning the future of the church and its mission in the world are discussed below.[15]

Resurgence of Cultural Traditions

Among all peoples of the world there is a resurgence of a sense of their cultural identity. This phenomenon is present in every continent and is manifested in a return to the roots of culture, to the original and living traditions, customs, understandings, values, and relationships—a return not for its own sake, but for the sake of rediscovering identity in order to cope with the modern world in ways that differ from one culture to another.

Inculturation is a process by which the gospel enters into a culture, takes from the culture all that is already gospelled, and is enriched by it. In addition to this, the gospel challenges the culture in those aspects that are un-gospelled and the culture challenges the gospel in those aspects which are merely Western and thus both are purified and universalized. So the dynamics between culture and gospel are such that each is enriched and challenged by the other. There is a call and a response. There is a rejection of elements of the culture that are contrary to the gospel, as well as a critique of and removal from the church of those elements that are not the genuine gospel but rather Westernized interpretations.

Christians today make up 33 percent of the world's population. Muslims, who in 2000 were almost 20 percent of the world's population, are among the fastest growing groups (with a growth rate of 2.15 percent per year). Within the Christian group, the Pentecostal-Charismatic churches are experiencing rapid growth, with a growth rate of 2.33 percent (compared to a 1.34 percent growth rate for Christians as a whole.[16] The growth of the Pentecostal-Charismatic churches seems to indicate that they respond most effectively to the desire of people for a personal encounter with God in their own culture and the need for community experiences based on their own values and customs.

Globalization

While not a radically new concept, globalization is particularly relevant in our day. Most of us accept the idea that humanity is rapidly becoming a global society. But this trend has to be treated in a critical fashion. Globalization is a double-edged sword, both a blessing and a curse—but it is here to stay. There are those who extol the virtues of globalization; they claim it is about tearing down borders and eliminating world poverty, uniting divided peoples and securing world

---

[15] The following ten points in this section are summarized from Anthony Bellagamba's *Mission and Ministry in a Global Church* (Maryknoll, New York: Orbis Books 1992), 1-9.

[16] Statistics are taken from the *World Christian Encyclopedia,* 2 vols., ed. David B. Barnett, George T. Kurian, and Todd M. Johnson (Oxford: Oxford University Press, 2000).

peace. But there is the seamy underside: the aim of globalization is often seen only in economic terms. As such, it tries to impose a single vision of how national economies should function and be structured; it is a modern neocolonial process by which global economic powers are securing their hold over the so-called developing world as well as the developed countries.

Positively, we have to appreciate the universal outlook globalization provides. Universalism means not only opening our windows to the outside but also keeping them wide open so that the mutuality among our church, other churches, religions, and all sorts of movements for the good of God's kingdom is not stopped but continues with unrelenting determination.

Revival of Religious Experiences

People are longing for personal religious experience: a hunger for the divine, a search for the absolute. Religious revival happens in all religions in the world. Churches, synagogues, temples, and all structural religions of today influence the lives of the people insofar as they provide an opportunity for genuine religious experiences. They will be judged unimportant if they become obstacles to this experience. As indicated above, the rapid growth of the Pentecostal churches today attests most clearly to what people expect from religious traditions in their quest for personal meaning as well as in their search for a community of equality and participation.

Basic Ecclesial Communities

With the support and encouragement of a small group, people find their way to God, and God finds a way to people. People long to experience God, to relate to God, and to share their own faith with others in freedom and spontaneity, in an atmosphere of confidence and trust.

The basic unit of the church, the parish, seems to fall short in this regard in many parts of the church. What is called for is the small faith community, which is today's response to the individual's quest for God and to personal meaningful involvement for the transformation of humanity.

Problems in Ministerial Structures

People's needs for God are no longer met in present structures of ministry. A whole range of new ministries is required. There are 400,000 priests. Of these, 68 percent care for the 40 percent of the Catholics who live in Europe and the United States and 32 percent minister on behalf of the remaining 60 percent.[17] There are not enough to take care of the sacramental needs, never mind mentioning other pastoral necessities. The church has to develop different ministries and

---

[17] Vatican, *Statistical Yearbook of the Church 1995* (Vatican City: Libraria Editrice Vaticana).

new styles of ministry. There has been a dramatic increase in nontraditional pastoral workers, from a few hundred in 1970 to almost half a million in 1995. The decline in traditional pastoral workers over the same twenty-five-year period amounts to almost 200,000.[18] The only observable increase in this latter category during this time span is the number of bishops. (Traditional pastoral workers include religious and secular bishops and priests, together with women religious and non-cleric religious men [brothers].)

The Western Church in Crisis

The Western church as an institution is in deep crisis. It is in crisis because it is Western, because it has modified the universality of its nature and defined itself in terms that may have been relevant to Westerners in the past but are irrelevant to them at the present, and are certainly irrelevant to non-Westerners. The ultimate reason for this crisis is that the church has become identified with an antiquated form of Western culture and expresses the mysteries of God, Jesus, community, and ministry in these terms; consequently, the church today appears irrelevant to its own Western members and totally alien to non-Westerners.

Many trends towards a global church have been developed not in the West but in the mission churches: liturgical renewal, ecumenism, interfaith dialogue, movements of inculturation, being true to one's own identity, and new understanding of ministry.

The Poor as the New Evangelizers

The poor are again at the center of our understanding of God's plan for humanity. Once more, God has chosen the poor to evangelize the world and to help the world to come to a new understanding of the gospel, of the real value of life, of the true value of community, and of the joy of sharing.

New Presence and Significance of Women

There is new awareness of the presence of women in the life of the church and society. Theology, spirituality, and ministry take on new dimensions where women enter the field. This will start a new era of evangelization and mission. What is asked for is equality, partnership, co-responsibility, and co-ministry.

New Frontiers for Mission

There is a rapid increase in the number of people who have not been exposed to the Christ event. It is projected that Christians will decrease from one-third of the population in 1970 to one-fifth in the year 2020. A whole new approach to mission outside and beyond the parameters of the church is a must.

---

[18] Ibid., see appropriate year.

Co-partnership with the Earth

The earth is the first sacrament of God's love for its inhabitants; it is the womb that gives life and nurtures it, a partner in the journey of humanity toward the kingdom. The earth can no longer be considered as an object to be controlled and dominated, or as a means to be used and misused as one pleases. The earth is part of humanity, and humans are part of the earth; they have a common destiny. To abuse the earth is to commit suicide, to misuse the earth is to threaten life, to respect the earth and to treasure it as one of God's greatest gifts is to ensure life. We need to develop a renewed theology of the earth and to promote ecology in all its aspects.

As a consequence of these new transformations an enormous number of books have been written; seminars, and meetings on inculturation and contextualization have taken place and continue to take place. As a consequence, two pastoral priorities seem to be emerging in the church today: contextualization and solidarity with the poor. Contextualization or inculturation follows theologically from Rahner's thesis. Inculturation has a particular urgency in Asia, with its great cultural and religious traditions. In Africa the church also is faced with the task of inculturating itself into the different African traditions. The second pastoral priority today is the church's solidarity with the poor, an option many regard as belonging to inculturation. We have to expect different views in theology stemming from the different situations in which the gospel is read and lived.[19]

THE FOUR SOURCES OF THEOLOGY

There are four sources from which theological insights are gained. They support one another and have to be viewed as a whole.

Bible, Tradition, and the Magisterium

"Holy Tradition, Holy Scripture, and the Church's magisterium are, according to God's wise design, so interconnected and united that none can stand without the others, and that all together effectively contribute, each in its own way, under the motion of the Holy Spirit, to the salvation of souls" (*Dei Verbum*, no. 10). The Bible is always seen as the *norma normans* and tradition as the official interpretation of our faith in the circumstances of the time. They contain, to use Lonergan's phrase, "God's say in the aims and purposes, the direction and development of human lives, human societies, human culture, human history."[20] We can look at the Bible as a book written centuries ago and regard it as "frozen evolution." But it has to be made alive so that it can speak to

---

[19] Robert J. Schreiter, *Constructing Local Theologies* (Maryknoll, New York: Orbis Books, 1985), 1.

[20] Bernard Lonergan, "Theology in Its New Context," in *Conversion,* ed. W. E. Conn (New York: Alba House, 1978), 9.

us again as God's word for our time and situation. After all, God's saving plan was revealed finally and definitely in the people of Israel, who had their particular culture, and in Jesus of Nazareth, who lived and understood his mission within this culture. The story of God's saving love presented in the Bible has to be told again and again so that we will be able to discover today the same God active in our own time. This is the question of biblical hermeneutics.

However, Vatican II did not put the Bible, tradition, and the magisterium on the same level but recognized that tradition and the magisterium are at the service of the word of God.[21] The relationship between the church's magisterium and scripture is seen in the following way:

> The task of providing an authentic interpretation of God's Word in Scripture or Tradition has been entrusted only to the Church's living magisterium whose authority is wielded in the name of Jesus Christ. Nevertheless, this magisterium is not above God's Word; it rather serves the Word, teaching only what has been transmitted, as, by divine mandate and with the Holy Spirit's assistance, it listens to God's Word with piety, keeps it in awe, and expounds it with fidelity (*Dei Verbum*, no. 10).

The Ongoing Life of the Worshiping Community

The committed Christian community is in itself the native soil and context of all theological reflection. It is here that God's revelation is preserved, transmitted, and, using a phrase of Edward Schillebeeckx, the "actualizing continuation" of the Bible happens. One must be a committed Christian, if one wants to understand what the Bible really is, God's word for us today. As Avery Dulles notes, "one has to share in the church's life, one has to participate, in order to get to know."[22] And as Pope Paul VI puts it, "The mystery of the church is not just an object of theological knowledge, it must be really lived by the faithful soul, who has as it were, a co-natural experience of it, even before he has a clear view of it" (*Ecclesiam Suam,* no. 37).

The recognition of the inner supernatural dimension of theological epistemology is regarded by Dulles as one of the major breakthroughs in our time: "Here we have a type of knowledge where theory and praxis are inseparably united."[23]

The Life Situation of the Committed Community

The contingent data of life in fact provide the categories, the language, the medium for theology. They are the concrete circumstances in which people

---

[21] On the relationship between scripture and magisterium in its different forms, see George H. Tavard, *The Church, Community of Salvation: An Ecumenical Ecclesiology* (Collegeville, Minnesota: The Liturgical Press, 1992), 153-70.

[22] Avery Dulles, *Models of the Church,* exp. ed. (Garden City, New York: Image Books, 1987), 25.

[23] Ibid.

have to live, their culture, their social, political and economic facts, as well as what we call the signs of the times. While we somehow always knew this, we have finally made the signs of the times the actual starting point of theological reflection.

The document of the first synod of bishops, *Justice in the World* (1972), regards as the most forceful sign of the time humankind's desire and clamoring for equality and participation. These are signs that ask for an interpretation in the light of our faith. This interpretation will in turn determine the priorities of the church and the direction it has to take in response to these signs (*Justice in the World*, nos. 44-45).

The official church has recognized that historical movements and concrete situations have to be seen and discerned as originating from God's entering into the process of history itself. Referring to the liberation movements that we have been witnessing over the last two hundred years, the *Instruction on Christian Freedom and Liberation* states: "Thus the quest for freedom and the aspiration to liberation, which are among the principal signs of the times in the modern world, have their first source in the Christian heritage. This remains true even in places where they assume erroneous forms and even oppose the Christian view of man and his destiny. Without this reference to the Gospel, the history of the recent centuries in the West cannot be understood" (no. 5). In line with this view, promoted by Vatican II, the Medellín conference formulated this statement:

> In the light of the faith that we profess as believers, we have undertaken to discover a plan of God in the "signs of the times." We interpret the aspirations and clamors of Latin America as signs that reveal the direction of the divine plan operating in the redeeming love of Christ which bases these aspirations on an awareness of fraternal solidarity. Faithful to this divine plan . . . we wish to offer . . . a global vision of man and humanity and the integral vision of Latin American man in development ("Message to the People," nos. 38-39).

The insistent stress on the concrete situation, the "contingent data," as the real starting point of theology became the origin of what is known today as contextualization or inculturation of theology.

The Presence of the Holy Spirit

The Holy Spirit is the great gift and the permanent promise that Jesus made to his church. If the Spirit was with the church in the past, the Spirit will be with us also today. The Spirit is the ultimate guarantee that we will remain basically faithful to the gospel preached by Christ. If we take this seriously, then we can be certain that the church can find an adequate self-understanding and will be an effective instrument of God's offer of salvation in any age and generation. But we can remain faithful to the Spirit only by truly discerning its will in the signs of the times; there is no "hot line" from here to the world beyond.

It is in the interaction and confrontation of the daily, historical life and the theological data of the tradition that we will find what God has to say to us today. The word of God is experienced in the contingent data, which in turn have to be seen and interpreted in the light of God's saving word spoken in the history of Israel and in the life and death of Jesus. To evaluate the contingent data in this way presupposes, of course, the conviction that God's mystery and self-communication to us realizes itself in history and in the world. It means insisting that the divine dimension is the deepest dimension of the *one* human reality. It means that the process of humanization is drawn into the eternal framework beyond the limits of the purely temporal. We need the theological data to be able to discover the deepest dimension of human reality. The ultimate reason for this is the biblical view of creation as oriented to Christ, the incarnation, and the resurrection as a transformation of this world already into the new creation.

The question often asked is this: What should have priority? Should we take the contingent data as the tools to interpret the theological or vice versa? The answer is simple. There is no either/or. It is in the interaction and confrontation of both the theological and the contingent that we will find who the God of history and the God of salvation really wants to be for us today.

6

The Use of Models in Ecclesiology

Since Vatican II different concepts and descriptions of the church have emerged. Some are the result of the council's own deliberations; others have emerged out of the experience of very concrete situations in which the church finds itself today. These new circumstances have given rise to various understandings of the church's essence and mission. Theologians have analyzed these different approaches and views and tried to synthesize them in order to come to grips with at least the main thrusts. In *Models of the Church* Avery Dulles outlines five descriptions of the church as most prevalent in the post-conciliar church.[1] Jerome P. Theisen presents nine models.[2] Richard McBrien, in his work *Catholicism*, sees three dominant models or ways of perceiving the church.[3]

WHAT IS A MODEL?

For the last thirty years the concept of the theological model has been used by theologians. Although this way of scientific investigation is primarily a tool employed by the empirical sciences, its use in theology has become acceptable. How such an empirical approach as model can be applied to theological topics at all is indicative of what has happened to theology over the last fifty years. In the words of Bernard Lonergan: "Theology has become largely an empirical science, in the sense that Scripture and Tradition are not premises but data. The steps from data to interpretation are long, arduous, and at best, probable. An empirical science accumulates information, develops understanding, masters

---

[1] Avery Dulles, *Models of the Church*, exp. ed. (Garden City, New York: Image Books, 1987).

[2] Jerome P. Theisen, *The Ultimate Church and the Promise of Salvation* (Collegeville, Minnesota: St. John's University Press, 1976).

[3] Richard P. McBrien, *Catholicism Study Edition* (London: Geoffrey Chapman, 1984), 710-14.

more of its material and, out of this, new insights and more comprehensive views will emerge."[4] Model thinking in theology can prevent us from making concepts and symbols into idols. It helps us realize that the infinite can never be captured in the finite structures of language. It opens almost unlimited possibility to theological development and, therefore, goes beyond any purely conceptual definition or symbolic representation.

Since Avery Dulles published *Models of the Church* in 1974, many other scholars have followed him in approaching theological topics with the hermeneutical tool of the model. Today we find books like *Models of Christology, Models in Moral Theology, Models of Original Sin, Models of Inculturation*, and so on. Howard A. Snyder has followed this line by investigating the biblical phrase "kingdom of God" under the theological concept of model.[5]

What is a model? A model is a conceptual and symbolic representation or system by which we try to grasp and express reality in whole or in part.[6] A model is to some degree an intentional abstraction from reality in order to clarify issues. It is a relatively simple, artificially constructed case, which is found useful and illuminating for dealing with realities that are more complex and differentiated.[7] Or, in the words of Luzbetak: "Models are simplified rough drafts, rough but effectively able to call up appropriate mental images. They are analogues around which inquiry can be usefully organized. Models have a great potential for expanding human knowledge. Their utility lies in the fact that they proceed pedagogically from the known to the unknown, not only summing up but, so to speak, dramatizing the implications of the particular analogy."[8]

Dulles distinguishes between the *explanatory* and the *exploratory* model: an explanatory model serves to synthesize what we already know or, at least, are inclined to believe. An exploratory model can lead to new theological insights. This kind of model is new, at least for theology, since it works more with hypothesis, which in turn depends on the data available.[9]

Another way of saying this is to distinguish between models *of* and models *for*. A model *of* symbolizes what a reality is, while a model *for* is like a blueprint for a new construction. Models *for* leave room for alterations and serve as guides for how to construct something in the concrete. The church, for example, is not just a model *of* communion but a model *for* a richer historical development of that communion in the settings of different cultures.

---

[4] Bernard Lonergan, "Theology in Its New Context," in *Conversion*, ed. W. E. Conn (New York: Alba House, 1978), 6.

[5] Howard A. Snyder, *Model of the Kingdom* (Nashville, Tennessee: Abingdon Press, 1991).

[6] Antonio B. Lambino, "A New Theological Model: Theology of Liberation," *Towards Doing Theology in the Philippine Context,* Loyola Papers 9 (Manila, 1977), 6.

[7] Snyder, *Model of the Kingdom*, 20.

[8] Louis J. Luzbetak, *The Church and Culture: New Perspectives in Missiological Anthropology* (Maryknoll, New York: Orbis Books, 1988), 136.

[9] Dulles, *Models of the Church*, 22-24.

Luzbetak sees a good model as having the following characteristics:

Good models will always be (1) *useful*, (2) *open*, (3) *fitting,* and (4) *stimulating*. By *useful* we mean that good models are well suited for organizing a body of knowledge. They explain a large quantity of data and allow few exceptions. Good models are useful also in the sense that they not only serve informational purposes but also help solve practical problems. By *open* we mean that good models recognize their limitations. Models are presented only as approximations of truth, only as tentative statements of reality, as hypotheses, and as invitations and challenges to further refinement and clarifications. By *fitting* we mean that good models are logical, consistent, and neat. That is, they are simple, clear, aesthetic, and balanced. By *stimulating* we mean that good models have a capacity to arouse the imagination and thus to contribute to further and deeper understanding.[10]

Models do not have to be exclusive. Various models balance or supplement each other. A chosen model has normally one or two secondary aspects and rejects only the polar opposite of the primary model. According to Antonio Lambino, when we choose a model, we should regard the following five points as important: (1) *Inadequacy* of all models: Each model comprehends only a different facet of reality; it does not exhaust it. Reality is always greater and richer than any model that tries to grasp it. (2) *Relativity* of models: Each model focuses on one aspect of reality. No single model can claim to be exhaustive or exclusive in the sense that it grasps and expresses the whole of reality completely. There is no model to end all models. Yet in the use of models, we need to be careful not to relativize everyone's position by contending that it is just another model and one model is as good as any other model. Likewise, we need to be careful to maintain the flexibility to work with several models at the same time, especially in times of rapid change, such as in our own days. (3) Models as *responsive to needs*: Each age of history and historical community tends to develop a model that best responds to its perceived needs. In that sense we can say that "a model is accepted/acceptable if it accounts for a large number of biblical and traditional data and accords with what history and experience tell us about the Christian Life."[11] When a model manages to synthesize what is already known, inspires new insights, and helps to solve various problems whose interconnectedness is not immediately apparent, it dominates previous models. Such a dominant model is often called a *paradigm*. (4) *Historicity* of models: When the historical situation changes, that is, if there is a shift in the human person's understanding of self, the need for new models arises. Often several models are used simultaneously to explain and explore different aspects of the same reality. In physics, light is often explained in terms of the movement of

---

[10] Luzbetak, *The Church and Culture*, 136-137.
[11] Dulles, *Models of the Church*, 24.

waves and of particles. And (5) *Time-limits* of models: In time every model reaches the limits of insight. New models will emerge.[12] However, theological models rarely disappear. In the natural sciences a dominant model that has been superseded by a newer paradigm generally dies away. For example, Ptolemy, Copernicus, Newton, and Einstein are a series of thinkers whose ideas about physics have been progressively superseded by later thinkers. In contrast, dominant models in theology are not usually vanquished as thoroughly as in the empirical sciences.

Hans Küng has described the way new models or paradigms in theology may come into existence by using parallels from natural science and existing theology. He mentions five links in the chain of reasoning, which may be summarized in his five theses.

1. As in natural science so also in theology there is a "normal science," the established position with its classic authors, textbooks, and teachers that is characterized by (a) a cumulative growth of knowledge; (b) a solving of remaining problems; and (c) resistance to everything that might lead to the alteration or replacement of the established model of understanding or paradigm.
2. As in natural science so also in theology, the awareness of a growing crisis is generally the point of departure for a crucial change in certain previously valid assumptions. This leads to breakthroughs in new interpretative models or paradigms. Where the available rules and methods fail, they prompt the search for new models.
3. As in natural science so also in theology an old model of understanding or paradigm is replaced when a new one is ready.
4. As in natural science so also in theology both scientific and nonscientific factors play a role in deciding whether a new paradigm will be adopted or rejected. Thus the transition to a new model cannot be forced by any rational process but rather entails what may be described as a conversion.
5. As in natural science so also in theology it is hard to predict, amid the great arguments of the day, whether a new model will be absorbed by the old one, or the old one replaced or archived. If it is accepted, the innovation solidifies into tradition.[13]

The positive result of such a process is that we gain new insights and ever more comprehensive views to the degree that the data increases. Exegesis has been proceeding that way for a long time. What we have gained today is more and more data. Out of this data theologians can construct a working hypothesis that they will have to substantiate with the data available to them. Today this procedure

---

[12] Lambino, "A New Theological Model," 6-7.

[13] Hans Küng, "Paradigm Change in Theology: A Proposal for Discussion," in *Paradigm Change in Theology: A Symposium for the Future*, ed. Hans Küng and David Tracy (Edinburgh: T&T Clark, 1989), 3-31.

is at the root of doing theology on the basis of models. All theologians agree that theology is not just an empirical science; we must keep in mind that it has an abiding norm in the past, a norm given to us once and for all in the revelation of Israel's history and ultimately in Jesus Christ.

There is no way back. The ultimate reason for this shift is the insight that the old dogmatic theology, with all its splendor and glory, misconceived history with its "classicist mode." It thought not in terms of evolution and development but rather in terms of universality and permanence.[14] The Second Vatican Council recognized this shift in this often quoted sentence from *Gaudium et Spes*: "And so mankind substitutes a dynamic and more evolutionary concept of nature for a static one, and the result is an immense series of new problems calling for a new endeavor of analysis and synthesis" (*GS,* no. 5).

What is new is the understanding that history itself becomes a means of revelation as well. As Lonergan put it: "There is a dimension in man which strives for meaning which makes culture possible. In bringing out this meaning in culture man makes himself the creator of his own history."[15] The different cultures must be taken more seriously if the gospel is to to reveal its universal significance for all nations and people. In his massive work on church and culture, Louis Luzbetak puts it this way when he writes about the church's mission in the future:

> The Church needs anthropology if it is to be able to evaluate and be in a position to offer to nations around the globe a two-thousand-year-old tradition, much of which is both spiritually and culturally precious, while much might best be described as mere trappings of history. The Church needs anthropology because it must be able to speak today as it did on that first Pentecost (Acts 2:1-12), in a way that all peoples of the world might understand. The Church ought to be able to speak in respective native tongues about the marvels God has accomplished—whether the people be Parthians, Medes, or Elamites; whether they be from Mesopotamia, Judea, Cappadocia, Pontus, or the province of Asia; from Phrygia, Pamphylia, Egypt, or Libya; whether they be Romans, Cretans, or Arabs. The Church must understand *all* peoples and be understood *by all,* despite deep cultural differences. It would be unfortunate indeed if the Church were to overlook the fact that it has today at its disposal, as never before, a vast treasury of human knowledge in the social sciences, not the least important of which is the Science of Human Beings called *Anthropology.*
>
> But even local churches *qua local* addressing their own people, with whom they share the same culture, need a *culturally oriented* approach to mission and therefore should avail themselves of the Science of Culture. As we have emphasized over and over again, there is no more effective or more genuine way of being Christian—that is to say, of being "of the

---

[14] Lonergan, "Theology in Its New Context," 7.
[15] Ibid., 8.

mind of Christ" (1 Cor 2:1 6)—than in terms of culture. The local church is not fully and effectively proclaiming the kingdom unless the gospel is preached in the cultural "language" of the community concerned: in other words, unless the proclamation of the Word, the participation in worship and manifestation of God's presence, and the specific forms of communication, fellowship, service and organization are all as closely as possible tailored to the culture and social situation of the time and place. What every local church needs is a truly local theology, local in understanding and local in practice.[16]

If it is true that all human beings are *cultural* beings, then Jesus must be *culturally* relevant if he is to be understood and appreciated. And so it is with the church; it must be culturally relevant if it is to be understood and appreciated. This is a most obvious fact but unfortunately one only too often overlooked.

DIFFERENT MODELS OF CHURCH

After Vatican II the church's interest gradually shifted toward the developing countries, whose voices were tolerated rather than seriously listened to during the council. Suddenly there emerged formidable theologians from continents like Latin America, Asia, and Africa who had not been present during the council. The first fruit of their effort to do theology from their situational and cultural background was the emergence of liberation theology. This was the first truly non-European systematic approach to theology; it brought movement into an otherwise very stable and fixed way of doing theology. The reaction of traditional theologians and the church's own teaching office ranged from outright condemnation to gradual acknowledgment as the years went by. The questions raised by these theologians could not be ignored, because traditional theology could not provide answers with its way of doing theology.

In the wake of these insights and developments after the council, different understandings and views concerning the church emerged. Theologians like Karl Rahner, Avery Dulles, Johann Metz, and Hans Küng realized that the emerging global church or world church would have to give way to different conceptions of church built on different cultural and sociological situations. Walbert Bühlmann, Leonardo Boff, Anthony Bellagamba, and most of the Latin American liberation theologians envisioned a church that would be able to respond to the changing situations in the world and, in turn, could help the traditional church in the West open itself to new situations that were emerging there as well.

Theologians have analyzed these different approaches and views and tried to synthesize them in order to come to grips with at least the main ones. Avery Dulles, in *Models of the Church*, sees five descriptions of the church in the

---

[16] Luzbetak, *The Church and Culture*, 374-375.

post-conciliar era. We will follow his models as a guide in our presentation but broaden his view where new emerging aspects ask for it.

The Church as Community of Disciples

In 1982, eight years after the publication of the *Models of the Church*, Dulles authored another major book on the church titled *A Church to Believe in: Discipleship and the Dynamics of Freedom*. In chapter 1 of this book Dulles proposed a new conception of the church in the light of which the five models he had presented earlier should be seen, reevaluated, and judged. He called this new conception of the church "community of disciples."[17] Behind this image we find an expression of the newly discovered realization that the basic vocation of any Christian is first and foremost to follow the Lord as he walked this earth (*Perfectae Caritatis,* no. 2).

The emphasis here is on following the Lord rather than following the church, on being constantly on the road rather than having already reached the goal. The church must be seen as the community of those who have made it their life's profession to follow the Lord and as such build a community that is called church.

The three basic elements of following the Lord in the New Testament are outlined best in Mark 3:3-15: called, to be with, and to be sent out. The stress in the vision of church as a *community of disciples* seems to be on the second aspect. To be a disciple means first and foremost to *be with the Lord*, to have been called by him into intimacy, to have firsthand knowledge of him. According to 1 John 1:1-4, to be a disciple means to have seen, touched, and lived with the Lord before one can be sent out. Mission means to witness to one's own experience of the Lord. This model would correspond most fittingly to John's understanding of the church as a community of disciples, in which all are kept in union because they experience individually the love, union, and intimacy of the Lord present in them through the Paraclete.[18]

John is worried that too much stress might be put on institution and succession and not enough on the individual Christ experience of the members in the community. Again in the words of Raymond Brown:

> There is much in Johannine theology that would relativize the importance of institution and office at the very time when that importance was being accentuated in other Christian communities (including those who spoke of apostolic foundation). Unlike Paul's image of the body and its members which is invoked in I Cor 12 to accommodate the multitude of

---

[17] Avery Dulles, *A Church to Believe In: Discipleship and the Dynamics of Freedom* (New York: Crossroad, 1982); M.-D. Chenu, "The New Awareness of the Trinitarian Basis of the Church," *Concilium* 146 (1981), 14-22.

[18] Raymond E. Brown, *The Community of the Beloved Disicple* (London: Geoffrey Chapman, 1979), 81-88.

charisms, the Johannine image of the vine and branches places emphasis on only one issue: dwelling on the vine or inherence in Jesus. (If John was interested in diversity of charism, he could have written of branches, twigs, leaves, and fruit, even as Paul wrote symbolically of foot, hand, ear, and eye.) The category of discipleship based on love makes any other distinction in the Johannine community relatively unimportant, so that even the well-known Petrine and presbyteral image of the shepherd is not introduced without the conditioning question, "Do you love me?" (21:15-17). . . .

The Fourth Gospel is best interpreted as voicing a warning against the dangers inherent in such developments by stressing what (for John) is truly essential, namely, the living presence of Jesus in the Christian through the Paraclete. No institution or structure can substitute for that. This outlook and emphasis would give Johannine ecclesiology a different tone from that of the Apostolic Christians known to us from other late first-century NT writings—a Johannine ecclesiology the peculiarity of which reflects the peculiarity of Johannine christology.[19]

The gospel of John airs a concern that many among the faithful share today. As necessary as institutions and structures may be, one of the most necessary elements felt to be indispensable for a spirituality of today is a personal experience of Jesus Christ alive.

Dulles, who does not refer here to John's gospel, regards the following elements as basic for such an image of church as community of disciples.

The Group around Jesus: Community of Disciples

Although this conception of church is not common in Catholic ecclesiology, it has a good biblical foundation, particularly in the Book of Acts, in which the primitive church is often called the "community of the disciples." This conception links the church to Jesus himself in the sense that the earthly Jesus founded the community of disciples, men and women whom the Father had called and given to him in order that he should lead them to a radical commitment to him and the kingdom he preached. They became the group that was to emerge after Easter as the church entrusted by the Risen Lord with the task to continue his mission to proclaim in word and deed the kingdom of God as God's saving will for all.

What all the gospels are concerned with is fellowship with the Lord. They could be called manuals of fellowship. It is difficult to decide to what degree we can say that the earthly Jesus founded a church. But we can say with certainty that Jesus deliberately formed and trained a band of disciples to whom he gave a share in his teaching and healing ministry. Therefore, we can say that Jesus

---

[19] Brown, *Community of the Beloved Disciple*, 86-88.

did found a community of disciples. The church that emerged after Easter should be understood and seen in continuity with that community of disciples that Jesus himself had created in his lifetime. This community is the place where authentic discipleship to Jesus himself and to his kingdom message becomes possible. In order to know what it means to be a disciple of Jesus, we have to look at these men and women whom Jesus chose, whom he called to follow him, and to learn from them what the Lord asked of them. This vision of church as a community of disciples seems to resonate with what many regard as their own experience of church today.

Like the first disciples, the present-day Christian has first to hear a personal call from the Lord and to respond to it in a free and self-conscious manner. This call must be heard as coming from the Lord of the church, not simply from the church, so that Christ himself is seen as the focal point of the Christian life. Dulles puts the stress on the personal experience of a call to become a Christian over against just being a Christian because one was born into a Christian church.

Discipleship: A Constant Becoming

According to the New Testament one is never a disciple but is always on the road to becoming a disciple. Discipleship is a precarious thing, something any of us can easily betray or deny. To remain in the company of Jesus requires a fresh grace from the Lord every day. The emphasis here is that being a disciple means to be on a journey toward discipleship. It means to be constantly learning strange words and deciphering puzzling experiences. It means "to go behind the Master" and let him determine the way, to let oneself be corrected every day. It is here that the community becomes quite important, because it is in the community that one finds support and discerns with others which way the Lord leads. Once again, it is not just a matter of receiving instruction only; rather, it is a question of learning and of actively participating in ministry and mission. This affirms what we said earlier about the identity-instilling power of the image of discipleship.[20]

This view follows closely the insight of the Latin American theologians for whom concrete fellowship with the Lord is the first step before any theory about the kingdom and the church can be brought forth. Only in the praxis of following Christ do we glimpse the mental categories that will enable us to grasp the real nature of the church and formulate it in a meaningful way.[21]

Disciples in Community

In the experience of our dependence on one another we come to realize that without community there would be neither scripture nor sacraments nor any

---

[20] Patricia Schoelles, "Liberation Theology and Discipleship: The Critical and Reforming Tendencies of Basic Christian Identity," *Louvain Studies* 19 (1994), 46-64.

[21] Jon Sobrino, *Christology at the Crossroads: A Latin American Approach* (Maryknoll, New York: Orbis Books, 1978), 60.

other means of access to Jesus himself. What counts is the experience of the individual disciple, who again needs the community of disciples for making and discerning this personal experience. It is a matter of staying in contact with the community, which goes back to the first disciples of Jesus and which was founded by them in order to come to know what authentic fellowship is all about.

This view is most explicitly presented in the gospel of Matthew. For him, the Sermon on the Mount is the new Rule and the new Law for the disciples. This Magna Carta of Christian behavior is to be understood as the new way of life for those who want to follow the Master. But Matthew makes it clear that the Sermon on the Mount presupposes the existence of a community of those already committed to the Lord, one in which the demands of the Sermon are practiced and lived. It presupposes a Christian community, we could even say the church. Without such a community we cannot live discipleship.

The Beatitudes show very clearly that the gospel is to be proclaimed and lived in a community in which the living out of the same Beatitudes is made possible through the community that provides the necessary support for the individual. The individual alone cannot live these virtues except as a member of a Christian community, and the Beatitudes assume that there are people in the community who have made them their rule of life. All the hard sayings in the Sermon on the Mount are meant to remind us that we cannot live without the support and trust of others. For Matthew, we can only be and remain disciples of Jesus by joining the community of disciples. Only the community can provide the atmosphere, the concern, the mutual love, and the experience of Christ risen and alive that will enable the disciple to live true discipleship. Outside of the community we cannot live discipleship.

Another feature of Jesus' ministry that Matthew emphasizes strongly and that expresses his idea of discipleship is Jesus' custom of sitting at table with his followers, who represent all kinds of people and always include the outcasts of society. Some authors even think that the Kingdom of God movement can best be summarized as a table community movement. The authors base the validity of this phrase on the undeniable fact that one of Jesus' basic behaviors was his frequent sharing of meals with the poor, the hungry, and the outcasts who made up the majority of his followers. What marks the community of Jesus' disciples is the continuous practice of sitting at table and remembering that Jesus will remain with them in this celebration until the day he will come again to fulfill it (Mt 26:29). But it is also the community which decides who can become a member and under what conditions an individual can remain a member of the community of disciples (Mt 18:15-18; 22:11-13).[22]

Disciple and Ministry

Dulles thinks that, in a church described as community of disciples, we will have to view ministry differently. Competence and authority should only be

---

[22] John Fuellenbach, *Throw Fire* (Manila: Logos Publication, 1998), 110-113; Herman Hendrickx, *A Key to the Gospel of Matthew* (Manila: Claretian Publications, 1992), 10-13.

invested in mature and faithful disciples. A leader selected and commissioned on the basis of proven discipleship may have a wide range of responsibilities, but authoritarianism of any kind needs to be outlawed in a community of disciples. However, this is possible only if the governing power in the church is no longer based solely on sacramental power. The ecclesiology of Vatican II seems to make such a distinction between the sacrament of orders and governing power theoretically possible. But as long as the liturgy, the place of the sacred, remains the only model for church organization, it will remain difficult to see how the community of disciples model would be allowed to develop at the grassroots level, by giving the laity a share in the government of the church, not on the basis of hierarchical delegation but on the basis of their own vocation.[23]

By seeing ministry as discipleship we can avoid making sharp distinctions between the disciples and become able to introduce into the church once again true equality among all. Discipleship is the common denominator that unites all, because all are followers and learners in relation to Jesus Christ. Walter Kirchschläger observes:

> The decisive criterion for ministry or a special task in the Jesus community, as well as in the early church, was personal bonding to Jesus Christ in existential commitment. This commitment is hidden behind the metaphor, found in the first three gospels, of "leaving everything" (Mk 1:16-20 par.; Mk 2:13-14), as well as in the later reflection about Simon's love of Christ in Jn 21. After Easter, this criterion was replaced by personal faith in Christ and the ability to witness (cf. Acts 1:15-26; 6:1-7; 1 Tm 3:1-7, 8-13; Ti 1:6-9). Definite presuppositions concerning one's gender or station in life were not relevant. Recent exegetical work has shown that women and married people were involved in the leadership structures of NT times. This work has corrected the onesided and dominant view that has obtained until now. The only pertinent exception is the circle of the Twelve who, as symbols of Israel's tribes, could be only males. Jacob had 12 sons, not 12 daughters. While this is correct, one should not fail to remember that there were women around Jesus who were a complement to the Twelve.[24]

Avery Dulles did not consider the vision of the church as community of disciples as a model in the proper sense. He saw it rather as a *preludium* to all models of church, something to be kept in mind when we conceptualize the church in various models. James D. G. Dunn shares this reservation. For him, the model of discipleship depends too much on the exceptional circumstances

---

[23] Christian Duquoc, *Provisional Churches: An Essay in Ecumenical Ecclesiology* (London: SCM Press, 1986), 101.

[24] Walter Kirchschläger, "Plurality and Creativity in Church Structure," *Theology Digest* 45 (1998), 249.

of Jesus' earthly ministry to provide a pattern for Christian community today. But he warns against putting this model aside as irrelevant:

> If "discipleship of Jesus" still has any meaning for today (and it certainly has) then the character of that discipleship, particularly of celebration and mission, of openness and service, should be a constant challenge to any ecclesiastical structure which does not positively promote such discipleship. The Church exists to enable the same quality of discipleship as that to which Jesus called his first followers.[25]

The Church as Institution

Cardinal Robert Bellarmine (+1621) proposed a definition of the church that became classical in Catholic tradition: "The one and true Church is the assembly of human persons bound together by the profession of the same Christian faith and the communion of the same sacraments, under the rule of legitimate pastors and in particular of the vicar of Christ on earth, the Roman Pontiff."[26] Pius XII took up this definition in his encyclical *Mystici Corporis*. However, far from being a real definition, it is actually a list of requirements necessary for belonging to the Catholic Church. It puts the stress on the exterior features, that is, on the visible form of the church, while the internal dimensions of membership are left aside. Clear and decisive as it may be for apologetical reasons, it is too external and minimalistic: external profession of faith, communion in the sacraments, and subordination to proper authority. These three criteria are determined by the central government, the Roman pontiff. They exclude from the church all those who do not correspond to these visible criteria, of which the central government is the author. Only Roman Catholics are true members of the church; others belong to her only by desire. As a consequence, the church of Christ "exists" only in the Roman Catholic Church. In such a model the power and functions of the church are divided into three: teaching, sanctifying, and governing. This leads to the distinctions between the church teaching and the church taught; the church sanctifying and the church sanctified; and the church governing and the church governed.

The result of such distinctions is that the church is identified with the governing body or the hierarchy. While the teaching and sanctifying functions of the hierarchy are seen as mediating the doctrine and grace of Christ, the governing function is perceived as being handled solely by the hierarchy.[27] This, in turn, leads to a strong hierarchical conception of authority. The church is conceived as a society in which the fullness of power is concentrated in the hands

---

[25] James D. G. Dunn, *The Christ and the Spirit*, vol. 2, *Pneumatology* (Edinburgh: T&T Clark, 1998), 247.

[26] Michael Schmaus, *The Church: Its Origin and Structure* (London: Sheed and Ward, 1977), 8.

[27] Dulles, *Models of the Church*, 34-46.

of the hierarchy and handed down through sacramental ordination. In extreme forms of such views there is hardly any room for active participation of the laity in the governing power of the church.

Bellarmine's definition has determined to a large degree the concept of the church still held today. This model sees the church primarily as a hierarchically structured, visible society that mediates salvation to its individual members through preaching and teaching of the word and administration of the sacraments. This was the dominant model in Roman Catholicism before the Second Vatican Council, and it inspired the first draft of the council's *Dogmatic Constitution on the Church (Lumen Gentium)*. The council fathers rejected such an approach to the mystery of the church as being too juridical and too rigid. What are we to say negatively and positively about the institutional model? At least the following: (1) It enjoys *strong endorsement* in many Church documents in the past and in Vatican II as well. The document *Lumen Gentium* remains ambiguous, since it adopted the hierarchical view without a serious attempt to reconcile the new with the old view. (2) It provides a strong sense of *corporate identity*, as each person knows his or her place and role in the church. (3) It is attentive to *historical continuity,* connecting the present church with the church of the past. It provides a feeling of security against any present theological uncertainty and theological fad.

On the other hand, the institutional model is based not so much on scripture as on a particular worldview with a definite understanding of the universe, of the human person, and of culture, which is composed of a set of meanings and values informing a common way of life. This view is a perfect expression of the classical worldview. It consists of a "dominant mentality" that enshrines a certain tradition; it implies certain presuppositions or assumptions; it regards certain concepts as fundamental. As a consequence, the church bases its authority not on the community but on the sacrament of orders. In democracy, authority rests with the people and is delegated by the people and is legitimate only to the degree that people give credit to it. In the church, authority derives its legitimation not from the people but from God or Christ. Democratic procedures for determining governing power in the church are, therefore, not possible. The ultimate reason given is the understanding that salvation comes to us from elsewhere and cannot be drawn from the grassroots. To say that all are equal does not affect the social organization of the church but is seen only as a spiritual reality. What might be rightly assumed in the secular world—that social and political equality is a basic human right—cannot be applied to the church in its organization. It might seem paradoxical for the church to defend the equality of social and political rights of men and women in the secular world and not to admit those same rights in the organization of the church.

Another paradox heard so often today is the claim of the church to be a historical anticipation of the kingdom of God in space and time now. The symbol kingdom itself stands for a community of brothers and sisters where there are neither rulers nor ruled, where all are equal and one in Christ (Gal 3:27-28). How does the church concretely witness to this kingdom of equals in its external structures? The Catholic Church finds itself in a constant dilemma: On the one hand, it defends social and political equality; on the other hand, it withholds this from its own members in the exercise of authority in the Christian community itself. The church firmly holds to the principle of authority based on the sacrament of orders, which is claimed to be the only principle to do justice to revelation as it was proclaimed in Jesus Christ.[28]

There are few passages in scripture that support this view. Even so, it sometimes seems that Catholic ecclesiology for many years knew only Matthew 16:17-19: "You are Peter and on this rock I will build my church." In Matthew 16:19 Jesus tells Peter that what he binds or looses on earth will be held as bound or loosed by God. But this statement is repeated in almost exactly the same words in 18:18 and applied to all the disciples or even to the church in general. Bas van Iersel observes: "It is only if we were to fail to read on after 16:18-20 that we might make the mistake of thinking that only Peter and his successors were permitted to make decisive pronouncements."[29] With the exception of the pastoral letters, the New Testament described the assembled community and not individual officials in the community as being ultimately responsible for making decisions in matters of doctrine and morals. Accordingly, the Christian community played a much more active role in any decision-making process in the early churches than we usually assume.[30]

The hierarchical and societal aspect is disproportionately stressed at the expense of the communitarian. The role of the ordained is exaggerated at the expense of the missionary responsibility of the entire church. The institutional structures are those that are regularly established, publicly recognized, stable, respectable, and uniform. Dulles singles out four categories of institutional structures in the church: (1) doctrines and doctrinal formulations that are normative for all the members such as creeds, dogmas, and canonical writings (scriptures, conciliar pronouncements); (2) forms of public worship, such as sacraments and other approved rituals; (3) structures of government, that is, offices with the powers and duties attached to them; and (4) laws and customs regulating the behavior of members.[31]

Finally, the scope of the church is limited to the Roman Catholic Church; the ecclesial reality of other churches is not recognized. The mission of the church is limited to the preaching of the word and the administration of the sacraments at the expense of the church's broader social and political responsibility. This is a real obstacle to creative and fruitful theology. Other essential ministries in the church, like the prophetic and teaching ministry, are entirely subjected to the magisterium. The charismatic ministries in the church are either ignored or presumed to have been legitimately taken over by the ministry of office.

---

[28] Duquoc, *Provisional Churches*, 6-7, 98-103.

[29] Bas van Iersel, "Who according to the New Testament Has the Say in the Church?" *Concilium* 148 (1981), 11.

[30] Ibid., 15-16.

[31] Dulles, *A Church to Believe In,* 22.

These are the main objections voiced against the institutional model as it has existed in practice and theory in the church since the Council of Trent.

The Council and the Hierarchical Model

The revolutionary vision of the church that emerged during the council put a stop to a church image that portrayed the church almost exclusively in terms of hierarchy. However, many theologians still think that, in spite of all the corrections the council made, the effective institutional and legal structures of the church seem to render this new vision of the church largely ineffective at the grassroots level. The old perception of the church still seems to be the image that prevails in many circles of the church up to the present. We may safely say, without being pessimistic, that the reform introduced by the council still has a long way to go.

The first question to be asked when correcting the hierarchical model will certainly be: How democratic or participatory can the church really be? Our time, with its passion for equality and participation, will use this as the litmus test to ascertain whether the church has a future or not. Its understanding of world order in hierarchical terms is alien for many people today. But can the church really be defined and understood as total equality of all, even in its very structure of authority and governing power?

Benedict Ashley in *Justice in the Church* introduces a distinction that might help us concerning the question of equality and inequality. He writes: "We must distinguish *functional* from *personal* equality and inequality. Functional inequality requires an order or hierarchy of functions if these functions are to be coordinated in a unified action."[32] How we understand hierarchy is important. As Ashley points out, there are two conceptions of hierarchy: one linear, the other nonlinear. The linear understanding conceives the universe as a linear order of entities emanating from the Divine One in which each entity totally contains all its inferiors and is totally contained by its superiors. The Christian Neo-Platonist Pseudo-Dionysius applied this linear conception to the celestial hierarchy of angelic spirits and to the ecclesiastical hierarchy of church offices. In such an ecclesiology members of the laity are totally dependent on their priests for all graces, the priests totally dependent on the bishops, the bishops on the pope, the pope on Christ, and Christ on God.[33]

Such a linear concept of hierarchy is not the way ecclesiological office needs to be conceived, although in practice this seems to be what occurred. This conception seems to be in the mind of those who today reject radically any hierarchical model as unacceptable to the modern mind and want to see it replaced by the principle of participation. Ashley quotes Sandra Schneiders, who writes:

---

[32] Benedict M. Ashley, *Justice in the Church: Gender and Participation* (Washington. D.C.: Catholic University Press, 1996), 10.

[33] Ibid., 11.

It is not that those in authority are exercising authority badly or that those who should be obeying lack faith, humility, or some other virtue (although both are sometimes true). It is that the principle of hierarchy, which is the nerve of both secular and religious obedience as they have been traditionally understood, is being radically questioned and the principle of participation is supplanting it in more and more sectors of life.[34]

Ashley thinks Schneiders sees authority linearly in her harsh judgment on authority and her demand for abolishing the principle of hierarchy altogether.

But there is another view of authority developed by Thomas Aquinas. This second model of hierarchy does not accept the linear conception of the order of being. Any entity in the chain of being is generically subordinated to its superior but not totally so, since it also has unique specific or individual characteristics not contained in any of the superiors except in the Creator. It likewise contains its inferiors only generically and not totally, so that they are in some respects superior to it. This view certainly does justice to a Christian anthropology, which sees every human being as absolutely unique insofar as it expresses something of God's very being that is not expressed in any other creature. The identity of a human person rests ultimately in his or her unique relationship with a personal God.[35]

This concept of hierarchy applied to an ecclesiology constitutes its members as functionally unequal, yet because each member functions to make a unique contribution to the common good, all members equally have a right to participate in the common good. Thus the *principle of hierarchy* and the *principle of participation* need not stand in opposition but can complement each other in an ecclesiology based on a nonlinear model. In such an ecclesiology, while the laity receives the broad range of graces through the church's official hierarchy, this general subordination of the laity to the hierarchy does not render the laity more distant from God because each Christian has unique graces directly from God, mediated only through Christ, his Divine Son, by Christ's Holy Spirit.[36] Ashley writes:

> The Christian view of justice does not confuse the personal equality due to all members of the church and of society because they are created in God's image with the necessarily hierarchical inequality of gifts, offices and kinds of status required for a community to achieve the common good of its members and to permit the maximum participation by all. Yet the inequality of function and status must always be in the service of personal equality, and must never override that more fundamental equality. The

---

[34] Sandra Schneiders, in ibid., 10.
[35] Fuellenbach, *Throw Fire*, 50-65.
[36] Ashley, *Justice in the Church*, 11-12.

Christian in whatever functional status must imitate Christ who came not to be served but to serve.[37]

But as long as all governing power remains practically, if not theoretically, linked to the sacrament of orders, the church will have great difficulty in coping with the charismatic element of the people of God, which in theory is not denied. The uniqueness of every person is revealed precisely in his or her having received a charism or charisms given to build up the Christian community (1 Cor 12). Therefore, the charismatic structure accounts for the functional inequality of every person.

Admittedly, charisms were of great importance for the infant church. But these charisms were rarely considered as belonging to the essence of the church, because the church is not primarily a merely charismatic movement but a hierarchical institution, founded on the apostles and their authority. But if we take Ashley's nonlinear model of hierarchy into consideration, the charisms are then to be understood as unique contributions made by the members of the church and are, as such, not contained in the office. And yet they belong to the essence of the church. Only if one sees hierarchy in the linear model can there be no unique contribution to be made through the charisms of the laity.

Paul's conception of the church as a charismatic entity entails a community that is kept alive through the charisms that the Holy Spirit gives to each member of the community for the well-being of the community and demands of the individual the full exercise of these unique contributions if the church will remain what it really is supposed to be: the anticipation of the kingdom community in which everyone will contribute to the happiness and full identity of every person.

Realizing the danger of neglecting the charismatic element in a highly structured church, Pius XII tried to show that the structures of the church contain both elements, hierarchic and charismatic, and that they can never be separated from each other.[38] Their mutual relationship is constantly explained in terms of *service* and *harmony*; consequently, there cannot be any conflict between the two. The historical reality of the church, however, has shown that these moral values will not do away with concrete conflicts and that it is too easy to put the blame on the factor of sin. In fact, the hierarchical remains so highly stressed that the connection between it and the charismatic element is neither seen nor reflected upon most of the time.[39] The ultimate reason seems to be once again the linear model of perceiving the hierarchical order.

Conscious of this danger, Vatican II tried to balance such a one-sided, exaggerated hierarchical picture of the church by reevaluating the charismatic elements. The council clearly states in *Lumen Gentium* that the church is built not only by institutional structures but also by the infinite variety of gifts that each

---

[37] Ibid., 164.

[38] Pius XII, *Mystici Corporis*, Acta Apostolica Sedis 35 (1943), 200 ff.

[39] Dulles, *A Church to Believe In*, 24-25.

person "has the right and duty to use . . . for the building of the Church" (*LG*, nos. 4, 12).[40]

By seeing the church as built on office *and* charisms, the council grounded a set of rights and duties for all Christians, among them the right to "receive in abundance the help of the spiritual goods of the Church, the right and at times the duty of the laity to express their views on Church matters, and the right to initiate activities in the service of the Church." In addition, it affirms the ability of the laity to engage in more immediate forms of cooperation in the apostolate of the hierarchy and to be appointed to some ecclesiastical office (*LG*, nos. 33, 35).

The relationship between office and charism is here conceived in such a way that the council regarded the church as being "a spiritual organism in which, from the early days, there have been permanent ministries and charismatic ministries, all regarded as gifts of the Spirit."[41]

The concrete question remains how these charismatic ministries can function effectively alongside the institutional ministries without being rendered ineffective by them.[42] Can we perceive of an institutional model that would give room for other ministries to function well? Many think that this is possible if the hierarchical model recognizes the proper importance and relative independence of these charismatic ministries from the ministry of office in the church. In terms of Ashley's nonlinear model of hierarchy, we need to acknowledge that the charisms are the unique contributions of the individual who, in exercising his or her charism, is *functionally unequal* with the hierarchy as the hierarchy is unequal to the laity in exercising its function for the well-being of the whole. This would require that government in the church not be based entirely on the sacramental dimension but on the charismatic element as well. What are these other ministries? We will deal here with only two, which are of great importance in the church as a whole: the prophetic ministry and the ministry of teaching.

In 1 Corinthians 12:28 and in Ephesians 4:11 Paul presents us with a list of ministries in the church that he arranges according to their importance by stating: "And God has appointed in the church first apostles, second prophets, third teachers, then workers of miracles, then healers, helpers, administrators, speakers in various kinds of tongues" (1 Cor 12:28); and in another text: "And his gifts were that some should be apostles, some prophets, some evangelists, some pastors and teachers" (Eph 4:11). Implied is that these ministries are supposed to be permanently present in the church. To the question of who succeeded the apostles in their ministry, the answer seems to be easy: the hierarchical ministries. The problem arises, however, with the other ministries. Are the prophets to be a permanent ministry visible and tangible in the church like that of the

---

[40] Enrique Nardoni, "Charism in the Early Church since Rudolph Sohm: An Ecumenical Challenge," *Theological Studies* 53 (1992), 655.

[41] Ibid., 662.

[42] On the whole issue of the charismatic element in the church and its relationship to the hierarchical element, see Karl Rahner, *The Dynamic Element in the Church* (New York: Herder and Herder, 1964), 42-83.

hierarchy? What about the ministry of teachers? Do these ministries have their own function? Or have they just been taken over by the hierarchy, whose members regard themselves as those called to discharge the ministry of the prophets and the teachers as well?

The following table identifies the three main ministries listed by Paul with some analysis of their continuing role in the church. Since the ministry of apostles is seen as continuing in the very visible and concrete ministry of the hierarchy, it will be useful to try to develop a fuller description of how the ministries of prophet and teacher continue in our day.

Table 6-1. The Church Is Built On (1 Cor 12:28; Eph 4:11)

APOSTLES	PROPHETS	TEACHERS
SUCCESSORS: - bishops	SUCCESSORS: - individual prophets - institutional groups	SUCCESSORS: - theologians
STATUS: ecclesiastical office	STATUS: charismatic ministry	STATUS: charismatic ministry
FUNCTION: - sound doctrine: apostolic tradition - ordered liturgy - administration of the sacraments - order and tradition - to assure unity of conviction in matters of faith and morals	FUNCTION: - to discern God's will for the church of today; to read the signs of the times - to present new models of following Christ in new social, political, and economic situations - to play a corrective role in the church's constant tendency to too much accommodation	FUNCTION: - responsible for passing on the tradition of the kerygma and the word of Jesus and for the continuity of Christian teaching - to interpret the tradition by providing new models of interpretation
DANGER: - to absorb the charismatic ministries into the ecclesial office - to become stagnated in traditional forms and ways and to end up in mere bureaucracy ministries	DANGER: - unwilling to let itself be "proven" and "tested" by the ecclesiastical office - to forget that this ministry is meant to serve the well-being of the whole church and not to dictate	DANGER: - to become only the mouthpiece of the hierarchy - to pretend to be the official teaching office of the church

Who Are the Successors of the Prophets?

The Christian understanding of prophetic ministry has its roots in the Old Testament where prophets arose as charismatic critics of the institution. Whenever established Israel forgot the covenant, with its demands for justice, and aligned itself too conveniently with the surrounding societies, the prophets appeared on the scene to protest. The classical prophets were among the most remarkable people who ever lived. They were verbal mediators between the two worlds of the primordial tradition. Their special characteristic was the passionate and critical involvement in the historical life of their people in their own time. They radically criticized their own culture in the name of God and called for an alternative consciousness contrary to the dominant consciousness of their culture.[43]

As a rule, the institutional representatives could not accept this critique. Since they could not ignore it, they always tried to domesticate it, that is, control it and integrate it into the institution. But there were always prophets who would not allow themselves to be domesticated. Prophets were always thorns in the flesh of the institution.

In Israel it was expected that in the end-time the prophetic spirit would be poured out on all; the whole messianic community would be prophetic (Jl 3). The perennial tension between institution and prophetic charism would finally cease. The early church was convinced that this was happening in its midst (Acts 2). If all were prophets, was there any need for a special prophetic ministry?

Ephesians 2:20 insists that the church is built on the "foundation of apostles and prophets," while in 1 Corinthians we read that "God has appointed in the church first apostles, second prophets, third teachers" (1 Cor 12:28). All three words—*apostles, prophets, teachers*—refer to persons having clearly defined roles and recognized ministries in the community.

Therefore we must distinguish between the recognized ministry of the prophet and the occasional gift of prophecy, as well as the general belief that in the New Testament everyone has received the prophetic spirit (Acts 2:17; 1 Jn 2:20; Jer 31:31-34; Ezek 36:24-28).

The question is: If this ministry belongs to the "foundation of the church," who has taken over the functions of the prophets and the teachers? Is there a succession of the prophets in the church? That the bishops are the successors of the apostles has long been an accepted thesis, but what about the prophets and teachers?

In the Catholic understanding of priesthood the three different ministries— prophet, teacher, and priest—seem to have once again been made into one. In the Old Testament the priest had three functions in the beginning. He was to proclaim

---

[43] Walter Brueggemann, *The Prophetic Imagination* (London: SCM Press, 1992), 44-79; Marcus Borg, *Jesus, a New Vision: Spirit, Culture, and the Life of Discipleship* (San Francisco: Harper & Row, 1987), 150-165.

God's will to people (Urim and Thumim); to teach as part of the levitical priest-hood (Dt 33:10), and to sacrifice and offer cultic offerings. However, the first function was taken over by the prophets, the second by the scribes. Sacrifice was the principal function left for the priest at the end of the Old Testament period.[44]

The New Testament started from a different perspective of priesthood than the Old Testament. Its understanding of priesthood emerged over a long period, and the different steps it took before it reached its present concept are difficult to delineate. The accumulation of a whole range of functions is historically explainable but hardly justifiable theologically. It is important that we come to see that these functions do not all belong by nature to the successors of the apostles, but that some are meant to be exercised by different people in the church and are to be regarded as their charisms.

Paul and Luke regard prophets as important members of the Christian com-munity. Paul lists them second after apostles (1 Cor 12:28), and they belong to the foundation of the church (Eph 2:20); to them the mystery of the calling of the Gentiles has been revealed (Eph 3:5); and they belong to the gifts of Christ to his church (Eph 4:11). Luke portrays the same view. There are five men whom he calls "prophets and leaders" (Acts 13:1-2) of the community at Antioch; Judas and Silas are named prophets (Acts 15:32) and are leading men among the brethren (Acts 15:22).

Accordingly, we must assume that, at a very early stage, charismatic, impul-sive prophecy became institutionalized and prophets were then seen as the holders of a spiritual office. This office had its own standing in the community between or on a par with apostles and teachers (1 Cor 12:28; Eph 4:11); next to apostles (Lk 11:49; Eph 2:20; 3:5; Did 11:3); next to teachers (Acts 13:1; Did 15:1); next to saints and apostles (Rv 18:20).

The Proper Functions of Prophets in the Early Church

We have to distinguish three groups possessing the prophetic spirit: (1) The eschatological community was convinced that each one had received the great gift of the end-time, the prophetic spirit (Acts 2:27; 1 Jn 2:20, 27). "But as for you, the anointing you received from him remains in you, and you do not need anyone to teach you; since the anointing he gave you teaches you everything, and since it is true, not false, remain in him just as it has taught you" (1 Jn 2:27). (2) There was "congregational prophecy," which describes the prophesying that was done by members of the early Christian communities who were not given the title prophets and who did not have the leading role in the community that those called prophets had.[45] (3) The ministry of the prophets became institution-alized and had its own standing in the community.

---

[44] Raymond E. Brown, *Priest and Bishop: Biblical Reflections* (New York: Paulist Press, 1970), 10-13.

[45] Francis A. Sullivan, *Charisms and Charismatic Renewal: A Biblical Theological Study* (Dublin: Gill and Macmillan, 1982), 95.

We are concerned with the last group and its function. The Letter to the Ephesians sees the prophetic role as mediation of revelation, receiving insights into mysteries and communicating them to the church. The prophet's role in Acts is a more practical one: giving direction to the church.[46]

More generally, their role was to encourage, edify, console, and call to repentance. They differ from the apostles in that they do not speak as official witnesses of the Risen Christ. In contrast to the teachers, they are not concerned with general points of doctrine but rather with urging the course to be taken in the present concrete situation.[47] James Dunn sees New Testament prophets functioning in line with the Old Testament prophets: they express warnings, admonish, give occasional premonitions and insights into the future, and are the mouthpiece of the Holy Spirit in giving guidance for the church's mission. Another very important function of the prophets in the early church was that they helped to interpret the prophecies of the Old Testament and the sayings of Jesus in the light of what happened (death, resurrection, and outpouring of the Spirit), and in relation to their own changing situation. Furthermore, it seems that the prophets delivered prophecies, not merely in the name of Jesus, but as the very word of Jesus, and in doing so they influenced the tradition of the kerygma of Jesus.[48]

Historical Development of Prophetic Ministry

In the first two centuries it was taken for granted that the ministry of prophecy was a permanent endowment of the church (Did 11-13). In all of the controversies of the second and third centuries with the Montanists, the fathers were adamant that the prophetic charism should not be suppressed in the church; for example, "The prophetic gift must, according to the teaching of the apostles, be maintained in the whole Church until the final advent" (Miltiades). "Some go so far in their zealous battle against false prophets that they reject the grace of true prophecy in the Church" (Irenaeus).

But the growth of clericalism in the church meant that prophecy faded into the background. From the third century on, prophecy belonged to the past and became the "Christian underground." Thomas Aquinas no longer knew what to do with prophecy as it was understood in the early church. The fruitful tension between apostolic succession and prophetic succession had to give way to an increasing sacerdotal, hierarchical church. During Vatican II Cardinal Ottaviani summed it up well when he declared that the early church did indeed have prophets and other charisms, but that with the death of the last apostles not only revelation but also the reality of these charisms ceased.

But prophecy in fact never died in the church. Great saints like Bernard of Clairvaux, Francis of Assisi, and Catherine of Siena show that the prophetic

---

[46] Ibid., 91-95.

[47] Avery Dulles, "The Succession of Prophets in the Church," *Concilium* 4 (April 1968), 28-32. Dulles quotes Hans Küng here.

[48] James D. G. Dunn, *Jesus and the Spirit* (London: SCM Press, 1975), 172-173.

role remained alive and in lively tension with the institutional church. Yet the church became less and less receptive to prophetic criticism. The history of the Reformation might have been different if the church had been open to the prophetic Spirit of the time. The whole history of Western Christianity after the Reformation is dominated by the struggle between the prophetism of the Reformation churches and the sacerdotalism of the Catholic tradition. Prophecy as disclosure of God's plans and purposes in history was almost totally disregarded and, as John Ronald Knox put it, "More than all other Christian churches, the Catholic Church became institutional."[49]

For the Catholic Church there could be no friction between prophets and magisterium. Prophecy was nothing more than the discharge of what was called the "prophetic office" of the church, which became identified with the magisterium. In short, the ministry of office had taken over the ministry of the prophets.

Prophets in the Church Today

Though Vatican II speaks fourteen times about charisms and recognizes their importance, nowhere does it state how they are related to the institutional element of the church. In the documents of the council we can hardly find anything that would come near to what the New Testament meant by this ministry. The crucial point, however, is that the church admits that God manifests God's presence and purpose in events of the present age. Only through the assistance of all can the church "hear, distinguish and interpret the many voices of our age and judge them in the light of the divine word" (*GS*, no. 44, see also no. 33). The question hotly debated during the council was whether or not the charismatic element in the church is distinct from the institutional. *Lumen Gentium* seems to imply a real distinction between the institutional and the charismatic, and the superiority of the latter over the former; for example, "[The Holy Spirit] furnishes and directs the church with various gifts, both hierarchical and charismatic" (no. 4) and "[The Holy Spirit] distributes special graces among the faithful of every rank. By these gifts the Spirit makes them fit and ready to undertake the various tasks or offices advantageous for the renewal and upbuilding of the Church" (no. 12, see also, nos. 7, 8).

But the council left the question open. Today most theologians say that the institutional and the charismatic are irreducible and distinct aspects of the church in its pilgrim condition. This means that the magisterium as such cannot appropriate this ministry and claim it as its own. In the nonlinear model of hierarchy this is obvious. Both are linked to service and are subordinated to the life of the Christian community as a whole. The ministry of prophecy belongs to the charismatic ministries and must be exercised. The church needs this ministry, that is, men and women capable of discerning God's hand in the history of our times.

---

[49] John Ronald Knox, *Enthusiasm* (Oxford, 1950), 590, quoted in Dulles, "The Succession of Prophets in the Church," 30.

Since prophets cannot appoint themselves as prophets but need to be recognized as such by others, prophetic movements stand in need of approval by the church at large. But officeholders are always tempted to suppress the prophetic element, for it is a disturbing element. By upsetting people's settled views and challenging their complacency, it continually threatens the unity and stability of the institutional church. Yet, "a Church in which the prophets have to keep silent declines and becomes a spiritless organization, and its pastors would become mere bureaucrats. . . . In such a Church people would be suffocated by the fumes of a decaying sacerdotalism. . . . History has shown that when prophets are not given their say within the Church they rise up to condemn it from outside."[50]

Prophets are essential not only for the church but for humankind as a whole as well. Only prophets engage in imagining different possibilities. They never ask whether their vision can be implemented. But there has to *be* a vision before it can be implemented. Modern cultures are normally competent enough to implement everything, but it seems impossible for them to imagine anything. The prophet's task is to keep alive the ministry of imagination, to keep on proposing alternative solutions and futures never thought of. The prophet has to propose new visions to enthuse and to energize people since it is the *not yet*, the promised, and that which is about to begin that can energize us, not what we already possess.[51]

Religious Orders as "Institutional Prophetic Ministry"

Is there a constant bearer of the prophetic ministry in the church? Or is this ministry totally sporadic, based on an ad hoc inspiration of the Holy Spirit without any permanence? There are individual prophets, but can there also be an institutional prophetic ministry? A number of theologians see religious life as a kind of institutional prophetic ministry.[52] Not all theologians share this view. While they accept that we do find prophetic orders and schools in scriptures as well as in the history of other religions, they insist that such institutions have rarely proven successful in the long run. "All they could do was to provide a discipline and an environment conducive to prophetic sensitivity."[53] Dulles does accept a *successio prophetarum*, but he defines it differently:

> Because prophecy is not ordinarily transmitted by continuous succession or by induction into office, prophets do not "succeed" their predecessors in an unbroken line as pastors commonly do. Yet when the prophetic

---

[50] Dulles, "The Succession of Prophets in the Church," 31-32.

[51] Brueggemann, *The Prophetic Imagination*, 11-14.

[52] Karl Rahner, *Spirit in the Church* (London: Burns and Oates, 1979), 35-73. Although Rahner does not use the word *prophetic*, from the content it is clear that he refers to religious life in the church as a prophetic dimension.

[53] Avery Dulles, "Successio Apostolorum," *Concilium* 148 (1981), 62.

charism is bestowed, the recipient can become not simply a successor of the prophets but a prophet in the succession. Thus a *successio prophetarum* exists, even though it be *discontinuous and unpredictable.*[54]

Thomas Merton held that prophetic witness was integral to monastic life. For him, the religious, called out of the world to live a life radically different from humanity at large, was well positioned to see the present from God's point of view and to discern the signs of the time more critically.[55] In 1993 the Congress on Religious Life had this to say:

> In the Church religious life forms a liminal group. That is, an alternative group, separated by its life style and ministry from the normal structures of society. It forms a liminal group by its life style of community celibacy, the option for the poor and permanent discernment in search of the will of God the Father. To live this way in all its radicality is to be in society in a manner distinct and somewhat distant from it. As Religious this is our prophecy. It is our way of being symbol of the Kingdom.[56]

With Jesus a new reality has entered this world: the kingdom of God. This is such a concrete and challenging reality that people are repeatedly drawn into its spell. In the end such people can do nothing else but dedicate themselves totally and unconditionally to this kingdom. In the words of the same congress: "Religious place themselves in the service of the kingdom. This they do with the intention of being transparent signs, living parables, messianic anticipations of the full realization of the kingdom. They attempt to re-present existentially the poor, obedient, chaste and compassionate Christ in the World."[57]

Since "radicalism" has not provided a completely adequate manner of distinguishing religious life from ordinary Christian life, authors such as Rahner, Schillebeeckx, and Gutiérrez have given different views as to how religious life might be seen in the church at large. Rahner favors a view of religious life that has been called *transcendentalism.* Religious life is seen as a way to realize the eschatological and transcendental dimensions of the Christian life. Schillebeeckx and Gutiérrez regard religious life as a particular *anthropological* form of Christian existence. Religious life offers authentic values. Some people turn toward these values, which normally are not chosen by the majority. This way of life is found in all great religions of the world. It is important to recognize today that religious life is not only a Christian phenomenon.

It has always been the role of religious persons to communicate their experience with the Holy. The role they play makes them distinct witnesses of precise

---

[54] Ibid., 65.

[55] Gerald Twomey, ed., *Thomas Merton: Prophet in the Belly of a Paradox* (New York: Paulist Press, 1978).

[56] Union of Superiors General, *Consecrated Life Today: Charisms in the Church for the World* (Montreal: St. Paul, 1994), 214.

[57] Ibid., 201.

human values like simplicity and austerity. They give witness to the centrality of relationship and encounter with the Holy, to compassion and nonviolence, to self-control and inner harmony with the cosmos and people living together. This way of life offers an alternative scale of values as a critical contrast to the status quo and will become a model of inspiration for society.

Latin American theologians propose the thesis that religious life is a way to realize "prophetic solidarity" with the people of God, especially the poor. They see religious life as a "prophetic exaggeration" of the fundamental call of every Christian to follow the Lord in concrete situations today. In the words of Indian theologian Michael Amaladoss:

> In the Church religious are a "prophetic pole," not only counter-cultural, but creatively prospective. Their prophecy is not only directed to the world, but also to the Church community. By radically living and/or promoting through their apostolic action some of the values of the Reign of God they are reminders of and invitations to a possible new world for all the People of God. They are also the cutting edge of the Church's mission to the world, in so far as they symbolize in a specially visible way the radicalism of the kingdom of God which is being proclaimed.[58]

Or, in the expressive language of Joan Chittister:

> It is not the loss of institutions that religious must fear; it is the loss of the fire/heat of the charism itself. It is the potential loss of prophetic presence that strikes at the root of religious life today. Religious life is to remind the world of what it can be, of what it must be, of what it most wants to be: deep down, at its best, at its most human core. Religious life lives at the edge of society to critique it, at the bottom of society to comfort it, at the epicenter of society to challenge it. Religious life is a reminder of the will of God for the world.[59]

Johann B. Metz has recently developed this view most strongly.[60] For him, part of a formal definition of the essential nature of religious orders is the fact that they are charismatic signs, resulting from the activity of the Spirit; in other words, they are charismatic institutions and movements.

The founders of religious orders like Francis, Dominic, Teresa of Avila, Ignatius, and others were often prophets, and their prophetic message remains present in the communities they founded. In the sense that the communities carry on the charismatic inspiration of the founders, we can speak of an "institutionalization" of a prophetic ministry without denying that individual prophets

---

[58] In ibid., 133.

[59] In ibid.

[60] Johann B. Metz, *Followers of Christ: The Religious Life and the Church* (New York: Paulist Press, 1978).

can arise at any time, without creating a community in which they "incarnate" their prophetic spirit. The danger for these charismatic movements is that they easily become domesticated. As Norbert Lohfink remarks: "Canonization, recognition of religious orders, even the development of canon law regarding religious orders, well-intentioned as they are, can have the effect of domesticating charism. Another way the Church, more than general society, tries to tame charism is to suppress and eliminate prophetism."[61]

The Origin of Religious Orders in Prophetic Protest[62]

Religious orders, as we understand them today, came into existence in the fourth century. But that does not mean that they had no antecedents. In the early church we find people who wanted to follow the Lord in a more radical way by renouncing possessions and marriage in order to be closer in fellowship with him. They lived in their respective Christian communities, in which they gave their witness that ultimately showed there can be no difference between being a disciple and being a Christian. Actually, they were following the general call of the Christian but felt the Lord inviting them to a different way of being his disciples, the way he himself had lived so radically.

The early Christian communities lived in a society that did not share their values; therefore, they became automatically what Lohfink calls a "contrast society,"[63] witnessing to a different set of values and a different way of being human.

This situation changed dramatically when the church became the state religion and people entered in droves. The church ceased to be a contrast society. By conforming itself to society, many felt that the Christian faith was compromised. At that moment the prophetic charism rose anew within the church and began to protest. Many scholars see a remarkable resemblance to the beginnings of the prophetic movement in the ninth century B.C., when established Israel had forgotten to live in covenant love with its God and in justice and peace with one another.

John Cassian comments that the first religious went apart "to practice those things which they had learned to have been ordered by the apostles throughout the body of the Church in general" (*Collationes* XVIII, chap. 5). According to him, monks formed communities to see that these ideals were not just talked about but lived. Religious life came into existence as a protest movement against a church that had conformed too much to society at large. Religious life was seen as following the model of the prophets in the Old Testament.

---

[61] Norbert Lohfink, "Where Are Today's Prophets?" *Theology Digest* 37 (1990), 107.

[62] Francis J. Moloney, *Disciples and Prophets: A Biblical Model for the Religious Life* (London: Darton, Longman, and Todd, 1980), 155-170.

[63] Norbert Lohfink, "Religious Orders: God's Therapy for the Church," *Theology Digest* 33 (1986), 208.

Many individual Christians at that time moved out into the desert and created new communities, which in turn took over the former mission of the church to be contrast society. These communities patterned themselves on the community model of the early church as described by Luke in Acts, in which everything was held in common by people of simple hearts who called themselves brothers and sisters.

Later, other communities took their orientation from the group that had followed Jesus when he walked this earth; in short, the disciples of Jesus. The best examples are the communities founded by Francis, Dominic, and Ignatius. Vatican II seems to have this pattern more in mind in its description of religious life.

No matter which pattern we consider that of contrast society or radical discipleship, both witness to the fact that there always seems to be a need within the church for healing and a reminder of our basic call; that is, religious orders have a therapeutic task to fulfill for the church. There seems to be a link between the church's task to be a contrast society and the existence in the church's history of monasteries and religious orders. Religious communities arose whenever the church forgot and betrayed its social mission. "It is not wrong to say that when the Church began to get sick, God ordained monks, nuns, and cloisters as its therapy. When the Church forgot that it was to be a contrast society, a contrast society was created in its midst."[64]

The Three Basic Functions of Religious Life in and for the Church

Metz sees the functional definition of religious life with regard to the life of both the church and society under two aspects: an innovative function and a corrective role. Both functions are prophetic.

The Innovative Function of Religious Life. What does it mean to say that religious life has to fulfill an innovative function for the church? The first mission or function of religious life consists in providing a clear reminder of the intimate link between being a Christian and following Christ. The general demand to follow Christ is too abstract. Its concrete meaning and content have to be demonstrated by means of very concrete models in every age and situation. The church as a whole and society at large need patterns, models, and visible forms that clearly and unmistakably reveal what the gospel demands of following Jesus mean today. Individual saints throughout the centuries most visibly exemplify the living out of the gospel demands in their times.

Who can provide these new patterns or models? Metz sees that the role of religious is to offer "productive models" for the church as a whole. These models should illustrate how fellowship with Christ is to be lived in the new social, economic, intellectual, and cultural situation of today. Following Christ is not

---

[64] Ibid.

just a subsequent application of the church's Christology to our life. Who Christ is can never be known unless we embark on the way of following him. Following Christ can never be a purely spiritual endeavor. It has to be lived and demonstrated in the concrete circumstances of our time.

To provide productive models means to show what being a disciple of Jesus is all about and to show what Jesus would do in the settings of our time. Their basic function should be to help the church move out of entrenched positions, to read the signs of the time and to show where the church's mission should move to now.

The Corrective Role or the Shock Therapy of Religious Life. The constant dangers of the church as a large-scale institution are accommodation and questionable compromise, the ever-present tendency of making the gospel livable in a consumer society and thereby watering down its radicalism to the point that it does not hurt any more. It is over and against a too nicely balanced view of things and too much compromise with the standards of the time that religious life is seen as having to play a corrective role.

A prophet is someone called and sent to recall to people God's saving interventions in the past, to challenge them to conversion from their disloyalty to God in the present and to urge them to build up a new humanity that is God's promise to people. It is a call to active hope based on experience and memory. It is a call to be a counter-culture not merely being critical and negative but proposing alternative ways of being and living community. The horizon of the prophetic mission of the Church is the Reign of God, a community and fellowship of justice and love.[65]

We can call it a prophetic role because religious life is not situated in the hierarchical office of the church but in its prophetic ministry. As such, it possesses a particular sensitivity to the signs of the time. After all, the prophet's task has always been to proclaim to the people of God the will of God for today. As Walter Brueggemann points out:

The task of prophetic ministry is to nurture, nourish, and to evoke an alternative to the consciousness and perception of the dominant culture around us. . . . The alternative consciousness to be nurtured, on the one hand, serves to criticize in dismantling the dominant consciousness. To that extent, it attempts to do what the liberal tendency has done, engage in a rejection and delegitimatizing of the present ordering of things. On the other hand, that alternative consciousness to be nurtured serves to energize persons and communities by its promise of another time and situation towards which the community of faith may move. To that extent it attempts to do what the conservative tendency has done, to live in

---

[65] Union of Superiors General, *Consecrated Life Today*, 131.

fervent anticipation of the newness that God has promised and will surely give.[66]

The prophetic task is a way of evoking, forming, and reforming an alternative community. The two key words are *critical* and *energizing*, two qualities that a prophetic ministry must hold together. The function of prophecy, therefore, is to upset at times the so-called balanced view and thus move the church out of stagnated perspectives and positions to fresh viewpoints and situations, toward the frontiers, into new circumstances and challenges. This task, however, is not a self-appointed ministry but a call to fulfill a function in and for the whole church. In this sense, Norbert Lohfink seems to be correct in calling religious orders "God's therapy for the church."[67]

Why should this be their task? It is because religious congregations are the heirs of great founders like Francis, Dominic, and Teresa, who upset the church of their times by demonstrating the uncompromising nature of the gospel and by moving the church, as a large-scale institution, into new situations and circumstances. They had to do this on the basis of their prophetic charism. One of the greatest (and perhaps the most deadly) temptations of religious life is to move too far into the middle ground, where everything is nicely balanced and moderate, and to forget to be a prophetic challenge in and for the church. To use Brueggemann's image, they are in danger of losing their imaginative powers and of becoming unable to envision new alternatives for the church that could help it out of the "only thinkable" solution born out of the present factual world. While many religious do excellent work in numerous institutions, very often we have to admit that they fulfill a role that society has assigned to them. They have been nicely integrated into society and are regarded as useful and appreciated for what they do as long as they stay where they are and do what they are "supposed to do": care for the old, serve in hospitals, run boarding schools, and so on. By no means are they to meddle in any way with issues of society.

But we should not forget that the prophetic ministry needs the ministry of office, from which it gets its approval and is discerned as being a movement in the church brought about by the Spirit for the benefit of the whole church. The whole church must recognize the relative independence of this ministry and listen to its voice and message. Both are meant for the well-being of the church although their functions differ.

The Witness of Community Living. There is a considerable number of spiritual writers who say that the priority of religious life today is the witness to community life. Religious life in community must be a clear sign that our Christian faith can create communities in which peace, justice, love, and true brotherhood and sisterhood are not just empty words but lived realities. As communities within the church, they serve as the visible and tangible anticipation of the final

---

[66] Brueggemann, *The Prophetic Imagination*, 13.
[67] Lohfink, "Religious Orders," 203-212.

community that God intends for the whole of creation. The reconciling power of the Holy Spirit creates a community that, already here on earth, reveals among men and women the unity and harmony that are to find their fullness at the end of time. Because of all the brokenness of human life and the impossibility of ever creating a perfect community, the sign that God's kingdom has broken into the world has to be demonstrated in our time.

This making the kingdom at least initially present in our world is the task of the whole church, but once again, religious communities should offer themselves as concrete test cases showing that the kingdom has indeed already appeared in this world. In a time when people hunger after signs of God's kingdom as present, the question is: Who can give this witness to real community if not the religious communities themselves? Who else can provide a more visible and tangible demonstration of the power of Christ's reconciling love in the church as a whole if not religious communities that claim to have made it their mission rather than "task" to follow the Lord more freely and to imitate him more exactly? Once again, the function of religious communities is seen as being a contrast society for our time.[68]

Conclusion: Prophetic Criticism Applied

The most genuine form of prophecy in the church comes in the form of communities that serve a prophetic function over against the entire church. Prophetic communities can actually exercise two functions. On the one hand, within the church itself they can provide prophetic criticism that questions accommodation to the world; on the other hand, they provide prophetic criticism over against the total society, which is the specific mission of the whole church.

Prophets are called, but no one can make himself or herself a prophet. If others proclaim us as prophets, then we can accept this and feel good about it, but not if we make ourselves into prophets. Prophets live in a given context to which they offer an alternative through their word, action, and life. Since they challenge ways of life, they have to reckon with opposition. They are outsiders and will have enemies. Prophets without enemies are no prophets. Their vocation is first a charism, not an office.

Several questions may be posed at this juncture: Are religious today really offering this prophetic critique to the church and to society as a whole? Have religious orders betrayed their calling so that God must devise other means to take up this task in the church? Is God's history of salvation moving in a different direction? These are difficult questions to answer. The drop in religious vocations raises such questions. We should not forget, however, that if we religious have failed, there is always the way of conversion.

However, many find the emergence of small communities and community movements in the church of today a hopeful sign that here God is furnishing the church with a new prophetic charism. Their very existence is a prophetic

---

[68] Ibid., 209-212.

criticism within the church, and they offer the much needed contrast society to society at large. In our world today the traditional forms of religious life might not suffice to serve as God's therapy for the church. Alongside the religious orders God might call other forms of community, including all of the faithful, to carry on God's therapy for the church. These communities, in turn, may well serve as a pattern after which religious orders will have to renew themselves if they do not wish to be bypassed in God's desire to reach all human beings and to make God's prophetic critique heard.

Corresponding to the reasons why there is a particularly urgent call for a prophetic ministry of religious orders, H. Arens thinks that the following stances could be taken by religious orders as forms of prophetic criticism within the church:[69]

The Crisis in the Church Itself. Over against a too hierarchically structured church, religious orders are to be more consensus-oriented, more fraternal, less hierarchically organized. The model of leadership within religious orders should be a challenge within the church for better cooperation and collegiality. Offices in religious orders are normally held for a limited period, which allows for more flexibility and protects against stagnation and immobility. Religious congregations today are trying to get away from clericalism by placing more emphasis on the common vocation. Consequently, there is a greater esteem for the lay person.

The Rift between Church and Society. Religious orders as prophetic communities offer to marginalized groups an alternative model wherein they feel more at home. Communities in which the faith is lived more holistically by taking into consideration all aspects of human life are extremely attractive. The option for the poor and marginalized is obviously a clear sign that a community will not have its role dictated by society but only by the gospel.

Consumerism and Materialism. The evangelical counsels, which promise a freedom from the concerns of this world, should enable the religious to let go, to be available, to be transferred, to change, and to die. It is the eschatological dimension of this way of life that relativizes all earthly values and should serve as a strong critique of a society that puts all of the stress on having and consuming.

Who are the Successors of the Teachers?

In Corinth there was a recognized group of teachers (1 Cor 12:28; Gal 6:6). They had a double function. First, they were to pass on the tradition that they themselves had received from the founding apostles, in particular, the tradition of kerygma and Jesus' words (Rom 16:17; 1 Cor 4:17; 11:2; Col 1:28; 2:7;

---

[69] Heribert Arens, "Das Prophetische am Ordensleben," *Ordenskorrespondenz* 33 (1992), 8-22.

2 Thess 2:15; 3:6). Second, they were to interpret the tradition and thus its development. New situations demanded such fresh interpretations. Concerning their authority within the community we can say: (1) The teaching function had more the character of "office" than any of the other regular ministries. Teachers were a more trained group who had the ability to retain, understand, and teach the tradition of the kerygma. (2) In comparison to the apostles, the teachers would only teach, while the apostles could demand and give orders. (3) As teachers moved beyond the simple passing on of tradition to its interpretation, they moved into the charismatic ministry, not unlike the prophet.

With regard to their relationship to the prophetic ministry we could say that "the teaching function provided an indispensable complement to prophecy; the normative role of the gospel and of Jesus' words provided an invaluable control on charismatic excess. Prophecy without teaching degenerates into fanaticism; teaching without prophecy solidifies into law."[70]

It seems obvious that the successors of the teachers are the theologians and the exegetes. Although the charism of theology, like the charism of prophecy, can never be adequately institutionalized, their ministry is to be a constitutive element in the church as well. The magisterium has often described their ministry in too narrow terms as the words of Pius XII show: "The noblest office of the theologian is to show how a doctrine defined by the church is contained in the source of revelation" (*Humani Generis*, no. 21). This task might fall under the first function of the teacher, but it ignores the second function of interpreting the tradition anew. Lately, the church has increasingly acknowledged that theology has a task independent from that of the magisterium.

Pope John Paul II states it quite clearly: "The Church wants independent theological research, which is distinct from the ecclesiastical magisterium, but knows itself responsible for the common service to the faith and the people of God. It will, however, not be possible to exclude all tension and conflicts between both."[71]

The pope sees this tension rooted in the limits of our mental capacity and the pilgrim state of the church. Dulles considers it the task of theologians "to reflect synthetically and critically on the Christian message, bringing out its meaning and coherence." Concerning the critical task of the theologians Dulles observes: "Yet the critical observations of theology are often no more enthusiastically welcomed than the denunciations of the prophets. Theologians, too, are at times suspected of disloyalty to the institutions."[72]

The teaching ministry is a task that must be exercised in the community and is not just an optional choice by those who have the talents and the gift for it. It belongs to the essence of the church. It contains a magisterium of its own, which

---

[70] Dunn, *The Christ and the Spirit*, 282-284.

[71] John Paul II, "Ansprache bei der Begegnung mit Theologieprofessoren im Kapuzinerkloster St. Konrad," *Verlautbarungen des Apostolischen Stuhles* 25A (Altoetting, 18 November 1980), 73.

[72] Dulles, "Successio Apostolorum," 63.

at times may not be in total agreement with the official teaching. This may even be necessary in order to explain scripture and tradition in new ways adaptable to the changing situation into which the church will have to proclaim its essential message of the kingdom now present. George Tavard notes:

> The necessity and the difficulty of reading documents—in order to know what they say and to determine the limits of their authority—establish a magisterium of theologians in the Church. For those who have the talents and the capacity also have the duty to serve the community through them. Teaching, then, is not optional. . . . It is a duty that pertains to the very structure of the Christian Church as a community of belief. Like all members of a community that is tied together by mutual service, the theologians are at the service of the community to which they must bring the fruits of their labors. And when theologians reach conclusions that they consider to be intrinsically normative, their ministerium becomes magisterium.[73]

Concluding Remarks on the Institutional Model

The institutional model of the church will be accepted only when the charismatic ministries are taken seriously once again. If the ministry of prophets, the ministry of teachers, and the other charisms are allowed to fulfill their functions, are given relative independence in the church, and can operate freely in the service of the whole church, then the Catholic Church will once again become a renewed church. These ministries are created and willed by the Spirit for the benefit of the whole. Tensions and conflicts may at times be unavoidable, but this belongs to the eschatological community that lives in the condition of this world. There will never be perfect harmony and peace; whoever wants peace at all costs among these different functions will only have the peace of a cemetery, where no life is left. Karl Rahner sees in the charismatic gifts in the church that element that might be called democratic over against the monarchical one of the office. Its acknowledgment as an essential part of the church's structure would make us see that authority and power are distributed to both in the church and to be shared by both in their proper ways.[74] Rahner points out that "if the structure of the Church is of this double kind [hierarchical and charismatic] and if its harmonious unity is ultimately guaranteed only by the Lord, then office-holders and institutional bodies must constantly remind themselves that it is not they alone who rule in the Church."[75]

The official church regards the charismatic elements in the church as belonging to the essence of the church. But statements made concerning the relationship

---

[73] George Tavard, *The Church, Community of Salvation: An Ecumenical Ecclesiology* (Collegeville, Minnesota: The Liturgical Press, 1992), 160.

[74] Rahner, *Spirit in the Church*, 62-63.

[75] Ibid., 60; see also, *The Dynamic Element in the Church*, 71-73.

between hierarchical and charismatic remain ambiguous. John C. Haughey comments that in *Lumen Gentium,* no. 4, the council contends that "the Spirit furnishes and directs the Church with various gifts both hierarchical and charismatic." This is potentially a very significant statement, but since it is not spelled out, its ecclesiological implications are not immediately obvious. Later in the same document it becomes even more obvious that there is considerable uncertainty about exactly where these charisms fit ecclesially.

[The Spirit] distributes special graces among the faithful of every rank. By these gifts He makes them fit and ready to undertake the various tasks or offices advantageous for the renewal and upbuilding of the Church. . . . These charismatic gifts, whether they be the most outstanding or the more simple and widely diffused, are to be received with thanksgiving and consolation for they are exceedingly suitable and useful for the needs of the Church (no. 12).

This passage is in no way clear about the relationship among graces, gifts, offices, and charisms; they are all jumbled together. What, for example, does it mean in practice for "the faithful of every rank" to be receiving gifts to "undertake the various tasks and offices for the upbuilding of the church"? The ecclesiological implications, while far-reaching, are not pursued here. *The Decree on the Apostolate of the Laity* again addresses the subject of the charisms and spells out the right and duty of the laity to exercise these for both church and world: "From the reception of these charisms or gifts . . . there arise for each believer the right and duty to use them in the Church and in the world for the good of mankind and for the upbuilding of the Church" (no. 3).

The question remains: How has the "right" to use these charisms in the church been made operational in the thirty-five years since the end of the council? *The Decree on the Ministry and Life of Priests* exhorts priests to discover "with the instinct of faith, acknowledge with joy, and foster with diligence the various humble and exalted charisms of the laity" (no. 9). How this important exhortation has been heeded in our parishes since Vatican II is an empirical question that is not likely to result in many affirmative answers.[76]

Not much is said about how these charisms should function and be exercised in the church. The fact is that the council was quite unprepared to deal with the subject of the charisms that entered in by the back door, so to speak. However, we are told that the church furnished with hierarchical agencies is an instrument of the "spiritual community . . . enriched with heavenly things [charisms]," forming "one interlocked reality which is comprised of a divine and a human element" (*LG,* no. 8). This statement seems to imply that the council accepted a

---

[76] John C. Haughey, S.J., "Charisms: An Ecclesiological Exploration," in *Retrieving Charisms for the Twenty-First Century,* ed. Doris Donnelly (Collegeville, Minnesota: The Liturgical Press, 1999), 3-5.

superiority of the charismatic over the hierarchical, which is regarded as an instrument of the charismatic dimension of the church. Here *office* is seen as a "necessary regulative for the charismatic." In this connection Karl Rahner sees the officeholder as "nurturing and discerning the charism" in the church by referring to 1 Thessalonians 5:19-20: "Do not stifle inspiration [other translations: quench the Spirit; suppress the Spirit; smother the Spirit; treat the gifts with contempt] but test everything and then keep what is good."

There is no way that the church can neglect the charisms; they are part of its very essence. Dominican theologian Christian Duquoc puts the matter crisply: "The charisms bear witness at the core of the institution to the fact that it is necessary for its very survival not to lock itself up in a legal order or a rationally planned institution. The charism constitutes a bridge between the Church as event and the Church as institution, or the gratuitous and the legal, or the unpredictable and what is planned, or the Spirit and the structure."[77]

To those who might think this issue of the charisms is being overstated, it is instructive to see the phenomenal growth of the churches that have the charisms as a constitutive part of their structures. The Pentecostal churches, for example, which started in the twentieth century, already claim approximately 500 million adherents, with very many of them former Catholics. These churches have developed a very charismatic ecclesiology, meaning they fully expect and train their members personally to discover and exercise the charisms of the Spirit.[78]

In the church there are two structures: the hierarchical and the charismatic. Both belong together. Charism without an ordering function disintegrates easily into turmoil, chaos, and division; order without charism results in conformism, indifference, and lifelessness. Keeping this dialectic between order and the charismatic gifts in balance is not easy. It is estimated there are over twenty thousand separate Christian denominations; we may well ask how many of these came into being because of the inability to keep charism and order in balance.

Yet as we observed earlier, as long as the church ties the exercise of governing power in the Christian community exclusively to the sacrament of orders, it hardly seems possible that the other ministries will be allowed to function independently and to participate in the governing power of the church. Can the Catholic church reform itself in this way? The answer can be affirmative only if the church takes its basic double structure seriously and explores how both ministries may be exercised in ways better suited to the new cultural and social situations, particularly how the charisms of the lay people in the church will be recognized in ways that enable them to share in the ruling power of the community.[79] Concerning the three ministries of office, prophecy, and teaching, Dulles writes: "For successful interaction, it is important that none of the three functions

---

[77] Christian Duquoc, "Charism as the Social Expression of the Unpredictable Nature of Grace," in *Charism and Church*, ed. Duquoc and Floristan (New York: Seabury, 1978), 93.

[78] Haughey, "Charisms," 6.

[79] Duquoc, *Provisional Churches*, 99.

usurp the specialization of the others or seek to reduce the others to innocuous servitude. For theology or prophecy to perform its distinctive task it must retain a certain measure of autonomy and critical distance from the official leadership, while at the same time accepting the latter's supervision."[80]

Each of these three ministries contains built-in hazards. The *apostolic leadership*, left to its own, tends to encourage passive conformity and blind conservatism. It suppresses troublesome questions and challenges and avoids any new and provocative issues. In practice, at least, many church leaders still hold to the view that they themselves have all these other charisms and that there is no real need for further charismatic ministries.[81] They think they will only complicate matters. *Prophetic leaders* can easily be caught up in their own insights. They can fall victim to the illusion that takes their own fantasies for the directives of the Holy Spirit. They forget that only false prophets can proclaim themselves prophets. *Teachers* can easily get caught up in their own world of speculations and proclaim their insights as *the* magisterium.

At the present moment there is a tendency to reaffirm the role of the hierarchy. This is understandable in the wake of excessive criticism of all authority in the church. Such an attitude of endemic suspicion can become destructive for the Catholic faith. The church cannot do without an authoritative ministry if it wants to remain faithful to its origin of apostolic tradition. In the words of Dulles:

> The Scriptures, the tradition, the creeds and the dogmas must be trusted, and so must ecclesiastical authorities who vouch for them. Dissent from authority cannot and should not be totally ruled out, but should be the exception rather than the rule. The presumption should be that Catholics accept the official teaching of the Church. Dissent, where it cannot be prevented, should be expressed in modest and discreet ways that do not undermine the very principle of authority. For the Church is by its very essence a community of faith and witness. The pastoral office exists in order to authenticate sound doctrine and to assure unity of conviction in matters of faith and morals.[82]

There is only one common goal for all hierarchical offices as well as for the charismatic ministries: to make the kingdom present in the midst of the church community and to continue the mission of Christ, which was the proclamation of the kingdom of God in word and deed as the ultimate goal of all creation. The kingdom that Jesus came to bring and that he entrusted to the disciples with the command to continue to proclaim it in his name is essential. The church has no

---

[80] Dulles, "Successio Apostolorum," 64.

[81] Rahner, *The Dynamic Element in the Church*, 52-53, 57. Rahner reacts here to the widespread idea that only the early church had an abundance of charisms but that with the end of the apostolic age these charisms vanished.

[82] Avery Dulles, "Ecclesial Futurology: Moving towards the 1990s," *CLSA Proceedings* (1985), 4.

other mission in God's unitary plan than to bring the whole of creation to its final goal: a sharing in the life of the community of the Trinity. This mission is entrusted to all the faithful on the basis of their baptism and their faith commitment to Christ and not just to the ministry of office in the church. As Tavard sees it:

> The ministry of all the faithful and by implication, the official ministry of the ordained are focused on the leadership of prayer, on the proclamation of the gospel in word and sacrament, on pastoral care or service, and on education or catechesis. The question is how does this fourfold pattern relate to the twofold division of lay and ordained and to the threefold hierarchy of bishops, priest and deacon. This is tantamount to asking at which point of this fourfold pattern ordination becomes necessary. Catholic theology says on the level of liturgy and the presidency of Eucharistic assemblies. Yet the fact is that this ordination has been extended to the leadership of prayer, to all preaching of the gospel, to the supervision of pastoral care and of catechesis. All this in spite of the fact that the faithful as such is competent to lead in prayer, that pastoral care can be adequately performed by trained lay counselors, and that the task of catechesis requires knowledge and pedagogical efficiency rather than sacramental grace.[83]

What is asked for today is how we can most effectively engage this common fourfold pattern of mission of all the faithful in a way that corresponds better to the gospel itself and the situations into which the mission of Christ has to be extended.

The issue is not to infringe on the ministry of office or even to question its validity as an office *over and against the community* concerned with the eucharist and the general government of the church. Rather, the issue is how to make the church's structure more suitable to serve its mission not only in the culture in which the present church structures evolved but in a world church with different cultures that have their own customs and ways of structuring authority and governing community affairs. There is no easy solution, but the insight of *Gaudium et Spes* must be applied to church structures as well. The text, referring to the enormous changes that affect our world today, concludes: "Thus, the human race has passed from a rather static concept of reality to a more dynamic, evolutionary one. In consequence, there has arisen a new series of problems, a series as important as can be, calling for new efforts of analysis and synthesis" (no. 5).

What this "analysis and synthesis" may ask for regarding a serious rethinking of church structures for the future has been proposed quite daringly by Walter Kirchschläger as follows:

> The decisive question of church structure at the turn of the millennium should no longer be the question of admission criteria to a level of church

---

[83] Tavard, *The Church, Community of Salvation*, 152.

ministry. Admitting married men as well as women to priestly ministry would not solve the problem of church structure, and it would be unfortunate if this were our only goal. The signs of the time call for a paradigm shift, and church history teaches us that it would not be the first! . . . We need to begin by thinking about the form of church structures and tasks on the basis of thorough reflection in various regions of the world, profiling what the needs are, and then formulating practical criteria. To do this we must find appropriate women and men to send into concrete service through prayer and the laying on of hands (which means ordination): catechists, worship and community leaders, pastoral care workers and deacons, as well as theologians.[84]

It is not a question of doing away with the hierarchical office of the church; it is, rather, a question of asking seriously if the three developed forms of consecrated ministry have to be maintained as the only form of the ministry confirmed through the laying on of hands. Cannot this ministry of office be ordered in another way that would include a broader range of ministries? For example, the introduction of the diaconate of married men in the church after the council may be useful for some parts of the church but in many parts—particularly in the third-world context—it just means reintroducing a former clerical caste and entrusting it with a ministry that ultimately every male or female can perform in the church today. Why not integrate into the office of ministry other services that many lay people are already performing and empower them for these ministries through the laying on of hands? This would really integrate the lay ministry into the life of the church and bridge the ever-widening gap between the state of the ordained and the lay state in the church. Which ministries should be integrated into the church's office would be up to the local churches to decide.

To illustrate the problem more clearly some data from the *Statistical Yearbook of the Church 1998* may give us a better picture: In 1998 there were in the church 4,439 bishops, 264,202 diocesan priests, and 140,000 religious priests, which amount to 408,641 ordained ministers. If we include permanent deacons (25,315) the total of the ordained equals 433,956. Non-ordained pastoral workers in the church comprise religious women (814,799), lay male religious (57,813), and members of secular institutes (30,102). In addition, there are 56,421 lay missionaries and 2,298,387 catechists. So the total of non-ordained pastoral workers in the church today equals 3,257,522.[85] These non-ordained pastoral workers are performing a ministry (except presiding over the eucharist) that is usually seen as preserved to the official ministry of the ordained: (1) leadership of prayer; (2) proclamation of the gospel in word and sacrament; (3) pastoral care or service; and (4) education or catechesis. Since non-ordained pastoral workers are on the increase in the church, the question of reevaluating their

---

[84] Walter Kirchschläger, "Plurality and Creativity in Church Structure," 252-253.

[85] *Statistical Yearbook of the Church 1998* (Vatican City: Libreria Editrice Vaticana, 2000), 98.

ministry and its relationship to the basic fourfold ministry of all the faithful cannot be postponed forever. To regard their ministry as a necessary response to an emergency situation (not enough ordained pastoral workers) means not to take seriously the situation and the circumstances in which the church is called today to fulfill its mission as a world church. The question is ultimately whether the church is willing to see the signs of the times and to discern them accordingly.

The Church as Communion[86]

This model perceives the church primarily as *koinonia* or community. The word *koinonia* appears nineteen times in the New Testament; thirteen of these are found in the Pauline writings. Community puts the stress on interpersonal relationship, whether to the Triune God or to the members themselves, rather than on describing the church in terms of an institution of salvation or a perfect society. It aims at personal growth through interpersonal relationships in the community.[87] The ecclesiology of communion has been hailed as one of *the* achievements of Vatican II. It could be called a *paradigm shift* in the understanding of church if one compares it with the dominant ecclesiology that prevailed in the century before the council. This approach to describe the church is known today as *communion ecclesiology*. It is delineated as follows:

> Communion ecclesiology represents an attempt to move beyond the merely juridical and institutional understandings by emphasizing the mystical, sacramental, and historical dimensions of the Church. It focuses on relationships, whether among the persons of the Trinity, among human beings and God, among the members of the Communion of Saints, among members of a parish, or among the bishops dispersed throughout the world. It emphasizes the dynamic interplay between the Church universal and the local churches. Communion ecclesiology stresses that the Church is not simply the receiver of revelation, but as the Mystical Body of Christ is bound up with revelation itself.[88]

Nowhere does the council's intention for a new approach at a deeper understanding of the mystery of the church show itself better than in the choice to perceive the church first and foremost as a community and not as an institution or as a perfect society. This called for a different conception of how the church should be envisioned also with regard to its organization.

The church should echo the interrelation between the three persons who together constitute the deity. The Church is called to be the kind of reality

---

[86] Dulles, *Models of the Church*, 48-62.
[87] Richard P. McBrien, *Catholicism* (London: Geoffrey Chapman, 1981), 712-713.
[88] Dennis M. Doyle, *Communion Ecclesiology: Vision and Versions* (Maryknoll, New York: Orbis Books, 2000), 13.

at a finite level that God is in eternity. Can further account be given to this analogy? Most obviously, it can be said that the doctrine of the Trinity is being used to suggest ways of allowing the eternal becoming of God—the eternally inter-animating energies of the three—to provide the basis for the personal dynamics of the community.[89]

The model has gained more and more attention in post-conciliar theology. Walter Kasper describes his approach to ecclesiology in these words: "For the Church there is only one way into the future: the way pointed out by the Council, the full implementation of the Council and its communion ecclesiology. This is the way which God's Spirit has shown us."[90]

The synod of bishops in 1985 affirmed that "the ecclesiology of communion is the central and fundamental idea of the council's documents."[91] And the Congregation for the Doctrine of Faith observed in 1992 that "the concept of communion can certainly be a key for the renewal of Catholic ecclesiology."[92] The synod links to this approach the biblical images that the council had used for church such as body of Christ, people of God, and temple of the Holy Spirit.

> The communal model views the Church as the Body of Christ, as the People of God, as a fellowship in Christ deeply committed to the well-being of its members. Theologically, the strength of this model lies in its deep Scriptural roots; anthropologically, its strength lies in a deeply in-grained human trait, the human need and subconscious craving for fellowship in almost everything we do as humans. The favorite model of Vatican II, as the Extraordinary Synod of Bishops of 1985 emphasized, was precisely this communal model, the Church as a People of God. The Church exists because human beings need each other: they need community.[93]

The *primary* meaning of communion in the council's documents refers to the intimate relationship the faithful have with the Triune God. The Christian community is regarded as the anticipation of God's ultimate plan with humanity and the whole of creation in union and communion with the Triune God. The church is seen as an icon of the Trinity. This is also called the *vertical* dimension of the primary meaning of *koinonia*. The *secondary* meaning of communion is its *horizontal* dimension, which refers to the relationship among the believers based on the prior communion with God.

---

[89] Colin Gunton, "The Church on Earth: The Roots of Community," in *On Being the Church: Essays on the Christian Community,* ed. Colin E. Gunton and Daniel W. Hardy (Edinburgh: T&T Clark, 1989), 78.

[90] Walter Kasper, *Theology and Church* (New York: Crossroad, 1989), 150.

[91] Extraordinary Synod of Bishops, "The Final Report," II,C,1 *Origins* 16 (1985), 448.

[92] Congregation of the Doctrine of the Faith, "Some Aspects of the Church Understood as Communion," *Origins* 21 (1992), 108.

[93] Luzbetak, *The Church and Culture*, 376.

Dennis M. Doyle sees four common elements in the various versions of communion ecclesiology which remain fairly constant:

> First, communion ecclesiology involves a retrieval of a vision of the Church presupposed by Christians of the first millennium, prior to the divisions among Eastern Orthodox and Roman Catholic and Protestant manifestations of Christianity. Second, communion ecclesiology emphasizes the element of spiritual fellowship or communion between human beings and God in contrast to juridical approaches that over-emphasize the institutional and legal aspects of the Church. Third, communion ecclesiology places a high value on the need for visible unity as symbolically realized through shared participation in the Eucharist. Fourth, communion ecclesiology promotes a dynamic and healthy interplay between unity and diversity in the church, between the Church universal and the local churches.[94]

In the ecumenical dialogue we can say the communion model is the one that is most congenial to both Orthodox and Protestants alike. In the words of the Faith and Order Commission:

> The notion of *koinonia* has become fundamental for revitalizing a common understanding of the nature of the Church and its visible unity. . . . The term is being reclaimed today in the ecumenical movement as a key to understanding the nature and purpose of the Church. Due to its richness of meaning, it is also a convenient notion for assessing the degree of communion in various forms already achieved among Christians within the ecumenical movement.[95]

This description of church is not new. When dealing with the church, St. Augustine and St. Thomas referred to *communion* frequently; the idea was taken up and further developed by the Protestant churches after the Reformation, often in contrast to the Catholic view with its heavy stress on institution. The whole theological controversy of charism against office, of "charismatic" against "legal," was often a question of how to perceive the church. Stronger emphasis on the charismatic dimension of the church over against a too hierarchically conceived church image led to a communion ecclesiology.

Among Catholic theologians, Yves Congar and Jerome Hamer in particular developed this model prior to the Second Vatican Council and laid the foundation for the council's renewed view of the church as communion. The church is seen here as a fellowship of persons—men and women in union with God and one another in Christ. As Congar puts it, "Church is the totality of means by

---

[94] Doyle, *Communion Ecclesiology*, 13.
[95] *The Nature and Purpose of the Church*, Faith and Order paper no. 181 (Bialystock, Poland: Ortdruck Orthodox Printing House, 1998), 48.

which this fellowship is produced and maintained—it is a community of salvation and not so much an institution of salvation."[96]

Strengths of the Communion Model

There is no need to prove the scriptural basis for this image of church once again. The ideas of election and covenant in the Old Testament and the three basic images in the New Testament—people of God, body of Christ, and temple of the Holy Spirit, consciously chosen by the council to show the Trinitarian dimension of the church—all clearly manifest how deeply the idea of community is imbedded in scripture.[97]

Augustine and Thomas preferred by far the image of community to describe the church. Augustine used the phrase "body of Christ" to stress the invisible community that embraces not only the members here on earth, but the heavenly beings as well. He was the first to talk about the "church since Abel." Thomas used the community aspect of the church to emphasize in particular the divine aspect or the vertical dimension of community.

Vatican I had intended to deal with two topics concerning the church: its internal form and its external form. The first preparatory documents were based on Adam Möhler's view of the church: "The church as Christ's Mystical Body" and the "church as a True, Perfect, Spiritual and Supernatural Community." Neither of the two documents was taken up during the council. Concerning the external structures of the church, only the questions of primacy and infallibility (which had not even been on the agenda of the council) were treated and became the *pars prima* in ecclesiology.

This view determined all treatises on the church up to Vatican II. In *Mystici Corporis* (1943) Pius XII wanted to complete what the council had left unfinished. The concept *Corpus Christi Mysticum* is here regarded as the most comprehensive and precise description of the church. The statement that the *mystical body* is identical with the Roman Catholic Church is critical. It almost sounds like a paradox: Pope Pius's intention was to soften the one-sided or exaggerated stress on external structures; yet by identifying the church with the physical body of Christ, he made the hierarchical structure even stronger. In spite of all the criticism of this encyclical, however, most of the impulses for a new ecclesiology before the Second Vatican Council were derived from it.

The Second Vatican Council took up the image once again. By dropping the word *mystical* and changing the phrase the church "exists in" to "subsists in" the Roman Catholic Church, it removed from the body of Christ image the triumphalism that was easily associated with it. By employing the third image,

---

[96] In Jean Rigal, "Toward an Ecclesiology of Communion," *Theology Digest* 47 (2000), 116-123.

[97] On the concept of communion ecclesiology prior to Vatican II and in the wake of the council, see Doyle, *Communion Ecclesiology.* He presents a vast range of theologians who have dealt with the topic explicitly.

church as the temple of the Holy Spirit, the council brought in the charismatic aspect of the church to counterbalance the hierarchical. The church according to this image is seen as an organism that is held together by the different functions of the members and organs that compose it. Each person or member of the community has received a charism which he or she is asked to exercise for the well-being of the whole. What keeps the community alive and healthy is the exercise of the charisms of the individual members. The Holy Spirit, as the creator of the church and as the sustainer of the Christian community, is powerfully expressed in this way. The Eastern churches were always particularly strong on this aspect. Their view of the church is first and foremost Trinitarian.

> As each human being is created according to the image of the Trinitarian God (Gen 1:26), so the church as a whole is an icon of God the Trinity, reproducing on earth the mystery of the unity in diversity. In the Holy Trinity the three Persons are one God, yet each is fully personal; in the church a multitude of human beings are united in one, yet each preserves his/her personal diversity unimpaired. The mutual indwelling of the persons of the Holy Trinity is paralleled by the coinherence of the members of the church. In the church there is no conflict between freedom and authority; there is only unity, but not totalitarianism. This conception of the church as an "icon" of the Holy Trinity has many further applications. "Unity in diversity"—just as each person of the Trinity is completely autonomous. The unity of the church is linked more particularly with the person of the church, its diversity with the person of the Holy Spirit.[98]

Dennis Doyle points out that theologians who promote communion ecclesiology emphasize that the church has its origin in the love shared among Jesus and the disciples. They stress that the love which is the core of Christian revelation is generated through the intimate connection of Jesus with the Father and is sustained through the sending of the Holy Spirit; the growth of the church is the spread of this divine love within Christian communities. To live in Christian community is to share in the life and love of the three Persons in one God.

In addition, almost all modern renewal movements that emerged in the church after Vatican II put strong emphasis on the church as community. The Charismatic Renewal movement, Better World movement, Neo-Catechumenate, and in particular the Basic Ecclesial Communities of the third-world church all adopted this model, very often unconsciously. The main reason for such a view on church is the fact that communion ecclesiology places its primary emphasis on relationship. Personal being and interconnectedness lie at the heart of what

---

[98] Gennadios Limouris, "The Church as Mystery and Sign in Relation to the Holy Trinity—in Ecclesiological Perspectives," in *Church—Kingdom—World: The Church as Mystery and Prophetic Sign*, Faith and Order paper no. 130, ed. Gennadios Limouris (Geneva: World Council of Churches, 1986), 37; see also Chenu, "The New Awareness of the Trinitarian Basis of the Church," 14-22.

the church is. Love, acceptance, forgiveness, commitment, and intimacy consti-tute the church's very fabric.

The church's responsibility toward the world is equally accepted. The church is seen as a community that guarantees not only the spiritual but also the human growth of the members. This model brings out very forcefully the church's abiding responsibility to be a sign of Christ's presence or of the kingdom of God present in the "already" form, by being a community in which justice, peace, and mutual love are realized and lived.

Weaknesses of the Communion Model

While granting the richness of the ecclesiology of communion, we should not overlook its inborn weaknesses. Luzbetak describes them in these words:

> The basic danger of this model is the fact that the image may lead people to become too introspective and not concerned enough about the world outside the church-community. To get lost in the joy and blessing of Chris-tian fellowship means to forget the kingdom for which the church exists; it is also to forget the church's mission. Furthermore using the images of Body of Christ and People of God we can become too mystical and possi-bly get lost in cliches and platitudes. One more danger with this model is that the communal character becomes so dominant that the institutional dimension of the church can be made to appear unimportant.[99]

Wherever this model is chosen consciously to offset a too hierarchically con-ceived church, the dangers are the following: (1) The relationship between the visible and spiritual dimension easily gets blurred. The church, seen purely in terms of "charismatic entity," easily leads to regarding the charism of office as useful but not absolutely necessary. The community can fulfill all its needs without an ordained minister. (2) The community model does not always clearly identify those elements that make such a community different from other com-munities. (3) A clear sense of identity is often missing in the sense that every-one can participate, irrespective of his or her affiliation (the best example is the charismatic groups). The three elements that make a Catholic a member of the church are often neglected. Orthodoxy is downplayed. (4) It tends to concen-trate on the values of the individual's growth at the expense of the social and political responsibility of the whole church and at the expense of the community's abiding commitment to the renewal and institutional reform of the church itself. (5) It easily looks at itself as an "exclusive community," tending toward an inwardness that keeps others out. Members of such communities often feel at home only among themselves and regard others as intruders. There is the dan-ger of looking at themselves as the perfect community, which then becomes the measure for judging the rest of the world.

---

[99] Luzbetak, *The Church and Culture*, 337.

In spite of its weaknesses this model seems to have become one of the most dominant and growing perceptions of the church at the moment. A church that takes community as its basic model will have to rethink its understanding of ecclesiastical office. The growing awareness in the church of the fact that charismatic ministries are constitutive of the church alongside ecclesiastical office will demand a new look at the functions that ecclesiastical office has to exercise in such a church. What is the role of an officeholder in a church that understands itself first as a charismatic entity in which everyone has a role to play? A few points could be outlined here:

First, officeholders have to make sure that the whole apostolic tradition entrusted to them will be proclaimed and lived in these communities. The precise purpose of the charism of office is to ensure that the apostolic tradition is being preached faithfully, not just partially.

Second, officeholders should have the gift of discernment, that is, the gift of being able to discover the many charisms in the congregation and letting them become active for the well-being of the whole community. The function of officeholders, then, is to discover charisms and to co-ordinate them for the good of the church. They should have an ability to dialogue and be able to sense the Spirit operative in the community rather than constantly acting as if they alone have the Spirit. As St. Paul wrote: "Do not stifle the Spirit, but discern everything and then keep what is good" (1 Thess 5:19-20). But the question has to be asked: Are future priests trained in this way? Is their suitability for this ministry judged by whether they have such abilities or not? Under what criteria are seminarians ordained and accepted to the priesthood for a church in which a communion ecclesiology is valued as the one most advocated by Vatican II?

Pope John Paul II in his post-synodal apostolic exhortation *Pastores Dabo Vobis* (1992) speaks explicitly about the necessary ability of cooperation for any candidate of the priesthood:

> The ordained ministry has a radical "communitarian form" and can only be carried out as "a collective work. . . . Of special importance is the capacity to relate to others. This is truly fundamental for a person who is called to be responsible to community and to be a "man of communion." . . . Awareness of the Church as "communion" will prepare the candidate for the priesthood to carry out his pastoral work with a community spirit, in heartfelt cooperation with the different members of the Church: priests and bishops, diocesan and religious priests, priests and lay people. Such a cooperation presupposes a knowledge and appreciation of the different gifts and charisms, of the diverse vocations and responsibilities which the Spirit offers and entrusts to the members of Christ's Body. . . . It is particularly important to prepare future priests for cooperation with the laity (nos. 17, 43, 59).

Third, on the basis of their own charism they have an obligation to prevent any community from closing in on itself. They have to present to them the universal aspect of the church. They, themselves, as members of the collegially structured charism of office, share in the church's universal pastoral ministry, although they are put in charge of a local community that demands of them a local pastoral ministry.

These three points do not define the ministry of office in the church conceived in the model of community, but they indicate which direction a rethinking of the priestly role in such a church must take. It seems that the renewal of the church through the Basic Ecclesial Communities in the third-world church will stimulate a thorough, vigorous, and even radical rethinking of the priestly ministry and its role in the church.[100] Dulles has made similar demands in his community of disciples model, in which he discusses the shape of a future ministry in such communities.[101]

The model of church as communion contains a number of aspects that are of particular importance for our age and time. First, the idea of communion is based on the human experience found in any culture of our globe. The need for sharing and intimacy is inborn in every human being. Theologically, the strength of this model lies in its deep scriptural roots; anthropologically, its strength lies in a deeply ingrained human trait, the human need and subconscious craving for fellowship in almost everything we do as humans.

Second, the communion model can bring together a whole range of theological issues. It can be used to relate the institutional and the spiritual dimensions of the church; deal with pluralism and unity; bring out the relationship of the universal church to the local churches; attend to the issue of primacy and episcopacy as well as the issue of evangelization and salvation. Yet the danger is that, since it can cover so many issues, it ends up having little meaning or no point of reference.

Third, since the communion model contains a vertical and a horizontal dimension, it can bring out the spiritual dimension of the individual as well as that of the community in its relationship with God on the one hand and with our fellow human beings on the other hand. It can help to realize that the *vertical-transcendent* and the *horizontal-communal* dimension of communion are of equal value and that any emphasis of one over the other will only result in a flawed vision of the church. And fourth, the model is well suited for ecumenical dialogue, since it is congenial to both Orthodox and Protestants alike.[102]

In view of the fact that the church must see itself and its mission in the service of the kingdom of God, the communion idea reveals most clearly what the kingdom is all about and what the church's mission consists of: the church is an anticipation in space and time of that great vision, spoken of by the prophet Isaiah and by Jesus himself, of the heavenly banquet at which all human beings

---

[100] Leonardo Boff, *Church, Charism, and Power: Liberation Theology and the Institutional Church* (London: SCM Press, 1985).

[101] Dulles, *A Church to Believe In*, 7-14.

[102] Patrick Granfield, "The Concept of the Church as Communion," *Origin* 28 (1999), 753.

will be united into one community of brothers and sisters in union with God and the whole of creation. It is the fulfillment of the age-old dream of all humanity for union with God and fellow human beings in justice, peace, and joy. The church's mission is to demonstrate this vision at least partially and to work for its coming about in all sectors of human life. The very phrase *kingdom of God* means communion, including all three aspects of the new transformed world: union with the Triune God, union with all creatures, and union with the whole cosmos.

The Faith and Order Commission described the church from this aspect as follows:

> It is God's design to gather all creation under the Lordship of Christ (Eph 2:10), and to bring humanity and all creation into communion. As a reflection of the communion in the Triune God, the Church is called by God to be the instrument in fulfilling this goal. The Church is called to manifest God's mercifulness to humanity, and to restore humanity's natural purpose—to praise and glorify God together with all the heavenly hosts. As such it is not an end in itself, but a gift given to the world in order that all may believe (John 17:21).[103]

The Church as Sacrament

Ecclesiologists hailed the notion of the church as sacrament as *the* achievement of the council as far as a theological definition of the church goes:

> The statement of the Second Vatican Council with regard to the total sacramentality of the Church is probably the most important pronouncement it made concerning the Church. . . . All the Council's other statements about the Church are affected by this insight. The key to the new understanding of the Church reached by the Council is the teaching of the christocentric character of the Church.[104]

This model of the church tries to come to grips with the divine and human elements of the church. It is the most theological view presented. Most moderate theologians accept this model as basic and most adequate because it expresses the essence of the church in traditional theological terminology. Henri de Lubac, Karl Rahner, Oscar Semmelroth, Edward Schillebeeckx, and Yves Congar all contributed to this model before and during the council. Vatican II used this description of the church for the first time in an official document of the church: "The Church is a kind of sacrament of intimate union with God and of the unity of all humankind, that is, it is a sign and instrument of such union and unity" (*LG*, nos. 1, 9, 48).

---

[103] *The Nature and Purpose of the Church,* 26.
[104] Michael Schmaus, *The Church as Sacrament* (London: Sheed and Ward, 1975), 5; see also Kasper, *Theology and Church,* 111-147.

After Vatican II the image of the church as sacrament gained momentum even in Protestant churches, which preferred the terminology "instrument and sign" rather than "sacrament."[105] The Faith and Order Commission expressed it as follows:

> The Church is the sign and instrument of God's design for the whole world. Being that part of humanity which already participates in the love and communion of God the Church is a prophetic sign which points beyond itself to the purpose of all creation, the fulfilment of the kingdom of God. . . . At the same time the Church is the instrument through which God wants to bring about what is signified by it: the salvation of the whole world, the renewal of the human community by the divine Word and the Holy Spirit, the communion of humanity with God and within itself.[106]

What Does It Mean to Say the Church Is a Sacrament?

As Christ is the sacrament of God, so the church is seen as the sacrament of Christ. It makes him present and tangible in this world until he comes again. Here the church signifies and effects the unity of humankind, one with the other and all with God in Jesus Christ, in virtue of being the "sign and instrument" that really contains the grace it confers.

Following Karl Rahner's argument, we can say that God created the world in order to lead it into God's own glory. All history must be seen and understood as manifesting and realizing the salvific plan that is the self-communication of God to all humankind. But history as such remains an ambiguous sign of this self-communication: the yes and the no each person gives to God. Only in the history of Jesus is the realization of the self-communication of God to all humankind achieved in an unambiguous way.

Christ the Sacrament of God

Jesus is the sacrament of God in history. Who God is and what he has in store for all creation become sacramentally visible in Christ. Jesus' life is marked by two essential aspects: *identification* and *representation*. He became one with us, by identifying himself with us and he is "God with us" (Phil 2). Christ is the "historically real and actual presence of the eschatologically victorious mercy of God."[107] He is God made visible and present to us with the aim of self-communicating once and for all to us. God has bound God's self to this person.

> From the moment the Logos assumes this human nature redemption cannot be canceled anymore, the grace of God no longer comes steeply down

---

[105] See Günther Grassmann, "The Church as Sacrament, Sign and Instrument," in *Church—Kingdom—World,* ed. Gennadios Limouris (Geneva: World Council of Churches, 1986), 1-16.

[106] *Nature and Purpose of the Church,* 43, 45.

[107] Rahner, *The Church and the Sacraments* (London: Burns and Oates, 1963), 18.

from on high, from God absolutely transcending the world and in a manner that is without history, purely episodic. The Logos is permanently in the world in tangible historical form, established in the flesh of Christ as part of the world of humanity and of its very history.[108]

Now it is possible to point to a visible, historically manifest fact, located in time and space. We can say: Here is a concrete sign that effects what it points to: God's self-communication to humankind. Having assumed our nature (identification), Jesus, who is God's union and communion with us and one of us as well, represents us to God; he is our union and communion with God. He said yes for us, once and for all, to God's self-communication, which has now become irreversible. God cannot withdraw from the world again. Therefore we say: *Christ is the sacrament of God.* He is an efficacious sign of our union with God and God's communion with us. He signifies this union, and he brings forth this union. A sacrament is a sign of something really present.

According to Trent, a sacrament is the "visible form of an invisible grace." Theologians would say a sacrament is an "efficacious sign; it produces or intensifies that which it signifies." The reality signified achieves an existential depth; it emerges into solid, tangible existence. All spiritual realities are accessible to us only through signs because of the incarnational structure of the human spirit. A sacrament as a sign of a spiritual reality contains the grace it signifies and confers the grace it contains. Jesus, God in human form (sacrament), signifies union with God and brings forth this union. This union of humankind with God is accomplished through the life, death, and resurrection of Christ. The transformation of the earthly Jesus by the Father through the power of the Holy Spirit (Rom 8:11; Eph 1:18-20) is the great breakthrough into the new creation, the final act in bringing about this union of humankind with God.

This new creation is the final accomplishment of God's salvific plan with humankind. The Risen Lord, in his identification with us, is already for us the final fulfillment of our future destiny. Anyone who comes in contact now with the Risen Lord is drawn into his sphere of life and is "already a new creation" (2 Cor 5:17).The question now is: How can this redemption accomplished in Jesus Christ become effectively present in time and space for every human being, since Christ is not physically present in the world in the way he was when he walked this earth? Or, how can we come in contact with him in a manner that is certain and reaches into this our world? Who represents him, the historically real and actual presence of the saving love of God? It is here that we have to locate the church.

The Church the Sacrament of Christ

We presuppose the principle that God touches men and women through other human beings and through tangible historical events. Salvation is mediated

---

[108] Ibid., 15.

through concrete historical-social realities. Hence, it is easy to see that the church becomes the sign of Christ present now in the world. It becomes his hands, his mouth, his body through which he communicates his words and saving actions to the world.[109] "The Church is for us the sacrament of Christ, she represents him, in the full and ancient meaning of the term, she really makes him present. She not only carries on his work but she is his very continuation, in a sense far more real than that in which it can be said that any human institution is its founder's continuation."[110]

Adam Möhler puts it this way: "The Church is the Son of God perpetually appearing in human form among men always renewing himself, eternally regenerating, his enduring incarnation, for the faithful are called in the Holy Scripture the Body of Christ."[111] The church in this view is conceived in terms of the mission of the Son in the Holy Spirit. The idea to perceive the church as sacrament takes on its full meaning within a Trinitarian perspective in which God's plan is revealed. In terms of content the kingdom of God means God's final revelation of who God is and the final fulfillment of every person's social destiny in union with the Triune God. In the words of Vatican II:

> Lifted up from the earth, Christ draws all men to himself (Jn 12:32). Risen from the dead, he has sent his life-giving Spirit upon the disciples and through the Spirit he has established his body, which is the Church as the universal sacrament of salvation. Sitting at the right hand of the Father he is at work in the world without ceasing to bring men to the Church, to join them more closely to himself through her (*LG,* no. 48; see also *Ad Gentes,* nos. 2-5; *GS,* no. 45).

Karl Rahner defines the church from this perspective as the "continuance, the contemporary presence of that real, eschatologically triumphant and irrevocably established presence in the world, in Christ, of God's salvific will."[112] The mission of the church is seen here as placing the world in the presence of the mystery of Christ in the Spirit. All its structures are completely subordinated to the mystery of Christ. In short, its mission is to bring people in contact with Christ and through him with the kingdom. It is a sacrament, for example, a sign that brings forth what it signifies. First, it is a sign of God's presence in the world; its mission is to bring people into contact with God and God's kingdom. Second, it is an anticipation of what is to come; it effectively mediates the salvation that is already present in it.

---

[109] Theisen, *The Ultimate Church and the Promise of Salvation,* 131.

[110] Henri de Lubac, S.J., *Catholicism: Christ and the Common Destiny of Man,* trans. Lancelot C. Sheppard and Elizabeth England (San Francisco: Ignatius Press, 1988), 29.

[111] Adam Möhler, *Symbolik* (Mainz: Kupferberg Verlag, 1864), 356.

[112] Rahner, *The Church and the Sacraments,* 18.

Church, Universal Sacrament of Salvation

The church is described as being by its very essence the *universal sacrament of salvation*. The description, which holds a prominent place in the *Dogmatic Constitution on the Church* (see *LG*, no. 48), is quoted both in the *Decree on the Church's Missionary Activity* (*AG*, no. 1) and in the *Pastoral Constitution on the Church in the Modern World* (*GS*, no. 45).

Since the church is seen as a universal sacrament, "an instrument for the redemption of all" (*LG*, no. 9), we must assume that the salvation of all human beings depends in some way on the church. The church is involved in the salvation of all who are saved (*LG*, no. 16). Whatever faiths and beliefs people may confess, we must assume that the grace which saves them is in a mysterious way linked to the church. In the words of the council, through this grace they are "ordered" to the church. That means the saving grace they receive outside the church gives them a positive inclination toward the church, so that all who live by God's grace are in a certain sense affiliated with the church.[113]

The question that arises is whether the church saves simply by being the reality toward which people are oriented, or whether the church acts to bring about the salvation of such persons. The perception of the church as "a universal instrument" of salvation (*LG*, no. 1) suggests that the church is actively at work in the salvific process but does not explain by what activities the church accomplishes this result.

Referring to the *Constitution on the Sacred Liturgy (Sacrosanctum Concilium)*, many theologians concur that it is through prayers and the eucharistic celebration that the church unceasingly intercedes with the Lord for the salvation of the entire world (*SC*, no. 83).[114]

The problem that arises when we state that the church is a "universal sacrament of salvation" is that it easily leads to an exclusive understanding of salvation as being totally *ecclesiocentric*. To avoid this danger, we constantly need to be reminded that God's saving grace cannot be restricted to the sacrament alone. There is grace outside the sacrament and, therefore, salvation outside of the church. Whatever interpretation is given to this definition, we may not interpret it so narrowly as to restrict all saving activity to that mediated through the church alone. The theological solution that is generally offered today is that it is through the Holy Spirit that the grace of salvation, linked to the incarnation, death, and resurrection of Christ, will reach all people in ways not known to us.[115] In the words of *Redemptoris Missio*:

---

[113] Avery Dulles, "Vatican II and the Church's Purpose," *Theology Digest* 32 (1985), 344-345.

[114] Francis A. Sullivan, *The Church We Believe In* (New York: Paulist Press, 1988), 128.

[115] J. Francis Stafford, "The Inscrutable Riches of Christ: The Catholic Church's Mission of Salvation," in *A Church for All People: Missionary Issues in a World Church*, ed. Eugene LaVerdiere (Collegeville, Minnesota: The Liturgical Press, 1993), 31-50.

The Spirit manifests himself in a special way in the Church and in her members. Nevertheless, his presence and activity are universal, limited neither by space nor time. . . . Thus the Spirit, who "blows where he wills" (cf. Jn 3:8), who "was already at work in the world before Christ was glorified" [and] who "has filled the world . . . holds all things together [and] knows what is said" (Wis 1:7), leads us to broaden our vision in order to ponder his activity in every time and place (*RM*, no. 29).

We already touched on this subject in the chapter on the church and the kingdom, and we will return to it in the chapter on the church's mission today.

Weaknesses of the Sacramental Model

First, there are very few passages in scripture that support this model at all, although Ephesians 5:32 is one possibility. Second, for some this model encloses the church within boundaries that remain introverted and cultic (sacramentalism). Others believe that by allotting to the world such a high degree of sacramentality (God's self-communication through history and matter), the church gets so immersed that it loses its own identity, since sacramentality is granted to all reality. Third, while this model explains (theoretically in words) the mystery of the church very beautifully, it does not offer concrete criteria by which to evaluate, judge, and discern the divine and the merely human in the church. Where, for example, is the divine in a church so human and so often defeated? Fourth, because the language explicating the church as sacrament is so technical and sophisticated, it is very difficult to preach about such a model. It remains basically a Catholic model only, although the World Council of Churches in Uppsala, in response to Vatican II, called the church "a sign of the coming unity of humankind."

The council wanted to be a pastoral council according to the intention of Pope John XXIII. This meant that all topics taken up by the council were to help the ordinary faithful see their faith in relation to the concrete situation in which they lived. The profound theological meaning and importance of the image of the church as sacrament makes this a model highly appreciated by theologians but hardly understood by the ordinary faithful. Yet, as Luzbetak points out, the important dimension of the church as universal sacrament is *ritual,* because religion is never divorced from ritual. Applying this to the church's missionary task, he concludes:

What is important to remember is that, just as in the case of community building, each culture has its own way of respecting an individual, bearing each others burden, listening, forgiving, caring, sharing, serving, and spending oneself for each other, so it is in the case of ritual: *each culture has its own set of ritual symbols and meanings that should be used as much as possible to make the local church even more recognizable as God's Universal Sacrament.*[116]

---

[116] Luzbetak, *The Church and Culture*, 382.

The sacramental charter of the church has been praised by all who commented on the council's view on the church. The church is regarded as the sacrament of Christ, sacrament of the Spirit, sacrament of the Trinity, sacrament of the kingdom, and universal sacrament of salvation. In the context of our treatise on the church, the best of these images seems to be to look at the church first as a sacrament of the kingdom. This view links it with the message of Jesus, in whom the kingdom that he came to communicate to all was made present. In the same way the church must be seen first and foremost as deeply linked to the kingdom of which it is a sign and a means in God's universal plan of saving the whole of creation. Looking at the church from this perspective will help us remain focused on the main message of Jesus: the kingdom of God. It is from this aspect that all theological topics ought to take their beginning and to which they should return.

The Church as Herald

The church as herald is a characteristically Protestant conception. This type of theology was highly developed by Barth, who relies heavily on Paul and Luther. For Barth, the fault of Catholic ecclesiology is that it concentrates too much on its own being with the result that it becomes triumphalistic. The correct attitude for the church must be to point away from itself, like John the Baptist, by pointing to Christ. The church is essentially a herald of the Lordship of Christ and a herald of the future kingdom.

According to Karl Barth, the church is the living community of the living Christ. God calls the church into being by divine grace and gives it life by means of the Word and Spirit, with a view to his kingdom. The church is not a permanent fact or an institution; it is an event constituted by the power of the word of God in scripture. There is no authority in the church except the word of God, which is to be let free to call into question the church itself. It is God's word that creates and renews the church and that urges it on to its mission: the constant proclamation of the salvific event, Jesus Christ, and the advent of the kingdom of God.

Rudolf Bultmann also promoted this view of the church strongly. The church is so much an event that it can have no solid sociological or institutional dimension. All historical forms that the church has to take are always provisional and even paradoxical. The word alone remains central and the only true reference point. There are three "catch words" concerning the church to which Bultmann constantly refers: *worship, eschatology,* and *vocation.* The church is first of all a community of worship in which the word is proclaimed. Second, it is an eschatological community, which means that God becomes present in the acceptance of Jesus by the believers. Third, the worshiping community becomes a community with a prophetic vocation, a kerygma that calls for a decision.

The mission of the church is to proclaim that which it has heard, believed, and been commissioned to proclaim. The emphasis is on faith and proclamation over interpersonal relations and mystical communion, which the community model stresses highly. This model is also called kerygmatic, for it looks upon the church as a herald, namely, one who receives an official message with the commission to pass it on. The biblical picture for this model is the herald of a king who comes to proclaim a royal decree in a public square.

This model is not strongly present in the documents of Vatican II as a whole, except in passages found in the *Decree on Ecumenism* and the *Dogmatic Constitution on Divine Revelation.* Catholic theology has accepted the importance of the word of God and regards the magisterium under the word and not above it. However, the hierarchy in particular has the responsibility of watching over the proclamation and interpretation of the word. In and for the community, the magisterium is to be seen as representing Christ's power and authority with regard to the fidelity to and continuity of his message. Among Catholic theologians Hans Küng has presented a similar view. For him, the church is the congregation that has been summoned (*ecclesia,* "being called out") by a herald. This gives to the church an "event character" rather than seeing it as an unchanging entity. *Ecclesia*, like *congregation,* means both the actual process of congregating and the congregated community.

The theology of the word of God has become central in the ecclesiological outlook of the Basic Ecclesial Communities (BECs). The word here has become the immediate point of reference and the source of inspiration. It is the primary catalyst of the community, since the word, unlike the sacraments, is always within reach. The word of God is here experienced in its direct relationship with life, since it is read, reflected upon, and meditated upon by the faithful almost daily. It is the foundation of the faith and the spirituality of the BECs. In the measure the BECs grow and develop in the church, this model will become more and more important and in need of being developed in the Catholic Church.

Strengths of the Herald Model

First, the herald model has a good and sound biblical foundation in the prophetic tradition of the Old Testament and in the theology of St. Paul. Second, it gives a clear sense of identity and mission to the church: a congregation that heralds the good news of Jesus Christ and is not afraid of being opposed by contrary views. Third, its spirituality focuses on God's sovereignty and humankind's infinite distance from God, which leads to virtues like humility, readiness for repentance, and reform. Fourth, it has given and can give rise to a very fruitful theology of the word. In comparison with the sacramental model, the word here "has a unique capacity to express not only what is present but what is absent, not only what is but also what is not, and hence to protest against what is actually given and to condemn it."[117]

Weaknesses of the Herald Model

The word of God appears *not* to have become flesh but simply word. From a Catholic point of view, the incarnational aspect is not seen and appreciated.

---

[117] Dulles, *Models of the Church*, 85.

Secondly, the "event character" is at times stressed so much that any "continuity" in time and space is questionable. The "permanence" of Christ's real presence as we see it in the sacramental model seems to be lost. This aspect is strongly stressed by the council in the *Constitution on the Sacred Liturgy* and in the *Dogmatic Constitution on Divine Revelation*. Third, the Catholic understanding of the church as a "stable community in history," one in which Christ continues to make himself present and available, leads to a different view of authority in the church. Fourth, the model focuses too exclusively on witness to the neglect of action. It has a very pessimistic outlook on the kingdom's power to change this world. Nor is much said about the Christian's obligation to create a new social order. The stress is too strongly placed on the kingdom as totally the work of God, entirely and exclusively produced at God's initiative. We humans can only patiently await its coming. The sociopolitical dimension of the gospel as a call to change this world is not taken seriously—nor is it even denied. Last, the model easily gives rise to biblical fundamentalism, one of the greatest threats to the gospel message today.

The Church as Servant

In all of the models up to now the church is seen as the active subject and the world as the object that the church acts upon or influences. The question formerly asked was: What can the world do to build up the church? Now the question is: What can the church do to make the world a better place in which to live? This view is based on the theological insight that the kingdom of God is meant for the world and that the church must see itself and its mission in the service of the kingdom. The *Pastoral Constitution on the Church in the Modern World* presents a completely new understanding of the relationship between the church and the world. After recognizing the world's legitimate autonomy, the council asserts that the church must consider itself as part of the total human family and as sharing the same concerns as the rest of all humankind.

The *Pastoral Constitution on the Church in the Modern World* point out that just as Christ came into the world not to be served but to serve, so the church, carrying on the mission of Christ, seeks to serve the world by fostering unity among all people (*GS*, nos. 3, 92). The disposition of the whole church is one of universal service to humanity as such, which is seen as one big family. Service becomes the central inspiration of ecclesiology. What is most important here is the theological method used in this type of theology. Dulles calls it "secular-dialogic," because the world is considered to be a properly theological source in order to discern the signs of the times. The "concrete situation" is taken as the starting point for theology, and only after an analysis of the situation is any theological reflection done. The method is "dialogic" because it seeks to operate on the frontier between the contemporary world and the Christian tradition. The model perceives the church primarily, but not exclusively, as an "agent of social change" in the name of the kingdom, which is coming among humankind, a kingdom of justice, peace, and joy as well as of holiness and grace.

Strengths of the Servant Model

The servant model helps the church to turn away from being overly concerned about its own internal affairs and to look at the world for which the kingdom is meant. This model underlines the principle that *diakonia*, which includes the struggle for a new social order, is as essential to, and even constitutive of, the mission of the church as are proclamation and sacramental celebration. The kingdom demands the transformation of all human reality, and the church must be an agent of this transformation. The church can give hope to a world stricken by war, injustice, and hatred by pointing constantly to the coming kingdom as having appeared already in Jesus Christ. It can give meaning to the small services all can do for a better world of justice, peace, and unity.

Howard A. Snyder sees three significant strengths in this model: First, its optimism provides motivational power for social change. Generally this model is a conscious critique of otherworldly viewpoints that see the kingdom either as irrelevant in present society or, worse, as encouraging passivity and discouraging Christian action on behalf of the public good. Second, it sees positive values in human culture. In its insistence that the kingdom is present and social, not just individual, this model stresses the good in human nature, in human cultural achievements and often in the physical environment. Rather than merely being a kingdom of darkness or a negative drag on the higher, nobler realm of nonmaterial spirit, the world in this view is a place of beauty and value within which Christians add their efforts to perfect society and heal its diseases. Third, this model stresses human action and responsibility. God has made us responsible creatures, capable actors in the world's drama. Not to accept this role is to fail to seek first God's kingdom and its justice. Sin is not just acts of personal immorality; it is failure to accept God-given responsibility for this world.[118]

Weaknesses of the Servant Model

First, only general biblical indications will support this model, since direct biblical references cannot be found. There are only references in a broader sense. The main argument is drawn from creation.

Second, the separation of kingdom and church, even if done by Vatican II, can easily lead to the assumption that the church is merely one of a number of agencies within history that are building up the future kingdom. Why should one belong to the church if one can work more effectively for justice and peace outside of it? What are the elements that make such an "agent of social change" distinct from other agents? We can easily lose sight of the Christocentric aspect of the kingdom, not to mention its ecclesiological dimension. This danger has been the worry and the constant concern of the magisterium in recent years, particularly expressed in the encyclical *Redemptoris Missio*, the document *Proclamation and Dialogue,* and the more recent *Dominus Iesus.*

---

[118] Snyder, *Models of the Kingdom*, 108-109.

Third, the stress on social or structural change can easily lead away from that necessary constant stress on personal conversion that the Bible demands. The cultic or celebrative aspect of the kingdom in this model is often rated secondary.

CONCLUDING REMARKS ON USING MODELS
IN ECCLESIOLOGY

We have been following the five models (or six if we include community of disciples as well) that Dulles presents in *Models of the Church*. Each model has its strengths and its weaknesses. The issue is not a matter of exclusiveness, but is rather a question of one's basic stance in looking at the church. For example, if I hold the sacramental model as my favorite, that does not mean I exclude the positive aspects of the other models. My image of church will basically be formed from the sacramental model, and I will modify this accordingly. My basic model, however, will remain the sacramental one. In the same way I can presume that someone who chooses the servant model as his or her basic model for perceiving the church does not exclude the aspects that are strongest in the sacramental model. To choose a model means I accept a particular vantage point from which to look at the church, while I keep in mind the valid features of the other models and thus allow myself to adjust my understanding of church. Accordingly, it follows that each of us has already chosen a model out of which to operate, whether we know it or not.

Is it possible to conceive a model that would contain the best of all models? Probably not. We can use different models to come up with a description of the church but to squeeze the idea of church into only one model would violate the very mystery of its being. We must be careful not to relativize any position by contending that it is "just another model" and that one model is "as good as any other." We need to maintain the flexibility to work with several models at the same time, especially in times of rapid change like our own; however, this does not mean that all models are of equal value at any time. Some models might give a more adequate answer to new emerging situations than others.

Richard P. McBrien uses Dulles's five models for his description of church, but he believes that they can be summarized in just three models: institution, community, and servant. For McBrien, the institutional model contains the sacrament and the herald models. McBrien sees these three models as complementary and comprehensive in order to understand the church and its mission adequately. He defines the church in the following way: "The Church is the whole body, or congregation, of persons who are called by God the Father to acknowledge the Lordship of Jesus the Son in Word and Sacrament, in witness and in service, and, through the power of the Holy Spirit, to collaborate with Jesus' historic mission for the sake of the Kingdom of God."[119]

---

[119] McBrien, *Catholicism,* 714.

McBrien outlines the mission of the church as follows: The *first task* of the church is to keep alive the memory of Jesus Christ in word and sacrament and to express hope in the world to come, a totally new creative manifestation of the future kingdom. The eucharist in particular presents the past and present aspect of the kingdom and creates hope in its future fulfillment. The *second task* of the church is to make the future present in its midst. The kingdom is a present reality and tangible in the community of disciples, and this reality must be made visible on the community level and not just individually. The *third task* of the church is to take up responsibility for the humanization of the world in its fullest sense. Because the kingdom of God is also a kingdom of justice, peace, and communion, and the church exists for the sake of the kingdom, this kingdom must be made visible in the form of anticipation of what is to come. Without this we cannot create or maintain a firm belief that the fullness of the new creation is not just "pie in the sky" but the ultimate fulfillment of God's grand design of creation and salvation.[120]

Although McBrien uses all five models to describe the essence and the mission of the church, it is obvious that he sees the church from the vantage point of the servant model. For him, the church must basically be understood from the central message of Jesus himself: the kingdom of God in the service of which the church must find its identity and its mission.

The church as described by the Faith and Order Commission contains almost all essential aspects of the different models mentioned above. But by emphasizing strongly the social mission of the church, the commission seems to give one model of church a particular preference, namely, that which highlights the social obligation of the church vis-à-vis the massive problems of poverty and injustices in the world today.

> The Church is the community of people called by God who, through the Holy Spirit, are united with Jesus Christ and sent as disciples to bear witness to God's reconciliation, healing and transformation of creation. The Church's relation to Christ entails that faith and community require discipleship in the sense of moral commitment. The integrity of the mission of the Church, therefore, is at stake in witness through proclamation and in concrete action for justice, peace and integrity of creation. The latter will often be undertaken with those outside the community of faith. This is a defining mark of *koinonia* central for our understanding of the church.[121]

---

[120] Ibid., 715-721.
[121] *Nature and Purpose of the Church,* 56.

7

Two Models for the Future Church

Basic Ecclesial Communities
and a Contrast Society

OVERVIEW OF THE PRESENT ECCLESIAL SITUATION

The current situation of the world is distinguished by two opposing characteristics. On the one hand, we have the phenomenon of globalization. The world
has become like a global village. It is not only financial information and resources that circle the globe electronically thousands of times every day, but
through the modern mass media we have almost immediate access to information from all over the world. The modern means of transportation convey people
and merchandise from one part of the planet to another in just a few hours.

On the other hand, globalization, which seems to bring the world closer together, creates new dependencies and injustices and establishes new forms of
domination by the strong and the powerful. Therefore, there are counter movements to globalization. People fear losing their identity and feel threatened by
the powerful, who try to impose on them "global culture" at the expense of their
traditional cultures. In order to preserve their identity, people look for their
roots, their original culture with its customs and norms of behavior.

This search for identity, however, often creates new problems. Whenever
people of different cultures move closer together, anxieties increase and can
produce hatred and violence, resulting in a rise in ethnic and cultural conflicts.
Many voices predict a "clash of civilizations"[1] and, in fact, in many places across

---

[1] Samuel P. Huntington, "The Clash of Civilizations?" *Foreign Affairs* (Summer 1993),
22-49. The basic assumption of the article is that the conflict between civilizations will
be the next phase in the evolution of conflict in the modern world. For the Western
world it will be the clash between Muslim civilization and Christian civilization. The
article stimulated a lot of discussion, which is still going on.

the world today such clashes are turning into bloodshed. We need only think of Northern Ireland, Rwanda, Sudan, Bosnia, Kosovo, and Afghanistan.[2]

This phenomenon of globalization calls for two responses on the part of the church. First, while globalization is a process that will go on and carries a number of great hopes for all of humanity, it has a negative impact on the poor and disadvantaged in all societies and creates great problems that are contrary to the whole gospel message. The church needs to take a courageous stand for justice and compassion in favor of all those who become the victims of this process. Second, globalization threatens the cultural identity of people. The reaction is that people, becoming concerned with their own identity, are looking to their cultural roots. The negative side of this is that the search for cultural roots can also lead to hatred and even war. The church must respond to this deep aspiration for identity but also to the negative byproducts that such search is creating by recognizing (1) the need for inculturation of the faith, and (2) the need to create a church community in which justice and compassion are the basic principles of action in face of a globalization process that leaves out the poor and the marginalized and often increases inequalities. The models of church that address these needs we will call *Basic Ecclesial Communities* and *contrast society*.

As we have described in the previous chapters, two basic images of the church were constantly in the forefront in the discussions on the church's identity and its mission during the council. The first image was the church as a hierarchically structured society, as it was generally understood up to then; Avery Dulles described this as an institutional model. The second image emerged during the council in reaction to the first one and in the attempt to counterbalance it. This image, called by Dulles the community model, came to be known after the council as communion ecclesiology and was regarded as one of the most important achievements of Vatican II.

In the years following the council different modifications developed out of these two basic images. The first, based on the institutional model, gradually unfolded into what some call today the neo-conservative model of the church. It is not just a revision of the old institutional model but takes the achievements of Vatican II seriously and addresses new experiences. The other modification that emerged out of the communion ecclesiology is called the *Basic Ecclesial Communities* (BECs). This model is growing in popularity, although mostly in Latin America, Asia, and Africa, where the future of the church will be found. It seems to have a dynamic that could lead to a new understanding of what it means to be church today. Since its environment is the local church, it seems to suit best the urgent necessity of the church to inculturate the gospel message more deeply into the culture of the local people.

We need to point out that we are not dealing here with the question of which of the two models (neo-conservative or Basic Ecclesial Community) is right

---

[2] Walter Kasper, "Relating Christ's Universality to Interreligious Dialogue," *Origins* 30 (2000), 321-323, 327.

and which is wrong. Both images agree with the council's achievements in such areas as awareness of the church as a community of local churches, the relative independence that goes with this awareness, and the ministry of the laity. Both views appeal to the authority of the council and justify their validity by quoting its documents.

Seemingly we are living out two different ecclesiologies found in the documents themselves without being able, at least for the present, to reconcile them with each other. Even during the council itself observers from the Eastern churches commented on the impossibility of living out simultaneously, on the one hand, the first two chapters of *Lumen Gentium,* which have as the basic image of the church the Pauline concept of people of God, and, on the other hand, the third chapter of the same document, which portrays the church in terms of a hierarchical entity.[3] The latter image, which became the dominant concept of the church after Vatican I, defines the church primarily in terms of a perfect hierarchical society.

The two models could be schematically presented as follows: The first model comprises these elements: (1) all power flows from the hierarchy; (2) the laity receives its ministry through delegation from the hierarchy; and (3) the hierarchy is the center around which everything revolves. The second model (BECs) has charism as its organizing principle. The basic images it uses are people of God (all are equal), body of Christ (living organism), and Creation of the Holy Spirit (charismatic entity). Thus we have two different models of society and communion, an older one challenged by a newer one, each with its own symbols and juridical structure. The issue, however, is not a matter of structures versus community. We know from the social sciences that society cannot be transformed into communities. Social groupings will search for community but, because of egoism and individualism, laws, order, and structures are necessary for any human community. The new model (BECs) seems to be concerned with the often forgotten fact that community has the primacy and that institution has to be regarded and treated as subordinated in the service of community and communion, not the other way around.

The new model (BECs) appeals particularly to new experiences and claims that it can make sense of these in ways the older model fails to do. The older model promises continuity, allows for change by internal modification, and claims to be able to integrate these new experiences quite easily without breaking out of its unchanging framework. It tries to accommodate what is felt to be important in these new experiences while, at the same time, it softens and limits their general impact. The BECs model faces the lacuna of not yet having an established framework and, therefore, struggles with forging its language, rituals and

---

[3] Joseph A. Komonchak, "The Significance of Vatican Council II for Ecclesiology," in *The Gift of the Church: A Textbook on Ecclesiology in Honor of Patrick Granfield, OSB,* ed. Peter Phan (Collegeville, Minnesota: The Liturgical Press, 2000), 69-92. Komonchak shows that Vatican II contained a variety of church images put side by side and that there was purposely no attempt to merge them into one single view.

juridical structures. A good example of juridical procedure in these images is the following: the old model allows the laity to form a pastoral council with consultative voice and the commissioning of ministers by the parish priest, while the new model operates on the concept of discernment of ministry by the whole community. Similarly with rituals, that is, while accommodation is made in terms of language and common celebration, the performance of the rituals remains strictly priestly and hierarchical in the older model. In sociological language we would say that we are faced with two different views of society: a hierarchical versus a more democratic or charismatic one. Or in theological language, the old model seems to have been organized around the axis of clergy-sacraments, while the new model seems to organize itself around the axis of gospel-laity.[4]

The first model has been called *neo-conservative* in line with the official church's attempt to restore the lost image of the church in the years following the council. Although bearing the characteristics of the institutional model, this image has conscientiously tried to incorporate the theology of Vatican II. Hence, it cannot simply be equated with an image of the church that existed prior to the council.[5]

The second image, basically built on the model of church as community, has come to us through the experience of many movements in the church today but most articulately through the Basic Ecclesial Communities of Latin America and the Small Christian Communities in Africa and Asia.

In spite of all the differences in this second model due to the divergent cultural, social, political, and economic situations in which it is embraced by the local churches, it contains a basic affinity wherever it can be found. Therefore we are justified in talking about a new model of church, since its commonality meets the requirements of a model to be (1) useful, (2) open, (3) fitting, and (4) stimulating without losing the flexibility to work with other models at the same time. It responds to the basic need of the common faithful to find and secure their identity as Christians in a community that takes their cultural background and their way of relating to one another seriously. In Africa and in Asia, where the nuclear family, the extended family, the clan, and the tribe still play dominant roles, the people will conceive of the church as community much more easily and even naturally, since it promises to understand and to express the gospel message in their own customs and culture.

In the so-called developed societies with their increasing loss of common values and fundamental convictions, *pluralism* has become the in word. The effect has been a loss of personal identity for the individual. Most people live in several very different worlds: family, job, leisure; private and public sectors;

---

[4] Lode L. Wostyn, *Exodus towards the Kingdom: A Survey of Latin American Liberation Theology* (Manila: Claretian Publications, 1986), 94.

[5] David N. Power, "A Theological Assessment of Ministries Today," in *Trends in Mission toward the Third Millennium*, ed. W. Jenkinson and H. O'Sullivan (Maryknoll, New York: Orbis Books, 1991), 197.

and domestic, economic, political, and cultural sectors. Each of these is often far removed from the others. "Many a time pluralism even results in a 'patchwork identity' and a syncretism of elements of the most diverse religious and cultural traditions."[6]

The desire for a community that will appreciate individuals and respects each person's uniqueness and value becomes more and more felt. The small communities that are arising in these churches are different from those in Asia and Africa, but they all are based on the insight that the Christian faith can only be grasped, personally experienced, and joyfully embraced in a community of people who reinforce one another in their commitment to the gospel. Nevertheless, it has to be admitted that this model has remained up to now a church model predominantly found in Latin America, Africa, and Asia. But we should keep in mind that these churches contain 70 percent of all Catholics in the world.[7]

Many Catholics still believe that the best way to face new experiences is to integrate them into the neo-conservative model; they continue to emphasize the hierarchical model of the church. At the moment we are experiencing a rather powerful resurgence of this model in the church, particularly in groups that have a great influence in society and public life. Qualities of the neo-conservative model include the following: (1) it is hierarchical in structure because its power does not come from the people but is held to come directly from Christ; (2) it is attentive to people and what they say; (3) it is centralized though ready to listen; and (4) it is interested in the concerns of its members. This model has attractive elements that appeal to many Catholics. For instance, it responds to a concern for the ordinary faithful who are considered unqualified to work out their own personal stand on matters of faith and morals and who need strong directions to enable them to live and deepen their faith. The mission and obligation of the hierarchy are to provide them with this direction. Second, there is presently a certain growing pessimism about accepting the world either as partner in dialogue or as a place of divine revelation. Although other cultures are appreciated, the main task of the church is still seen as that of bringing the faith to the people. The goal of mission work is the building up of a Christian culture. This culture then stands as an expression of a socially attainable faith and also as a directive for personal and public life, which provides symbols, rituals, office, custom, and teaching. These offer guidelines and directives as well as a clear and distinct Christian identity.[8]

The European Synod of 1991 on new evangelization brought up the question of faith and inculturation very forcefully. The issue was the "Re-christianization of Europe." The fact that evangelization never occurs outside of a specific culture places great stress on the relationship between culture and evangelization.

---

[6] Kasper, "Relating Christ's Universality to Interreligious Dialogue," 223.

[7] *Statistical Yearbook of the Church 1998* (Vatican City: Libreria Editrice Vaticana, 2000), 42.

[8] Power, "A Theological Assessment of Ministries Today," 197-199.

People are shaped by the historically determined value systems and thought patterns of their culture, which surround and limit them. In addition, each person is born into a specific social system and participates in a specific lifestyle. Our present technological and industrial culture is determined in its intelligent pursuits by a strong focus on whatever can be clearly mapped out and realized. For this reason, new evangelization does not aim only at an adaptation of the good news to the respective culture but also at its transformation.

The concrete question at the synod was how to envision such an evangelization of culture. Shall we support an evangelization of culture only because it is necessary in order to bring the good news to each individual? Or should we say that the evangelization of culture is an integral element of the proclamation of God's word? We also have to admit that the creation of a more human society and culture is not a tool or a tactical move of the church in order to secure its own interests. A more human culture is good in itself and not only good because it is a means to an end. This, in turn, presupposes respect for other views and for the freedom of the individual to express these views unhampered.

This gives rise to a very basic challenge: the presumption that modern culture is being built on the philosophical basis of relativism. How can this respect for other views be reconciled with the claims of the Catholic Church to be the sole possessor of the truth? The pope himself, without watering down the claim to absolute right of truth, supports dialogue and sincere listening among all in the spirit of discernment and courage. Serious inculturation of the faith demands more than the imposition or even the creation of a Christian culture, which can easily be perceived as a new way of colonization by the dialogue partners of other cultures and religious traditions.

Third, the church, visible as a clearly identifiable body with social power, guarantees an effectiveness in working together that can never be obtained through small communities whose members insert themselves into the fabric of social life. If the church's mission is the transformation of all social and political realities toward the kingdom, then it is extremely important that the church be heard and exert its influence in public, in places where politics and decisions are made that affect human society as a whole. This has to be regarded as a constitutive element of its mission.

How the church can make its voice heard in public and how it can influence legislation on all levels of society are challenges that call for new forms of mission strategy today. We have come to realize that the church must be present in the decision-making processes that affect the whole human race. Since one of the most successful forms of influencing decision-making bodies in democracies is a lobby, many feel that the church must be present at political centers of power with competent and well-informed people to make its view known and respected for the well-being of all. Worldwide religious communities have recognized the chance to participate in New York and around the world in UN specialized agencies and world conferences, and a number of them have applied for and received UN consultative status. This should be regarded as a way of evangelization through advocacy. What has been done already and what possibilities there are can be seen in the reports given by a number of authors.[9]

A church with a visible organized structure, well-defined leadership, and clear doctrine is in a much better position to make its views and concerns heard in society and politics than an organization composed of small communities. This is the great advantage of a well-organized institution such as the Catholic Church, which still speaks with one authoritative voice, the pope. The influence of the church as a large-scale institution may be waning, but it still is a formidable voice in the world today. Therefore, we are not advocating the church model of BECs as a substitute for the institutional model but rather as its counterbalance. As we noted earlier, models are not exclusive; they supplement one another. The question is: What serves as the best model to look at the church in today's world and to use as a standard to evaluate other models?

CHURCH AS BASIC ECCLESIAL COMMUNITIES

Although the official church accepted the emergence of BECs, often with great enthusiasm, and regarded this phenomenon as the working of the Holy Spirit, particularly in Latin America, the BECs have also experienced stubborn resistance or at least strong resentment from some official church leaders. Most often this is due to their link with liberation theology, in which the BECs are rooted. Twenty years ago José Marins pointed out:

> Some authorities are not happy that the BEC make the people participate, that they decentralize decision-making, that they create a new style of priests, that they make the faith bear on real life. . . . A part of the Church feels uneasy with that trend, which is in conflict with their theological vision which shocks their clerical way of life, and so some bishops become spokesmen of that mentality and try to disparage the communities.[10]

Reflecting on the church in Latin America more than thirty years after the bishops' conference in Medellín (1968) enthusiastically praised the emergence of BECs as the hope for the Latin American continent, Clodovis Boff sees both

---

[9] See Brother Ignacio Harding, OFM, "Franciscans International [a Non-governmental Organization with General Consultative Status with the Economic and Social Council of the United Nations]—International Advocacy as Integral Evangelization: Possibilities and Limitations," *Sedos Bulletin* 31 (January 1999), 3-9; see also Brother Reynolds and Sean Healy, "Transformation of Society and the Role of Advocacy—An Irish Case Study," *Sedos Bulletin* 31 (January 1999), 10-19.

[10] Quoted in Joseph Healey, "Evolving a New Model of Church: A Comparison of the Basic Christian Communities in Latin America and the Small Christian Communities in Eastern Africa," *Verbum SVD* (1985), 215.

church models operating in Brazil today. In his judgment it is the neo-conservative model that has gained considerable ground over the last decades.

> There is a double dynamic at work in the Churches of Latin America today: the dynamic of participation, coming from Medellín and Puebla, which finds expression especially in the base communities, and the dynamic of order and authority, of commands, discipline and obedience, with everything coming from the top down. Unfortunately, this latter dynamic seems to be growing but at the same time the experience of base communities is something which is irreversible in our churches, there is no going back. . . . There has been a tendency recently to incorporate them into the parish structure and restrict their activity to the renewal of the parishes, as a kind of auxiliary service in the parishes, whereas their original thrust and inspiration was to transform the parish into a dynamic center of community, to decentralize and desacramentalize the parish.[11]

Clodovis Boff's comment affirms the general observation that the official church of Latin America is in the pursuit of harnessing if not stamping out entirely liberation theology and tries very hard to get these vibrant base communities under control and to incorporate them into the existing structures once again. How these communities will develop under this restraint is hard to predict.

The BECs model is built on three important theological principles developed either during the council or immediately afterward, when the bishops tried to adapt the council's vision of the church and its mission in the world to their respective churches. These principles can be summarized as follows: First, the church must be understood in relation to the world. We must take into consideration not only theological sources but also secular sciences, history, and the world in which we live. All attempts to understand the church that do not take into account its relation to the world are inadequate, one-sided, and faulty. Second, the church is not the center of the world; God's salvific will goes beyond the boundaries of the church. Third, the church has a concrete role to play in the sociopolitical liberation of human beings in the world. This in no way implies a negation of human secular autonomy but must be regarded as an assertion of Christian responsibility.[12]

Latin American theologians have written extensively about these communities.[13] They believe it is from these communities that we can gain a true and genuine understanding of what church means today, both in its essence as well

---

[11] Clodovis Boff, "The Church in Latin America: Between Perplexity and Creativity," *Sedos Bulletin* 27 (1998), 136-137.

[12] Roger Haight, *An Alternative Vision: An Interpretation of Liberation Theology* (New York: Paulist Press, 1985), 163-165.

[13] See Leonardo Boff, *Ecclesiogenesis: The Base Communities Reinvent the Church* (Maryknoll, New York: Orbis Books, 1986); idem, *Church, Charism, and Power: Liberation Theology and the Institutional Church* (London: SCM; New York: Crossroad, 1985), 117-123.

as in its mission. Leonardo Boff has set forth his most challenging ideas in *Church, Charism, and Power*. He regards the church as a sacrament of the Holy Spirit and thus charism becomes the organizing principle of the church. As a sacrament of the Spirit, the church becomes precisely the sacramental realization of the kingdom in the world and the instrument of its mediation in history.

Charism is understood as the manifestation of the Spirit's presence in each individual member of the community and directing everything for the good of all. Each member of the church is charismatic, exercising a particular function in the community and enjoying a fundamental equality with other members. As the organizing principle, charism includes the hierarchy. The charism of office is that of exercising leadership within the community. This charism is of prime importance by virtue of the fact that it is responsible for harmony among the many and the diverse charisms within the community. But, nevertheless, the hierarchy is to be seen as possessing one ministry among many other charisms that together built up the whole church.[14] Boff's view of charism as the basic structure of the church confirms in another way Benedict Ashley's view on the distinction between functional and personal equality and inequality of all members in the church, as we saw in chapter 6.

The BECs are understood as the entities in which the kingdom makes itself present in its community-creating aspect. These communities consciously seek to practice and live out those features that characterize the kingdom: equality, participation, fellowship, and communion—or, in the words of the Bible, justice, peace, and joy (Rom 14:17)—as the basic elements of the kingdom historically anticipated.[15] BECs are the soil from which a new understanding of church is emerging because they challenge the way in which the church traditionally has been perceived.[16] In the words of Joseph Healey:

> The establishment of Basic Small Christian Communities has had a great influence on the Post Vatican II Church especially in the Third World—as a new model of Church, as a dynamic force for conscientization and as a process for lay people to become active participants in ministry and evangelization. Quite independently of one another, three areas of the Church in the Third World—Latin America, Africa, and Asia—have experienced the extraordinary growth of these communities.[17]

The New Testament Background: House Churches

A number of authors believe that the emergence of BECs all over the world has a foundation in the New Testament itself. Two words, *oikos* and *oikia,* are

---

[14] Leonardo Boff, *Church, Charism, and Power,* 154-164; idem, *Ecclesiogenesis,* 23-30.

[15] Leonardo Boff, *Church, Charism, and Power,* 145f.

[16] Wostyn, *Exodus towards the Kingdom,* 91-100.

[17] Healey, "Evolving a New Model of Church," 211.

used approximately two hundred times in the New Testament. The reality behind these concepts can best be translated with "household" or "house church." "Household" and its related terms describe the very foundation and context of the Christian movement. According to Herman Hendrickx:

> Religiously, the movement originated in and owed its growth either to the conversion of entire households or of certain individuals within households. Generally cultic activities like the Eucharist were celebrated in the house. Economically, the household comprised the context for the sharing of resources among the co-believers as well as the wandering charismatics. Socially, the household provided a practical basis and theoretical model for the Christian organization as well as its preaching.[18]

The house church was the genesis of the church in any city. Paul's missionary strategy in particular seems to have been to get a foothold in a family whose house he would then use as a meeting place and as a center for further missionary work in the town.[19] The converted household provided space for the preaching of the word and for worship, as well as for social and eucharistic table-sharing. The Greco-Roman household included not only members of the immediate family and their slaves, but also freed persons, laborers, and tenants. These household communities comprised men and women working as partners in ministry.

Essential for the house churches were these four characteristics without which a gathering could not and cannot be called church: (1) *koinonia*/community, which means that the members are concerned about one another's welfare and have a sense of belonging and being interconnected with all the other house churches; (2) *diakonia*/service or mission, which means all must serve each other in all needs that may arise, since all are brothers and sisters in Christ; (3) *kerygma*/gospel-rooted, which is the name for the Christian story, whose proclamation gathers together a people of faith, for it is the proclaimed great story that every true church shares with every other true church; and (4) *liturgia*/eucharist, which means each gathering unit of Christians is a eucharist-celebrating unit.[20]

Since the community met "in households" it was obvious that the *domina* or mistress of the house, for example, Prisca and Priscilla (1 Cor 16:19), was fully responsible for that community and its gathering in the house church. This raises once again the question of who actually presided over the eucharistic celebration in such households gatherings. Others note, however, that

---

[18] Herman Hendrickx, *The Household of God: The Communities behind the New Testament Writings* (Quezon City: Claretian Publications, 1992), 2.

[19] Rafael Aguirre, "Early Christian House Churches," *Theology Digest* 32 (1985), 151-155.

[20] Bernard J. Lee and Michael A. Cowan, *Dangerous Memories: House Churches and Our American Story* (Kansas City, Missouri: Sheed and Ward, 1986), 24-28.

In Roman and Hellenistic society the father of the house exercised the authority for all. The structure in ancient times was clearly hierarchical with a patriarchal order. Initially, the Christian community broke with a patriarchal structure since the community consisted of brothers and sisters, united in one faith, one Lord and one baptism. This would have made eminent sense in an enthusiastic movement. Eventually the hierarchical and patriarchal model predominated as the Church developed specific structures even as early as the end of the first century.[21]

The early Christian vision of "discipleship of equals," concretely practiced in the house church, especially attracted women and slaves to Christianity. This soon led to tensions and conflict with the dominant cultural ethos of the patriarchal household. The historical fact is that the house church did not survive beyond the first century. The new "household of freedom," which we find in the letters of St. Paul, had to give way to the old patriarchal pattern found in the normal home of the surrounding culture. The church adjusted quickly to the Greco-Roman culture, and the household of freedom soon belonged to the past. The patriarchal pattern became the pattern not only for structuring the house church but for the universal church as well. Adaptation to culture does not always coincide with Christian norms.[22]

The Council's View of the Church as Local Church:
Theological Background

Although the council adopted a universal perspective most of the time when it talked about the church, it asserted quite strongly in *Lumen Gentium* that it is only in and out of the particular churches that the one and single Catholic Church exists (*LG*, no. 23). This has been called by some theologians the most important ecclesiological formula of the council.

It guarantees, or should guarantee, that the relationship between the whole church and the individual churches is seen as one of reciprocal or mutual inclusion, that individual churches are not considered administrative subdivisions of a pre-existent reality, nor is the one church a subsequent federation of individual churches. The many churches are not churches except in the one church; the one church does not exist except in and out of the many churches. Since Vatican II, these carefully nuanced and mutually conditioning statements have prompted what some called a *Copernican revolution* in ecclesiology and a renewed interest in the local churches, whose communion is the whole church.[23]

---

[21] John F. O'Grady, *The Roman Catholic Church: Its Origin and Nature* (New York: Paulist Press, 1997), 69-70.
[22] Hendrickx, *The Household of God,* 129-130.
[23] Joseph Komonchak, "Ecclesiology of Vatican II," *Origin* 28 (1999), 765.

This view of church is the second most important theological reason for the emergence of the phenomenon called the Basic Ecclesial Community.

Experience with Basic Ecclesial Communities

In Latin America the emergence of BECs was neither programmed nor did it follow specific pastoral planning. Rather, BECs emerged in response to specific needs, namely, the lack of priests, the advancement of sectarian churches, social and economic oppression and dependence, and the feeling that, if the people did not take matters into their own hands, the faith might just disappear. In hindsight it is obvious that the ultimate inspiration came from the Holy Spirit. In Africa, in contrast to Latin America, BECs were introduced from the top, that is, from the official church through statements of the bishops. However, this was a response to the growing awareness of the people's need to express their own values of community, harmony, and solidarity in the context of their Christian faith.[24]

The local hierarchy, in response to the request of the council to implement the documents of Vatican II, came to realize that the inculturation and the localization of the church were among the most immediate tasks for their churches. The then-emerging BECs were soon regarded to be one of the best tools at hand for this task. They were seen as a sign of the times, indicating the way the Spirit was moving in the churches.

Evidence of this new model has been derived particularly from the experience of BECs in Latin America and in Asia, as well as from the Small Christian Communities in Africa.[25] Medellín defined the base communities in these words:

> The Christian ought to find the living of the communion to which he or she has been called, in the "base community," that is to say, in a community, local or environmental, which corresponds to the reality of the homogeneous group and whose size allows for personal fraternal contact among its members. Consequently, the Church's pastoral efforts must be oriented towards the transformation of these communities into a "family of God," beginning by making itself present among them as a leaven by means of a nucleus, although it be small, which creates a community of faith, hope and charity. Thus the Christian base community is the first fundamental ecclesiastical nucleus, which on its own level must make itself responsible for the richness and expansion of the faith, as well as of the cult which is its expression. This community becomes then the initial cell of the ecclesiastical structures and the focus of evangelization, and it currently serves as the most important source of human advancement and

---

[24] Healey, "Evolving a New Model of Church," 218.

[25] Marcello Azevedo, S.J., "Basic Ecclesial Communities: A Meeting Point of Ecclesiologies," *Theological Studies* 46 (1985), 601-620.

development. The essential element for the existence of Christian base communities are the leaders or directors. These can be priests, deacons, men or women religious, or laymen.[26]

The "base communities" are seen here as the "initial cell of the ecclesiastical structures" in terms of the greater institutional church. A definition of BECs given by the permanent Council of the Conference of Brazilian Bishops in a statement issued in 1982 readily lends itself to practical applications: "Basic Christian Communities are formed by families, adults and youth, in a tight interpersonal relationship of faith. . . . They celebrate the word of God and are nourished by the Eucharist. . . . They enjoy solidarity and a common commitment. . . . They are cells of a greater community."

The Federation of Asian Bishops' Conference (FABC) describes the Basic Christian Communities as follows:

> In parts of Asia today the need for forming Basic Christian Communities is becoming more strongly felt. The people are expressing their need for some kind of basic social grouping whose members can express real interpersonal relationships and feel a sense of communal belonging. Many different forms are evolving, leading to a fuller participation in Christian living. These groups are not the only way of participating in the life of the church; still the Spirit seems to be moving the church strongly in this direction.
>
> These Basic Christian Communities have arisen as a response to different needs and situations, such as: (1) Existing parish structures sometimes are not conducive to intensive Christian life. They can become inadequate to ministering to the growing needs of people. (2) Our people are too many and too spread out for the number of priests available to minister to them. (3) The people need a sense of belonging and support, especially in a non-Christian environment. (4) People are taking more and more responsibility for their church and are responding to new ministries to serve their small Christian communities. (5) There is growing urgency for genuine Christian witness in community among the ideological struggles taking place in Asia.
>
> A group of people is described as a basic community when the number of members is such that they can really know one another, meet with one another, relate to one another. The members are not too far apart to come together fairly frequently. There is a certain degree of permanence among the members. There is also mutual caring, sharing and support. The community strives for common goals and concerns. There is unity and togetherness.

---

[26] Medellín Document, *The Church in the Present Day Transformation of Latin America in the Light of the Council* (Washington, D.C.: Catholic Bishops Conference, 1970), 226.

A basic community becomes a Christian community when its inspiration, model and center is Jesus, the Risen Lord. There is openness to the charisms of the Holy Spirit, a praying and worshiping together. The members of the community share the Word of God, integrate it into their daily lives and proclaim it to others. "No Christian community, however, can be built up unless it has its basis and center in the celebration of the most Holy Eucharist." Thus the members of the community must have the Eucharistic celebration as the source of its Christian life.[27]

The East African bishops also speak of such faith communities:

A SCC [Small Christian Community] is a caring, sharing, faith-reflecting, praying and serving community in which ongoing Christian formation takes place. It may consist of an existing community, a neighborhood grouping of five to fifteen families, people with common interests or activities, and so on. It is a natural community or grouping based on geographical proximity, blood relationship, occupation, social ties or other affinities. It is the basic place of evangelization and catechesis.[28]

At a plenary session of AMECEA held in Nairobi in 1976, the bishops held a study day on Small Christian Communities. As a result, they set themselves the task of building these communities as a pastoral priority.[29] At a further plenary session in 1979 they reiterated this policy, stating, "We have been able to clarify, deepen and confirm our conviction that the pastoral option we have taken is indeed one that holds great promise for the Church in Eastern Africa." This policy represents the most appropriate way of expressing the mystery of the church as a communion of faith, hope, and love, as well as being an excellent means of involving all the members of the people of God in the common task of continuing the reconciling mission of Christ in the world.

In this document the bishops describe Small Christian Communities as "the most local incarnation of the one, holy, Catholic, and apostolic Church." The universal church "must be really present to Christians in their own locality," and the most appropriate way is through the existence of these communities. Through them "the Church is brought down to the daily life and concerns of people to where they actually live. In them the Church takes on flesh and blood in the life situations of people." Christians are able to reflect together on their experiences and can place them under the light of the gospel. The gifts given

---

[27] *For All the People of Asia: Federation of Asian Bishops' Conferences Documents from 1970-1991*, ed. Gaudencio B. Rosales and C. G. Arevalo (Maryknoll, New York: Orbis Books, 1992), 76-77.

[28] Compilation of AMECEA [Association of Member Episcopal Conferences in Eastern Africa] statements in Joseph Healey, *A Fifth Gospel: The Experience of Black Christian Values* (Maryknoll, New York: Orbis Books, 1981), 37.

[29] 1976 AMECEA Plenary, "Building Christian Communities," *Afer* 18 (1976), 250.

by the Holy Spirit are for service and the upbuilding of the church. In Small Christian Communities everyone is able to take part in the life of the church and so make full use of their gifts. The role of the ordained minister is "to recognize, encourage, and coordinate the various gifts of the Spirit."[30]

For the bishops, the resolve to base Christian life and witness on Small Christian Communities is not just one way among many possible ones; it is not just following a passing fad in the church today. It is a basic commitment, a serious shift in pastoral emphasis. It is deliberately intended to modify deeply our pastoral system, policy, and practice. Up until now, the avowed common system was to base the life of the church on the parish level rather than on the sub-parish level. In these circumstances of Eastern Africa, what we call missions or parishes cannot be taken as the basic units of the local church. If they are, the church is doomed to failure. We need to adopt a new system, whereby the basic units of the church are those smaller communities where the ordinary life of the people takes place.[31] The similarity and closeness to the New Testament term "house church" seems obvious.

The description by the bishops of AMECEA of Small Christian Communities as "the most local incarnation" of the church points to a shift in ecclesiology within the Roman Catholic Church. Traditionally, a local community of believers belonged to the church on the basis of its unity with the bishop and through him to Rome. The church universal is the church at its fullest. The local church, which in the language of the Second Vatican Council refers to the diocesan church united to its bishop (*LG*, no. 26), receives its authenticity from its union with the universal church. While preserving this link with the wider church, the bishops of AMECEA now believe that a small community—a division of the parish, which is in turn a division of the diocese—is a manifestation of the church itself. In practice, this means that in looking at those gathered in such a community, we are seeing the church.

The Brazilian bishops mention six elements in particular that are worth incorporating into any renewal of community life in the church. (1) The church in such communities is considered as the "people of God" and "a creation of the Holy Spirit" according to 1 Corinthians 12:7, in which "to each is given some manifestation of the Spirit for the common good." (2) The church is considered as sacrament, sign, and instrument of a profound union with God and of the unity of the human race (*LG*, no. 1). In this context, the church is not considered primarily as a society with a visible structure. (3) The role of the laity, considered in itself and not just as a participation in the ministry of the priest, is deemed constitutive in the life and mission of the church. Lay people have a ministry of their own, and not just through delegation from the hierarchy. (4) The communities possess a holistic view of history; the story of humanity and the story of salvation are seen as intrinsically interconnected. This view makes the quest for

---

[30] AMECEA Pastoral Institute, *Communities Called Church* (Eldoret: Gaba Publications, 1979), 265.

[31] 1976 AMECEA Plenary, "Building Christian Communities," 266-267.

justice and liberation a constitutive element of evangelization. (5) These communities are the churches *of* the poor, not *for* the poor. Ministry and leadership as well as the social force of these communities come from the poor and are exercised by the poor. This constitutes a new form of being a force for social change. (6) The prayer and the ministries of these communities derive much from the forms in which the general religious experience of the people in the culture is expressed and nurtured. Even if we accept cultural differences and allow for historical diversities, we can still take these communities as the key to an understanding of how church life may develop in this present age. Here the local church is allowed to develop a new relation to itself, to the world, and to the universal church. These communities still feel the need for an ordained ministry but no longer see a need for a clergy/laity distinction. Charism is seen as the basic organizing principle that gives to each one a function on the basis of being a member of the community. The center and source of these communities is their prayer life.[32]

This prayer is marked by six qualities. (1) Fundamentally, it is listening to the word of God. The Bible plays a decisive role in the prayer meetings of these communities. (2) The power of the word of God is experienced in their daily life and the people become conscious of it. It is a word that is alive and addressed to their real problems. When hope is shared with others in a hopeless situation, the Bible comes alive. The Bible is seen as their own book rather than the book reserved for the clergy to be read to the laity.

> The Gospel is the calling card of the base ecclesial community. The Gospel is heard, shared, and believed in the community and it is in its light that the participants reflect on the problems of their life. This is a typical feature of the community; the Gospel is always confronted with life, with the concrete situation of the community. It is not simply a marvelous and consoling message; above all, it is light and leaven. The Gospel is seen as good news, as a message of hope, promise, and joy for the real situation of the poor.[33]

(3) It is a common prayer in which the freely expressed voice of everyone is welcomed and not hindered by class distinction, whether social or ecclesiastical. (4) The prayer finds its expression in the experiences and things available to the people: food, drink, songs, meeting places, all those things they themselves have made. (5) It is a prayer in which the poor are present and active with their popular religiosity, their native religious experience and expression. These are not just pious prayer groups that sit around and reflect together. As faith moves to actions, a deep process takes place. Most BECs use the classic observe-judge-act model of reflection. Beginning with its local reality, the community evaluates and critiques its experience through discernment and then

---

[32] Power, "A Theological Assessment of Ministries Today," 193-194.

[33] Leonardo Boff, *Church, Charism, and Power*, 127.

moves on. (6) It is joyful and festive, with a joy that springs from the experience of the kingdom present and the awareness of the power of freedom that the Spirit can give. As it is practiced in these communities, leadership is not guaranteed by office, delegation, or title of power, but by charism, discernment, and public affirmation within the community.[34]

What kind of community do we have here? We have, first of all, a community in which the poor of the society feel at home, are free to express themselves, and are able to contribute to the life of others.

> The base ecclesial community is also the place where true democracy of the people is practiced, where everything is discussed and decided together, where critical thought is encouraged. For a people who have been oppressed for centuries, whose "say" has always been denied, the simple fact of having a say is the first stage in taking control and sharing their own destiny. The "comunidas eclesial de base" thus transcends its religious meaning and takes on a highly political one.[35]

Second, we have a community where there is no class distinction. The mission to the world is seen as the responsibility of the whole community as such and not of the laity as distinct from the clergy. The holistic view of reality takes this world seriously and results in an awareness of the gratuity of life and of all living things.

> Political commitment is born of the reflection of faith that demands change. ... The base ecclesial community does not become a political entity. It remains what it is: a place for the reflection and celebration of faith. But at the same time, it is the place where human situations are judged ethically in the light of God. The Christian community and the political community are two open spheres where what is properly Christian circulates.[36]

Finally, mission to the world is undertaken with sensitivity and in an openness to those not of the community. There is an awareness that the church does not possess all the answers but can suggest some solutions through listening to the Word of God and being open to the Spirit.[37]

On closer analysis, we find three elements that enable the people to hear what the word of God is saying: the Bible, the community, and the real-life situation of the people vis-à-vis the surrounding world. In a concrete case it does not matter where one starts. One can begin with the Bible, or with the

---

[34] Inacio Neutzling, "Celebrationes dans les Communautes de Base," *Spiritus* 24 (1983), 115-155.

[35] Leonardo Boff, *Church, Charism, and Power,* 9.

[36] Ibid., 8-9.

[37] Healey, "Evolving a New Model of Church," 213. Healey lists here the five similar characteristics as proposed by J. Marins.

given community, or with the real-life situation of the people and their problems. The important thing is to ensure the inclusion of all three factors.[38]

Problems These Communities Have to Face

Since these communities do not as yet have explicit juridical structures, these are the main difficulties they have to face: (1) The process of discernment is difficult, whether it is a matter of reading the signs of the times, seeing God's presence in a real-life situation, or discerning charisms and ministries. (2) There is the constant risk of substituting democratization for discernment, especially in choosing leaders. The natural leader is not ipso facto the best and Spirit-filled leader of a BEC. This is an insight many BECs had to reach through painful experiences. (3) Some communities, especially when they undertake the work of social liberation, can find themselves victims of ideologies of power. This is a concern constantly voiced by the official church but, at times, exaggeratedly so. The accusation has been made that these communities are at times mere social and political action groups used by ideologies that have no religious bearings at all. Marxism in particular has been seen as having dangerously invaded and undermined these communities. The reality of church at the grassroots level has been seriously questioned. (4) The independence of local churches that might arise out of this model of church could easily lead to fragmentation if bonds between churches are not fostered. (5) Given the persistence of mass religion and the genuine piety and need of those who adhere to it, the Christian community has yet to work out its responsibility toward those not interested in accepting its invitation to membership, while at the same time it holds onto the sacraments and other forms of religious expression.

Renewal of the Parish Church through Small Christian Communities in Africa

SCCs, the African counterpart to the BECs of Latin America, evolved in the context of pastoral planning.

> The concept of Small Christian Communities developed as a result of an attempt to put the ecclesiology of Vatican II into practice. The African bishops opted for the SCC pastoral priority as the best way to build up local Churches that are truly self-ministering, self-propagating, and self-supporting. The AMECEA Pastoral Priority of SCCs has effectively questioned the whole system by which pastoral ministry is carried out. . . . The SCCs are the best means for developing African Christianity . . . "small

---

[38] Carlos Mesters, "The Use of the Bible in Christian Communities of the Common People," in *The Bible and Liberation*, ed. N. K. Gottwalk and R. A. Horsley (Maryknoll, New York: Orbis Books, 1993), 119-133.

communities also seem to be the most effective means of making the Gospel message truly relevant to African traditions."[39]

The Africans were more concerned with inculturating the gospel message into the fiber of the African community, while the BECs in Latin America were more concerned with the liberation of the oppressed from injustices. Although they exercise many ministries, all of them are tied directly into the work of liberation.

On the basis of the bishops' option for SCC and the African pastoral experience, the Lumko Institute in South Africa has developed a method to build SCC in the local parishes that could lead to a renewal of the African church. They envision five stages of church growth that aim at enabling members of a congregation to assess their own stage of growth.[40] In addition, knowing where they have come from, they gain a clearer picture of where they are going. This historical survey is presented in the following five stages.[41]

The First Stage: The Provided-for Church

The dominant person in the parish is the priest who organizes everything himself and offers the laity all the necessary means of salvation. This is the role described for the laity by the Code of Canon Law of 1917. They have the right "to receive from the clerics spiritual goods and strong help for salvation" (Canon 682).

The Second Stage: A Pastoral Council Church

The laity is recognized as sharing in the mission and work of the church by working alongside the priest. One way of doing this is through shared leadership in the parish council. At this stage the laity are still often treated as "helpers of the priest" rather than carrying their own responsibility. Although for the first time in history the church introduced the parish pastoral council as a legal entity after Vatican II (Canon 536), these pastoral councils are only "optional," that is, it depends on the bishop if he wants them in the diocese or not and, in addition, the members of these councils have only a "consultative" vote.

The Third Stage: The Awakening Church

This is a positive title for what is, for many people, both cleric and lay, a negative experience. As more lay people become involved in church life through the exercise of their Spirit-given gifts, the issue of responsibility arises. This, in

---

[39] Anselm Prior, *Towards a Community Church* (Gemiston: Lumko Publication, 1991), 7.
[40] Ibid., 17-27.
[41] Anselm Prior, *Towards a Community Church*, 2d ed., the Training for Community Ministries series, no. 28T (Natal, South Africa: Lumko Publications, 1997).

turn, raises the issues of power and control. While this can generate a lot of tension in the parish, it can also lead to the non-ordained taking true responsibility and, as true equals, finding a new way of working alongside the ordained.

The Fourth Stage: The Task-Group Church

Having accepted the commitment that arises from their baptism, the laity take responsibility for all that needs to be done, both within the congregation and beyond its boundaries. With the needs of parishioners and their neighbors now being met, many would accept this as a fine model for the parish—a church at worship and in the service of others. However, the African bishops want parishes to go one step further.

The Fifth and Final Stage: The Communion of Communities

At this stage all the believers of a parish are invited to be active members of a SCC, which is situated in their neighborhood. Their regular meetings are based on gospel sharing and always include reports on their activities since the last meeting and plans for further action on behalf of others. These communities are part of the structure of the parish. One of their number is a member of the parish council and all of them are engaged in various liturgical and other activities that keep them linked together and in union with the wider church.

In the traditional model of church, the Sunday eucharist is often the only time for believers to nourish their faith, pray, and listen to the scriptures. This one hour in church on Sundays is supposed to carry them through the following week as committed Christians. In a church based on many SCCs, the people will come to the Sunday eucharist with their faith already alive and nurtured.

The Lumko Institute presents four marks that describe SCCs:

At Lumko we do not define Small Christian Communities. Definitions can be restrictive and limiting, whereas we know that each Small Christian Community is a living reality and is distinguishable from every other one. Relying on our experience in many countries, though especially in Africa, we prefer to describe these communities and we do so under what we regard as the four essentials, or the four marks by which Small Christian Communities can be recognized and evaluated.

Firstly, they meet in their homes. Sodalities usually meet in the church or hall. The members of the Small Christian Communities meet on a neighborhood basis and usually rotate their place of gathering so that each has a turn in hosting the group. The meetings need to be held on a regular basis—you cannot form community by meeting once a year! Usually the core members gather once a week, or once a fortnight.

Secondly, the most important activity of their meeting is gospel sharing. Through common reflection and sharing they meet the person of Jesus

Himself. They become ever more aware of the presence of the Risen Lord in their midst and in each other. This regular sharing on the Word leads them into a personal relationship with Christ who truly is the foundation of their community. This also leads to a deeper sense of community among themselves. Thus, gospel sharing also gives rise to a spirit of openness and trust in the group. The members come to know each other as brothers and sisters.

While they do not use texts from the gospels only, it is recommended that they begin with these as the four gospels are the consequence of the mature reflection by the early church on the person and mission of Jesus Christ. Once they have imbibed this Good News they can then use the other books of the New Testament as well as texts from Old Testament books, which they reflect on in the light of the person of Christ whom they have met in the gospels.

Thirdly, the members of a Small Christian Community look to one another's needs. They see that the lonely, the sick and impoverished of their neighborhood experience the caring love of the Lord through His disciples. They are involved in the affairs of their locality as they wish to put into practice the love they have received from Christ through another.

Fourthly, each Small Christian Community is in unity with the universal church. Visits are made between the communities. They take turns in preparing and leading the Sunday liturgy. They sometimes meet to work or discuss together. Also, each community is in close contact with the central parish. They have a representative on the parish pastoral council. They engage in training and join others for days of recollection and prayer. The full-time pastoral ministers regularly visit the small communities so as to strengthen their ties with the parish as a whole as well as with the universal church.

The church as a Communion of Communities is an ideal which will never be fully achieved. However, like the Christian challenge to live and forgive, it remains as a guiding star on which we set our sights. It is also a standard by which we can measure all our pastoral programs and activity.[42]

In short, we could say that the Small Christian Community is a caring, sharing, faith-reflecting, praying, and serving community in which ongoing Christian formation takes place. It may consist of an existing community, a neighborhood grouping of five to fifteen families, people with common interests or activities, and so on. It is a natural community or grouping based on geographical proximity, blood relationship, occupation, social ties, or other affinities. It is the basic place for evangelization and catechesis.

The African Synod (1994) adopted as a model the church as family of God to describe the reality of the church in Africa. The synod fathers preferred this

---

[42] Prior, *Towards a Community Church,* 42-43.

model because of the prominent position the family holds in the African society in spite of all the upheavals that affect the family in this continent. They regarded this model as a challenge for the church to become what it aspires to, *the family of God.* The church's goal in Africa is

> to be a Christ-centered, vibrant and people-oriented Church where the African sense of the family is experienced by all. The ideal African family is based on the extended family system where members are united in a common ancestry which gives each person his/her identity. It is also a center for passing on traditions and culture as well as a place where reconciliation and healing of wounds are facilitated. The Church in Africa must, therefore become a family in the African sense where the family is an oasis of rest, security and identity. To do this, it must create an atmosphere of openness, stability, warmth, forgiveness and solidarity in the spheres of human operation.[43]

We can regard the family of God model as the African nuance to the Basic Ecclesial Community model. But it is important to be alert to the differences, which are culturally conditioned and indicate that the BEC as a model cannot just be exported or imported to other local churches in spite of many similarities.

How Do Ministries Arise in These Communities?

One of the most important issues of this new ecclesiology is the status of leadership in the SCCs. The most local manifestation of the church in present practice is the parish, which is headed by a priest. The priest is ordained and appointed by the bishop, who is head of a particular church in which the one, holy, catholic, and apostolic church of Christ is truly present and active. Does this mean that the leaders of the SCCs must also be appointed "from above"? And what of their non-ordained status? Even if it were acceptable for these leaders to be elected by the members of the SCCs themselves, whether that election is ratified by a central authority or not, the question of a community headed by a non-ordained leader introduces a new concept of church into Roman Catholic theology.

The matter of training for leadership is a further pastoral implication. Holding authority over a local church, albeit a neighborhood community that has its vital link with the parish through the Sunday celebration of the eucharist, these leaders represent more than the members of their small community. They need to be trained in this wider perspective. To leave the content and method of this training to the choice of the local parish priest or animators, and thus open up the possibility of it never taking place, would be to give it insufficient emphasis and open the church to potential fragmentation.

---

[43] Mary Gerard Nwagwu, "Communion and Self-Reliance: Signs of Church as God's Family in Africa," *Afer* 42 (2000), 23.

Every ministry arises from the effective participation of the people in the life and mission of the church and from the needs to which the ecclesial community consciously seeks to respond. The awareness of the needs and the election of the persons to respond to those needs give rise to the ministries and to the corresponding ministers. Normally, the process of formation follows these steps: occasional collaboration, permanent collaboration, becoming conscious of one's role, becoming conscious of one's ministry, confirmation by the community (and by the priest or bishop).

This raises a question we discussed earlier: Is the traditional structuring of the church still sufficient to deal with the present situation? Can the hierarchical threefold structuring of office not be done in different ways? Could, for example, the leadership charism (and others as well), which is essential in BECs/SCCs, not be integrated into the charism of office and give it an empowering through the laying on of hands? This would truly integrate the lay ministry into the life of the church and bridge the gap between the ordained and the lay state in the church.

Or does the understanding of church in this model not ask for a different type of priest altogether? A type of priest who comes from the community and is ordained for the community similar to the local leaders of the early church, who were appointed by the apostles and remained permanently in their own communities?

In *Like His Brothers and Sisters: Ordaining Community Leaders*, Bishop Franz Lobinger, the co-founder of the Lumko Institute in South Africa, argues precisely for such ordained community leaders, people who are married, live in their community, and provide for their own living. This type of priest existed at one time in the early church alongside the "Paul-type" priest. Lobinger calls them "Corinth-priests." They were called elders in the early church. They took care of the local churches and provided all their sacramental needs. Following his view of church, which is elaborated in the Pastoral Institute for South Africa in terms of BECs/SCCs, Lobinger presents a thesis for discussion. He argues that every mature Christian Community should have several ordained community leaders, as in the early church, who would celebrate all the sacraments the community needs to be a mature church community. His concern is the mature Christian community, and his basic argument is based on the scriptures as well as on the signs of the time.

> The process of becoming a mature faith community includes many aspects, and one of these is that the community develops the ability to fulfill all its essential tasks by itself. An immature community is either unwilling or unable to do so, or prevented from doing it. The New Testament communities provide the models for a mature community. They were quickly enabled to assume all responsibilities even to presiding over their sacramental celebrations. However they still welcomed and wanted the periodic visits of an apostle to ensure that their community life was complete and genuine. The congregation which says: "We are able to do most

things for ourselves, but for the authenticity of the Word and presiding over the sacraments we prefer to wait for somebody to be sent to us" cannot be considered as leading a complete or mature community life. In recent years we have experienced an increased need to stress community building and self-reliance. Many efforts are being made to lead congregations from the stage of being provided for by outsiders to one of maturity. We should continue this evolution and guide the communities to that maturity where some of their own members can be ordained to preside over the proclamation of the Word and the celebration of the sacraments.[44]

In Lobinger's view this would lead us away from "the passive, anonymous congregation to one where the members consciously come together, have a sense of belonging to one another, and act as a community. Therefore it is most fitting that the presiding ministers of the liturgical rites should be members of the celebrating community. In other words we should aim at some of its members being ordained for presiding over its own celebrations." For him, the present practice of exercising the priestly function in the church leads only to harmful confusion. He remarks:

It is harmful to continue with our present contradictory way of explaining that laity do not exercise official ministry when in fact they do, and that priests exercise all pastoral ministry when it is evident to everyone that lay people do most of it. Lay leaders who are able to express themselves clearly have made it known that they suffer under this lack of clarity. Their motivation is impaired because they feel they are asked to undertake Church tasks beyond their rights. This is particularly true of those who conduct a Service of the Word on Sundays or who practically bear a presiding responsibility for the whole community. Concerning other liturgical tasks, it is often only theologians who take note of the confusion, not the laity who conduct liturgies, preach homilies and lead communities; but this very unawareness of confusion is all the more reason to strive to resolve the dilemma. People call many functions "lay ministry," which are actually something else, but we hesitate to use the correct terms, such as "presiding over the community" because we fear that we might lessen the status of the only existing kind of priesthood. Many Church leaders overreact by speaking of "clericalizing the laity and laicizing the clergy" while in fact the problem lies elsewhere. It is the result of not allowing the normal development of natural forms of pastoral ministries to take place. Some priests see their role becoming ambiguous. They have to ask others to share duties which were exclusively theirs while officially stating that this should not be done.[45]

---

[44] Franz Lobinger, *Like His Brothers and Sisters: Ordaining Community Leaders* (Quezon City, Manila: Claretian Publication, 1998), 87-88.

[45] Ibid., 89.

Lobinger's solution for the shortage of priests is not just to ordain married men *(viri probati)*, but to start from a new understanding of Church in which the community takes care of itself. Simply ordaining married men to overcome the present shortage of priests is no solution because it would keep the whole struc-ture as it is. For Lobinger, it is the mature Christian community with its many charismatic gifts, which enable it to take care of itself, that is basic for the type of priest called an ordained community leader. "The proven community leaders are the more natural kind of candidates and it would therefore be more appro-priate to ask 'why not proven members of the community? Why restrict ordina-tion to those who are not members of the local community, are not following an average profession, and do not have a family?'"[46] It is clear that such a solution must prove itself first before it could be adapted to any kind of Church. Many Churches are not ready for such a view because it presupposes a community whose vision of Church is more the BEC type.

Summing Up

The basic question still remains: does this model have a future? Will not the general trend in the church today toward a more conservative reevaluation of the Christian faith hamper the further development of such a model? Those involved with this kind of church are still optimistic. They hold that these commu-nities "are writing a narrative theology of liberation and inculturation. A certain searching, experimenting, dying and rising will continue as the grassroots tries to evolve a new model of Church and the seed of a new model of society."[47]

Clodovis Boff, addressing the enormous loss of Catholics in Latin America, estimates that every year some 3,500,000 people leave the Latin American Catho-lic Church for the Pentecostal churches. Some say that twenty years from now most of the population of Latin America will belong to Pentecostal churches and that the largest Catholic continent will lose its religious hegemony. Since these "new churches" are found everywhere in the world today, it might be im-portant to ask why are they so successful. Boff presents the following subjective and objective reasons for their attractiveness, which may also have a dark side.

Subjective Factors. The *direct experience of God,* overflowing with emotions, with wonder; an experience of rebirth, a change of life. They are churches of conversion, which one joins at one's free will. Next to these aspects there is emotionalism, which at times leads to mass hysteria. *People feel welcome.* A poor person, a miserable person, an outcast who is despised, socially humili-ated, finds in the new churches hospitality, comfort, the good news, and this helps people become rooted in the community. The question remains: To what extent can these new churches be considered communities? For instance, the universal church of the kingdom of God does not create a community; it has

---

[46] Ibid., 87.
[47] Healey, "Evolving a New Model of Church," 223.

patrons, it is like a huge religious supermarket. The new churches convey a strong *sense of identity.* They say: "We are believers, chosen, saints, elected by God." This generates self-esteem, pride, a sense of dignity. The dark side of this is the arrogance of the pure, contempt of others, a sectarian spirit. There is *community participation.* The very animated celebrations, with beautiful songs, filled with enthusiasm, fervor, spontaneous prayer. Participation in services: one-third of the faithful have an assignment in their church. They are active participants, not patrons. They have a vital *Christ-centered message.* Christ the Lord, the Savior, the Bible, which is at the center of everything, the Spirit that is infused into everyone. Here too we see the shadow of Biblicist fundamentalism, a lack of theological culture. They demand *ethical rigor.* They offer a new model of life, a healthier, more dignified, clean life. Leaders appear as wholesome, decent people. This attracts simple people. Finally, people are driven by their *enthusiasm in proclaiming the gospel.* They have energy, they believe what they say. The dark side here is the spirit of conquest, proselytism, fanaticism, psychological blackmail. But there is no denying their profound conviction and the energy with which they proclaim Jesus Christ.

Objective Factors. They have *high penetration* in the poorest social groups, the outcasts; they reach out to the poorest among the poor, more so than the Catholic Church and BECs. The dark side is that they manipulate the miserable, the defenseless, the ignorant. They are charismatic churches with *institutional flexibility.* They are decentralized and do not have a cumbersome apparatus. They are light, streamlined structures. The training of the ministers is very practical, straightforward. A period of six months is sufficient for training a good minister. The dark side lies in the poor education of many; they are ignorant ministers. The churches easily splinter, become fragmented. They have *good communication.* They are capable of communicating the core message effectively, and they are convincing. A debate between a minister and a bishop is a disaster for the bishop, whose language is based on dogmas and canon law, while the minister is free and focuses entirely on the Holy Spirit, the Bible, and Jesus Christ. Many talk, but they repeat the same things over and over again—variations on the Spirit, on Christ the Savior, on salvific faith.

In addition to these subjective and objective points of attraction, some with their dark side (such as fundamentalism, emotionalism, proselytism), Boff feels three other quite negative aspects should also be mentioned: (1) the financial abuse of the poor, which at times becomes exploitation; (2) frequently they do not lead people toward social commitment. Rather, they relate to society in a sectarian manner; and (3) they do not dialogue with either Catholics or the popular religion or the culture; they are iconoclasts.[48]

Boff holds that one of the most effective ways to deal with this challenge and to help people to find in the Catholic faith what they seemingly find in these

---

[48] Clodovis Boff, "The Catholic Church and the New Churches in Latin America," *Sedos Bulletin* 31 (1999), 197-199.

fundamentalist sects is the BEC movement. The BECs, he writes, "do not flow into sects; rather, they represent a dam to hold back sects, a defense against them. In my diocese, Rio de Janeiro, which is the most religious because it is exceedingly traditionalist, sects grow more than in other Brazilian dioceses. So, religious ministry alone cannot solve this problem." It is the affinity in many aspects to the new churches that makes the BECs so important. He continues:

> Basic ecclesial communities [BECs] are one answer to this fundamental problem: there is a great affinity between the basic communities and the new churches. There is a structural analogy between BECs and the new churches: (1) the centrality of the Bible, even though in BECs it is not read in a fundamentalistic way; (2) the community experience, although BECs are less charismatic and more democratic communities; (3) participation in the ministries, in church services; (4) missionary spirit, BECs are spreading, they preach the gospel and reach out to those who have distanced themselves. Obviously, there are some differences as well. For instance, BECs encourage social and political awareness, they have a very clear social commitment, which is to transform the system, they are open to ecumenical dialogue, not only in terms of traditional ecumenism but also in terms of macro-ecumenism: dialogue with Afro-Brazilian religions, other indigenous religions, etc.
>
> It is clear that the BECs lack something which the new churches have: for example, the emotional aspect which is integrated into the experience of faith. What is missed the most is institutional freedom: BECs operate within the framework of parishes, dioceses, under the control of the bishop and of the parish priest, and if the bishop or the parish priest does not want them there is nothing they can do.[49]

The Need for Spirituality in BECs

BECs have often been accused of being merely social action groups. There were cases in which this might have been true, but basically BECs are worshiping communities in which people experience the presence of Christ and deepen their own personal Christ experience. In a talk entitled "The Search for Justice and Solidarity: Meeting the 'New Churches,'" Clodovis Boff reemphasized this dimension as most important today for any BEC, particularly in Latin America, where the church faces the challenge of Pentecostal churches:

> We have to think of a new model of action that no longer presents the heavy, rigid, Marxist features of the past. It has to be a militant model that is more charismatic, more spiritual, more integrated, more flexible. This type of action would not only be more appreciated by the Pentecostals but

---

[49] Ibid., 200-201.

would also be more biblical, more Christian, more spiritual. It may be that in this way dynamic dialogue and ecumenical growth can be begun.[50]

Twenty years ago liberation theologian Segundo Galilea pleaded for a stronger stress on the spiritual dimension of the Christian commitment with regard to the secularism that was invading Latin America's society:

> The "contemplative" woman or man today is the one who has an experience of God, who is capable of meeting God in history, in politics, in his brothers and sisters, and most fully through prayer. In the future you will no longer be able to be a Christian without being a contemplative and you cannot be a contemplative without having an experience of Christ and his Kingdom in history. In this sense, Christian contemplation will guarantee the survival of faith in a secularized or politicized world of the future.[51]

Karl Rahner, envisioning the church of the future, voiced the same concern. Facing the crisis of the church in Europe, he insisted that the members of that church would have to be "mystics." What he meant was that in a world of secularism only those who had a deep personal experience of God and who in their lives could make this experience accessible to a totally secularized world could survive in their faith. Secularism is a worldwide phenomenon and affects every society.

> Secularism may stem from explicit unbelief, the denial of the existence of God or of any religious dimension to human life. Such unbelief is rarely the product of a formal, atheistic, rational philosophy. More often, it is an allegiance to a popular myth of science as the ultimate theory of everything, a conviction that the only truths are those which are accessible to scientific observation and experiment. Basically, it is a faith in unlimited human progress, apparently confirmed by the spectacular achievements of Western technology.[52]

In the face of secularism the model of small faith communities can be seen as one answer to help the individual believers to preserve their faith. As the saying goes, faith that is not shared dies. Individuals may not be able to maintain their enthusiasm for Christ and his message without the support of a community that shares with them that enthusiasm and joy which come with a true encounter with Christ and his Spirit. Is it not just this aspect that makes so many sectarian groups attractive to many mainline Christians today?

---

[50] Clodovis Boff, "The Search for Justice and Solidarity: Meeting the New Churches," *Sedos Bulletin* 31 (1999), 205.

[51] Segundo Galilea, *Following Jesus* (Maryknoll, New York: Orbis Books, 1981).

[52] Ludwig Bertsch, "Inculturation in Europe's Societal Situation: An Introduction," in *Yearbook of Contextual Theologies* (Aachen: Missio Institute, 1993/94), 104.

Aylward Shorter, referring to African intellectuals, has this to say concerning the spread of secularism:

> Consumer materialism is nowadays the most common cause of secularism. Rather than formal unbelief, it is a religious indifferentism induced by the preoccupation with material things. As Mary Douglas points out, it is the product of a world of impersonal things, a world in which personal relationships are at a minimum and in which symbolism and ritual are discounted as forms of expression in the interpretation of reality.[53]

Concluding Remarks on BECs

The question is how to cope with this all-pervasive secularism, which shapes young and old alike. CEBs are different in structures and outlook depending on the situations in which they have emerged. But as a model for an answer to urgent needs, they could be equally relevant to the church in the First World. Here, as well, the need for such small faith communities becomes more and more felt and articulated. They will definitely be different from those in Asia, Latin America, or Africa. People feel that the parish structures will not be sufficient for the faith even to survive. What is asked for are communities in which the faith is expressed in a more personal way, where all participate and share their faith, where all feel equal and are respected not on the level of what they achieve but on the level of being persons. The model of a church made up of CEBs may well be the one that can address this deeply felt need for inculturation and localization of the church. In the words of the Asian Bishops' Conference:

> Now *the Church cannot fulfill her mission of service without being local.* For the Church becomes Church only when she is *incarnated in a people and culture,* in a *particular place and time.* The mystery is one, total and universal, but its concrete realization is varied, multiple, and particular. This localization and concretization of the Church is necessary in view of fulfilling her mission and realizing her universality. It is only in her solidarity with the world and by her insertion into history's movement that the Church can be taken in earnest as a community of service to the world. This means that the Church must incarnate herself in the socio-cultural and religious traditions of the peoples as well as in their modern concern to create a just and human society.
>
> It is to be noted however that the local church is not a partial church nor merely a division or a viable unit of administration within the vast domain of the universal Church. It must and does contain the whole mystery of the Church and as such every local church is the microcosm of the whole reality of the Church.

---

[53] Aylward Shorter, "Secularism in Africa," *Sedos Bulletin* 30 (1998), 11.

The *localization and concretization of the Church* find *expression* in what is called the *Basic Christian Community.* As an ecclesial community at the grassroots it should embody the full reality of the Church. It is a visible community of the disciples of Christ gathered together and embodying the Spirit of their master. It is a community of persons in authentic interpersonal relationship with a mutual sense of belonging and concern, in a fellowship open and extending to all, and in an outreach of humble service. It is a *community of faith, hope and love* in its function of effective witness and humble service.[54]

How will the church look in the near future? This is not a question that is easy to answer. At times we may ask as did the Lord God, who, while looking at Israel, asked his prophet Ezekiel, "Mortal, can these dry bones still live?" The prophet had his doubts but it was the Lord God who gave him the answer: "Yes, they will, I will put my Spirit into them and they shall live" (Ezek 37:1-14). But when the Lord pours out the Spirit anew over the church, it may look quite different from what we are used to. Its survival will depend on whether it becomes a world church, as Karl Rahner anticipated, and whether it will commit itself to take the side of the poor, who make up almost 70 percent of the world's population. As a world church, it will have to embrace all cultures and express the Christian message of God's kingdom in their values and customs. As advocate of the poor, its principles of action must remain those of its master, Jesus himself: compassion and justice.

To the first challenge there seems to be no better model available than to see and understand the church in the model of CEBs. This does not exclude other models, because there is no one model that expresses the mystery of the church fully. The use of models depends also on the situation in which the church finds itself. To the second challenge of globalization and the increase of the poor in today's world, the model of church as a contrast society seems to be best suited to respond to its commitment to the kingdom, which is ultimately defined as a matter of "justice, peace, and joy in the Holy Spirit" (Rom 14:17).

THE CHURCH AS A CONTRAST SOCIETY

The brothers Gerhard and Norbert Lohfink proposed a model of the church that they called a "contrast society." While the phrase is not found in scripture, it is a metaphor proposing God's view of how human beings are to live together and what values are to be basic to any given social reality as an alternative to a history that is marred by violence, oppression, and injustice. In short, it is seen as a model of how God imagines human society. In spite of all the discussions and the controversies that the term has created among exegetes and theologians, the image highlights certain aspects that are needed to understand the church

---

[54] Rosales and Arevalo, *For All The People of Asia,* 148-149.

today, aspects which seem to fulfill all Louis J. Luzbetak's requirements for a good model, that is, that it is useful, open, fitting, and stimulating.[55] The model provides us with a clear idea of how we as church should see and understand ourselves in a globalized society with its own value system. In this understanding the church is conceived as a community that is based on a different set of values that it must live and uphold over against a society that does not share these primary values. So perceived, the church is seen primarily as a community in which justice and compassion are the basic rules of conduct, which must be demanded from society at large as well if the church wants to fulfill its primary mission to lead all human societies into the kingdom of God now and to come.

Biblical Basis

In analyzing the biblical origin of the people of Israel we saw that Yahweh's intention was to create this nation as a contrast society. Since the Christian community stands in direct succession to the Old Testament people, the church finds its identity in defining itself precisely as a contrast society.[56] Jesus definitely saw Israel as a chosen people that God had made into a contrast society in the midst of all other nations. He understood his mission as gathering the true eschatological Israel into a society in which the values and the social order of the kingdom of God would be fully lived. It was not holiness and purity that should determine social reality, since this option had only created a fragmentation of the covenant idea and had ostracized half of the people as renegades and sinners. Jesus demanded a social reality in which justice and compassion would determine social reality so that God's kingdom could clearly shine through and all would become the great community of God where there would no longer be a distinction between male or female, Jew or Gentile, ruler or ruled, but all would be one family under the fatherhood of God.[57]

The community of disciples Jesus envisioned would be different from the Old Testament community as it had evolved in his time. It would be Israel renewed, standing in contrast to all other communities because in it God would reign and the principle for action and behavior would definitely be Jesus' own principles of action: justice and compassion.

The Early Church as a Contrast Society

Did the early communities also understand themselves as contrast societies in relation to the social milieu around them? Certainly, the experience of the

---

[55] Louis J. Luzbetak, *The Church and Culture: New Perspectives in Missiological Anthropology* (Maryknoll, New York: Orbis Books, 1988), 136-137.

[56] Gerhard Lohfink, *Does God Need the Church?: Toward a Theology of the People of God* (Collegeville, Minnesota: The Liturgical Press, 1999), 51-120; Norbert Lohfink, *Option for the Poor: The Basic Principle of Liberation Theology in the Light of the Bible* (Berkeley, California: Bibal Press, 1987), 48-52.

[57] John Fuellenbach, *Throw Fire* (Manila: Logos Publications, 1998), 193-218.

kingdom as present in their midst definitely set them apart from the way of life found in the society in which they lived. There are a number of texts, particularly in the writings of St. Paul, that support a positive answer to these questions. They attest, first of all, to the experience of being one in Christ and living in a community in which all are equal and class distinctions exist no more: "So there is no difference between Jews and Gentiles, between slaves and free men, between men and women; you are all one in union with Christ" (Gal 3:28). And in Acts: "The group of the believers was one in mind and heart. No one said that any of his belongings was his own, but they all shared with one another everything they had" (Acts 4:32).

It is obvious from these texts that the church is intended to transcend all other bases of unity such as being of the same race, sharing the same occupation or economic status, adhering to a particular political doctrine, belonging to a certain social class, or sharing the same level of education.

> The political novelty which God brings into the world is a community of those who serve instead of ruling, who suffer instead of inflicting suffering, whose fellowship crosses social lines instead of reinforcing them. This new Christian community, in which the walls are broken down not by human idealism or democratic legalism but by the work of Christ, is not only a vehicle of the Gospel or fruit of the Gospel; it is good news. It is not merely the agent of mission or the constituency of a mission agency. This is the mission.[58]

Thus the early communities did experience themselves as being in contrast with the rest of society. Their whole value system was different. Paul's admonition to the community was: "Do not make yourself like the structures (form) of this age, but be transformed by the renewal of your mind" (Rom 12:2). According to Gerhard Lohfink this text states that the form and spirit of the churches must not be adapted to the form and spirit of the rest of society.[59]

But the moment the church became the "Christian society," the question of a contrast society ceased to be asked. When the church became the "official society" under Constantine, there seemed to be no need any longer for the church to be a contrast society. But it did not take too long for the church to realize that its new status was a mixed blessing. The idea of the church as a contrast society was then taken up by groups like religious orders and sectarian movements, which either silently or openly protested against a church that had paid dearly for becoming an agent of the state and had, by necessity and for the sake of convenience, compromised the gospel's demands.[60]

---

[58] John Howard Yoder, "A People in the World: Theological Interpretation," in *The Concept of the Believer's Church*, ed. James Leo Garrett (Scottdale, Pennsylvania: Herald, 1969), 274.

[59] Gerhard Lohfink, *Jesus and Community* (London: SPCK Press, 1985), 122-132.

[60] Francis J. Moloney, *Disciples and Prophets: A Biblical Model for the Religious Life* (London: Darton, Longman, and Todd, 1980), 155-170.

CAN THE CHURCH BE A CONTRAST SOCIETY TODAY?

In our time the question concerning the conception of church as a contrast society poses a different problem. Critics ask, Doesn't such a view of church contradict the very purpose of the church? Doesn't being a contrast society automatically close the church off from the rest of society? Isn't it the church's mission to be in the world and in its societies in order to transform them? One author, for example, writes: "The question arises: if we define the church as 'contrast society' are we not declaring the church to be a separated unity from the world which it wants to serve? Will the church not become by necessity a sectarian entity, which would contradict the whole mission of the church?"[61]

Gerhard Lohfink answers such objections as follows. In the way the church conceives of how God wants people to live in society, it does not see itself as "counter to" or "against" society, as such, but as a "contrast" or "protest" against a society that does not live up to what it is supposed to be in the eyes of God. The church poses an alternative, much as the Old Testament people did, in order to fulfill its mission for the world. The idea of church as a contrast society aims at the constant attempt by many, inside and outside the church, to limit the church and its activity to the purely spiritual, the inner realm of the person, and so deny the church any right to get involved in the public realm and to claim a say in how society and the state have to order their affairs. There is the constant tendency on the part of those authors to make the kingdom of God "atopic," meaning "everywhere and nowhere, as being not located in space and time at all."[62] For them, the kingdom is purely spiritual and an entirely transcendent reality.

Against the second accusation that the definition of church as a contrast society would mean to form it into a community of the pure elite, those who help one another to become morally better and then regard themselves as superior to the rest, Lohfink counters: "Church as contrast society does not come into existence because Christians live more determined, more heroic and morally better lives than the rest of humanity. . . . Church as contrast society emerges only when people let themselves be caught by God's Kingdom present now, including their weaknesses and guilt."[63] We are not living anymore in the cultural setting in which Jesus preached his message. The social reality of Jesus' time was determined by two values: holiness and purity.[64] The values that shape modern society and gain prestige and fame are competition and success. The effects of such social reality in our world today are the same as in the time of Jesus: they necessarily lead to exclusion and marginalization of millions of people. But our opportunity as Christians lies just here: to show the world that a

---

[61] Marian Machinek, "Die Vieldeutigkeit der Rede von Kirche als Kontrastgesellschaft und ihre moraltheologische Implikationen," *Forum Katholischer Theologie* 15 (1999), 134-146.

[62] Gerhard Lohfink, *Wem gilt die Bergpredigt?* (Freiberg: Herder, 1988), 147-160.

[63] Ibid., 159-60.

[64] Fuellenbach, *Throw Fire*, 200-206.

different form of society is possible, one that, however, is not accomplished through words and doctrine but only through concrete practice.

Whatever definition and understanding we may propose for the church, if it wants to remain faithful to its Master, it has no alternative but to conceive itself as a society in which the ultimate norm for social and communal structures must be justice and compassion. These are the indispensable principles for action that Jesus demanded from his eschatological community. To create a community in which justice and compassion would reign meant for Jesus the final bringing about of God's plan of salvation for Israel and the whole world. In this, he saw the mission for which he was sent.

That Jesus wanted a community that includes all and would not develop into an esoteric group concerned only with its own members can be seen in Jesus' own behavior. In bringing about the kingdom, three options were available to Jesus, two of which had already been chosen by others: the revolutionary, the sectarian, and the worldly.[65]

For revolutionaries, the battle cry has always been "radical change." They want to change the present by overthrowing those who rule and so bring in God's reign by force. This option was open to Jesus, but he neither authorized nor accepted it. Sectarians, following the motto, "Let us create it," insisted on total withdrawal from society and the creation of a new model of community in which the covenant would be realized to the full. This was the option of the Qumran community and has been the option of many movements in the church through the centuries. This option abandons the world because it is seen as being beyond repair. Jesus did not choose this option either. He did not join the Qumran community but stayed where the people were and used their marketplaces for his preaching and his actions. Jesus chose what Dunn called the worldly option, with its command "Live it!" He showed that the kingdom is happening now in the midst of human affairs and that human actions may become the carrier of this kingdom. To accept the kingdom meant for Jesus to celebrate its presence now in this world, not in withdrawal. Jesus' option can be called worldly, because it asks us to live wholly immersed in this world yet according to otherworldly values that challenge it to let itself be transformed by what Jesus came to bring. Consequently, the church, in the footsteps of Jesus, cannot withdraw from the world and close itself up like an esoteric community that cares only for the salvation of its own members. Its mission is the whole world, because the biblical concept of election always contains the mandate to engage actively in God's plan of salvation, which aims at saving all.

Every church community must understand itself from this vantage point and define its mission accordingly: to be a community whose basic principle for action is compassion and justice in contrast to the wider society in which it lives. To be sure, we need to keep in mind other considerations when we define the church and its mission, but if we forget this essential aspect, the church has nothing to say to many people today, particularly to the poor and marginalized of our time.

---

[65] James D. G. Dunn, *Jesus' Call to Discipleship* (Cambridge: Cambridge University Press, 1992), 44-52.

Globalization and a Contrast Society

There are many reasons today for the church to opt to become again a contrast society. One reason in particular is the process of globalization. It is one of the most important and widely discussed processes taking place in the world today.

Usually, globalization refers to the process of growing and intensifying interaction of all levels of society in world trade, foreign investment and capital markets. It is supported by technological advances in transport and communications, and by a rapid liberalization and deregulation of trade and capital flows, both nationally and internationally, leading to one global market. International contacts and exchange are of course nothing new. Migration flows took place in the ancient world. International trading companies existed in the time of the Phoenicians. European colonization (often accompanied by missionary enterprises) started at the end of the 15th century. Present-day globalization differs from these earlier processes both in nature (its emphasis on liberalization and deregulation) and in scope and intensity. But like colonialism, globalization mostly benefits the powerful economic interests.[66]

To be sure, globalization does not affect all human populations in identical ways. It has structured the world into haves and have-nots, and it has created two zones on this globe whose interaction is one of exploitation and dependency. It has also created a new social class: the expendables, also called garbage people, namely, those who do not produce and who will not consume. Vast groups of people in many developing countries feel the negative impact of globalization the most. In the words of Indian theologian Felix Wilfred:

> Globalization seems to carry the whole world along. But in fact, it leaves more and more behind it in the desert of misery. It uproots people with the promise of plenty, but in fact it saps them mercilessly and allows them to dry out and die. The poor and the weak in our society are increasingly deprived of the security their traditional occupations, however low and menial these may be, provide. They are incapable of competing in a system whose very nature is to leave behind many as it progresses. The agricultural sector has experienced the heaviest blow of globalization.[67]

At the root of globalization is the *ethic of competitiveness*, which is being promoted as the fundamental and compelling guide for our actions. It shows its devastating effect mostly in poor countries, where it only increases the misery of the majority.

---

[66] Rob van Drimmelen, *Faith in a Global Economy: A Primer for Christians,* Risk Books series (Geneva: World Council of Churches, 1998), 8-9.

[67] Felix Wilfred, "No Salvation outside of Globalization," *Euntes-Digest* 29 (September 1996), 137.

Economic globalization is based on the exclusion of a growing number of "useless" persons who do not even have the "privilege" of being exploited. There are progressively more poor in the global village; never before in human history are there so many poor and so poor like in the actual situation. The presence of more poor in the world continues to challenge Christianity and theology.[68]

What seems so frightening for many is the way globalization is presented as a religious belief about how the whole world has to be structured and what values have to be promoted as being absolute.

Globalization is a mechanistic process (and therefore most easily manipulable by the wielders of power) in the face of which there is no choice, no alternative. The most insidious aspect of this ideology is that it could present itself as the only way. It creates a certain sense of inevitability and absoluteness. In this sense it is akin to the Semitic religious traditions which have the strong tendency for absoluteness and dogmatism.[69]

We do not have to evaluate globalization in negative terms only. If globalization could grow into global *solidarity and cooperation* also with the poor and marginalized, then it would mean greater unity among the peoples of the earth and a greater respect for the person, who is created in God's image. It is exactly in this context that the church today must once again consider itself as a contrast society, which, in contrast to a society of competition and success, will understand itself as being on the side of those who drop out of this process since they can neither produce nor consume. The challenge of the church today is to be a society of justice and compassion like the one Jesus envisioned in the context of his culture and time.

We are, of course, not the only ones who look with critical eyes at globalization and its effects on the poor in the world. Many international groups make their protest heard. These internationalists see clearly how devastating a purely economic approach to international reality can be:

Today's globalizers basically accept world economic developments as inevitable, while internationalists want to shape and influence these developments through political intervention. Globalizers applaud the absorption of all countries and systems into one, whereas internationalists speak of other forms of integration and pay special attention to the poor and the marginalized. While internationalism has always aimed at improving relationships between nations, the present process of globalization undermines the very concept of the nation-state. Internationalism is based on the conviction that citizens should be able to influence government poli-

---

[68] Armando Lampe, "The Globalization of Poverty," *Sedos Bulletin* 32 (2000), 132.
[69] Wilfred, "No Salvation outside of Globalization," 136.

cies; globalization erodes national sovereignty and can in the end threaten democracy and people's participation.[70]

In order to make our concern heard we should realize the kingdom with its demand of basic human values like justice and compassion needs to make itself heard outside the confines of the church as well. In supporting and at times joining these groups we give support and recognition to the kingdom of God that is at work wherever people stand up for the values of this kingdom.

The Challenge to the Church of the Contrast Society Model

To be a contrast society does not entail living behind closed doors. Rather, it calls for a community with open borders and, at the same time, a burning center. The issue is: given this view of church, how can we preserve an identity that calls for clear lines and limits and yet is open to those who are committed to gospel values? How can we remain Catholics, with our clearly defined doctrines and morals, and yet welcome those who want to come in on their own terms and understanding? Without a burning center and a closeness to Christ and his vision of the kingdom, such a community will be swallowed up by the values and standards of the society that surrounds it. As a contrast society, the church is, above all else, a worshiping community. Only a constant experience of the kingdom present in their midst enables the community and the individual to see the presence of God's kingdom in society at large as well. No mission into the world is possible without a constant union with the Lord who called and sent us. The church as contrast society is not a social action group but a community of those who want to follow the Lord and proclaim his kingdom, as one finds in the Gospel of Thomas: "Whoever is near me is near the fire, and whoever is far from me is far from the kingdom" (Saying 82).

One need not be a prophet to foresee that, in the near future, the church will more and more become a minority group in a society that for the most part will not share its values and concerns. In the measure that this happens, the conception of the church as a contrast society or alternative community will gain new support and strength and could give the church a new identity and new enthusiasm for its mission in the world.

The perception of the church as a contrast society is, of course, more readily embraced either by those Christians who live as minorities among other religious traditions and value systems (for example, in Asia and Africa) or by those who find themselves in situations of oppression and dependence or else in surroundings that hardly reflect Christian values anymore (as in parts of Latin America and many first-world countries).

The new Christian communities emerging all over the world are precisely the offspring of such a view of church. They want to offer a contrast society with a set of values different from those held in the surrounding society. How-

---

[70] Van Drimmelen, *Faith in a Global Economy*, 9.

ever, in order that such church communities remain truly bound to the universal church and not deteriorate into hundreds of diverse sectarian groups, we will have to see and appreciate the need for universal structures and the gift of the Petrine ministry of unity.

The Theological Value of Such a Conception of Church

The theological insight gained from such a conception of the church indicates once again that the kingdom will remain linked to a community that must see itself in the service of God's ultimate plan of salvation for all. Jesus linked the reign of God, previously belonging to the people of Israel, to the community of his disciples. With this new election of a community, God's purpose for the Old Testament people is now enlarged into the new people composed of Jews and Gentiles. They are now to become a visible sign of God's intention for the world and the active carrier of God's salvation. They are called out of the nations to take up a mission for the nations. They will fulfill this mission precisely as a contrast society in the midst of human societies.[71]

From this perspective the church is vital for the continuation of the kingdom in the world. "It is the community which has begun to taste (even only in foretaste) the reality of the Kingdom which alone can provide the hermeneutic of the message. . . . Without the hermeneutic of such a living community, the message of the Kingdom can only become an ideology and a program, it will not be a Gospel."[72] In *Models of the Kingdom,* Howard A. Snyder offers eight models of interpreting the kingdom of God.[73] One such model he calls the "counter system," which comes closest to the model of the church as a contrast society. The kingdom is seen as a counter system, that is, a way of conceiving and organizing society that is counter to its present dominant form. This model could also be called the *subversive kingdom,* because it consciously seeks to replace society's dominant values and structures. The kingdom is a reality and a set of values to be lived out now, in the present order in radical obedience to the Gospel and in opposition to the powers of the present age. This model sees the kingdom as a call to justice in society according to the values of the kingdom. It shows a particular concern for the poor and oppressed, the victims of society. It reminds the Church of God's special care for the widow, the orphan, and the alien. This view is strongly Christocentric in the sense that Jesus' life and his call to discipleship become the focus of attention. The Church's mission is to be countercultural in faithfulness to Jesus Christ. In the words of John Howard Yoder: "The alternative community discharges a modeling mission. The Church is called to be now what the world is called to be ultimately. . . . The Church is

---

[71] Gerhard Lohfink, *Jesus and Community,* 17-29.

[72] Lesslie Newbegin, *Sign of the Kingdom* (Grand Rapids, Michigan: Eerdmans, 1980), 19.

[73] Howard A. Snyder, *Models of the Kingdom* (Nashville, Tennessee: Abingdon Press, 1991), 77-85.

therefore not chaplain or priest for the powers running the world: she is called to be a microcosm of the wider society, not only as an idea but also in her function."[74]

Fidelity to Christ is the most important sign of the kingdom now. To the degree that the values of the kingdom—justice, peace, and joy (see Rom 14:17)—are realized now on earth, the kingdom makes itself felt. The final goal of the kingdom is peace and justice on earth and in all creation. This eschatological reign begins now but will be fully manifested only when God's reign comes in glory. Its strongest feature is its affirmation of God's Kingdom as both present and future and as both individual and social. It does so without compromising either the power or the gentleness of the Kingdom.

Concluding Remarks on the Contrast Society Model

The two major challenges the church faces today are inculturation and solidarity with the poor. Both elements assume different urgency and shape in different situations. Both have been regarded by the church itself as constitutive elements of our Christian faith. Both demand a dialogue with the world of different cultures and religious traditions. Dialogue, not monologue, is called for because the kingdom is already present among the dialogue partners and can therefore offer to the church something which it might not yet have. There are many ways to conduct this dialogue in the church. The two models of church that have been presented here as the most promising for the future address themselves particularly to the two most urgent challenges today.

First, the Christian faith must incarnate itself into different cultures at the grassroots so that people can experience and celebrate God's love and concern for them in their own values and customs and so come to know what God has in store for them.

Second, all humans are brothers and sisters bound together by a basic human solidarity. In today's world, where this truth seems swallowed up by economic and political values that extol competitiveness and success as ultimately determining social reality, the church must offer a different view of society, one in which all those who cannot compete will be regarded first as brothers and sisters in a society in which the ultimate values will be compassion and justice. These are the values Jesus chose and died for in order to bring God's dream of a society into the world: the great community where everyone counts and everyone is brother or sister to the others. The church today must become a contrast society in which the values of the kingdom count and are not compromised for other values no matter how appealingly these values may be presented.

From the perspective of the Indian church, Felix Wilfred writes:

---

[74] John Howard Yoder, *The Priestly Kingdom: Social Ethics as Gospel* (Notre Dame, Indiana: University of Notre Dame Press, 1984), 124-125.

The lure of globalization and the comforts and the goodies it offers are too powerful to resist. But the real test for the Church is here: Whether it wants to go along with the values, tastes and priorities of the middle and upper classes very much in line with globalization, or whether it wants to be a Church of the poor—making its own the struggles and concerns of the victims. The present-day developments taking place in the country are bound to look very different when seen through the eyes of the poor. Seeing societies through the eyes of the poor and to convert itself to their cause in the age of globalization is the need of the hour, the call of the Gospel which Jesus preached to the poor. The deeply meditated prayer of our great poet Tagore can become the prayer of conversion for every committed Christian and for the whole Church in the country:

This is my prayer to thee, my Lord—strike, strike at the root of penury in my heart. . . . Give me the strength never to disown the poor or bend my knees before insolent might.

The poet brings to our mind the two great temptations today: namely to disown the poor and to prostrate before the powers that be. And that is exactly what globalization and economic liberalization do. It is ready to compromise millions of poor for some profit, for some power. Strength is what is required to side with rather than own the victims of our society and to be their voice; strength is what is required before all those powers. When the poet speaks of striking at the root of penury, is he not pointing out the need to radically transform our consciousness and to attune ourselves to the voices of the poor?

In addition to calling for conversion, radical commitment to the cause of the poor also calls for *witnessing*. The glamour of globalization and liberalization can easily make us forget the victims they produce. But the passion of the Lord is an actual reality in the life and struggles of the millions of this country. It is a contemporary experience for a committed Christian and church. We respond by our witnessing incarnated in deeds. Like Joseph of Aramathea we need to take the poor from the cross on which they are nailed. Even more, we can no more allow any such inhumanity be done to the weaker ones whom God loves in a special way. And that brings to my mind the challenging words of Ashok Mehta:

If it is the claim of the Christians that even to this day they feel the agony of Christ on the cross whenever humanity suffers, as it were, it has to be proved in action, not by any statement.[75]

We are called in our world to bring God's kingdom as God's final design for all. It is this world in which we are called to create communities in which God's presence is experienced and God's kingdom of justice, peace, and joy shows its

---

[75] Felix Wilfred, "Church's Commitment to the Poor in the Age of Globalization," *Vidyajyoti* 62 (1998), 95.

first "budding forth" (*LG*, no. 4). This is the world in which God's kingdom is already present and within the reach of all those who open themselves to the Spirit that Jesus released like a fire when he sent us the Spirit. Our experience of the kingdom is not something we can hold for ourselves; our mission is to share this experience so that all may come to see and discover where God is making God's plan come true. And where we see its presence, we are to celebrate it in order to keep the fire burning and to give expression to our indestructible faith that the power of God's kingdom is at work to make God's dream for creation come true, no matter how this world may look at the present.

8

Mission of the Church

The concern of Jesus was the kingdom, God's dream for creation. To bring this Kingdom to bear on this world and to transform it into God's final design, Jesus chose justice and compassion as his life principles. What counted was a basic human solidarity that would not exclude anyone from God's love and would guarantee that all would be treated as brothers and sisters in the great family of God.[1]

Jesus gave his life to make this vision come true. In order to continue his work until the end of time he elected disciples and told them "as the Father has sent me, so I am sending you" (Jn 20:21). The mission of the church must be seen and understood from this perspective: totally in the service of God's Kingdom designed for the transformation of the whole of creation. Once the church is no longer seen as the sole holder of the Kingdom, it does not have to define itself any longer as the kingdom of God under siege by the powers of this world. Since Vatican II the church sees itself more as *leaven* of the Kingdom or in the *service of* the Kingdom, which is broader than the church. In other words, a theology of transcendence gives way to a theology of transformation. With such a view of church and kingdom in mind, the mission of the church is outlined as follows.

THREEFOLD MISSION

To proclaim in word and sacrament that the kingdom of God has come in the person of Jesus of Nazareth

Sacrament means that the church symbolically opens up the everyday world to the ultimate, the kingdom of God. But, in doing so, the church is also forced to accept its own provisional character. In the words of Edward Schillebeeckx:

---

[1] Albert Nolan, *Jesus before Christianity* (Maryknoll, New York: Orbis Books, 1978), 21-29, 59-67.

208

The Church is not the Kingdom of God, but bears symbolic witness to the Kingdom through word and sacrament, and her practice effectively anticipates that Kingdom. She does so by doing for men and women here and now, in new situations (different from those in Jesus' time), what Jesus did in his time: raising them up for the coming Kingdom of God; opening up communication among them; caring for the poor and outcast; establishing communal ties within the household of the faithful and serving all men and women in solidarity.[2]

To create church communities (local churches) everywhere and, in so doing, present the church community as a place where the kingdom of God makes itself visible.

These communities will offer themselves as test cases of the kingdom present now in two ways. (1) The disciples in such communities are to celebrate the presence of God's kingdom in their midst and let themselves be set on fire again and again. Especially when they remember the Lord in the table fellowship of the eucharist, the disciples should make present once again that compassion of God that Jesus showed in such feasts to be the heart of his own experience of God. The kingdom can therefore never be separated from the church, which, after all, is God's chosen instrument for God's kingdom here on earth. The following quotation of Johannes Verkuyl is strong but it is also correct:

> The Kingdom is, of course, far broader than the Church alone. God's Kingdom is all-embracing in respect of both points of view and purpose; it signifies the consummation of the whole of history; it has cosmic proportions and fulfills time and eternity. Meanwhile, the Church, the believing and active community of Christ, is raised up by God among all nations to share in the salvation and suffering service of the Kingdom. The Church consists of those whom God has called to stand at His side to act out with Him the drama of the revelation of the Kingdom come and coming.
>
> The Church constitutes the firstling, the early harvest of the Kingdom. Thus, though not limited to the Church, the Kingdom is unthinkable *without* the Church. Conversely, growth and expansion of the Church should not be viewed as ends but rather as means to be used in the service of the Kingdom. The Church, in other words, is not a goal in and of itself; but neither is it, as some at present would seem to imply, a contemptible entity that should feel ashamed of its calling and seek its redemption in self-destruction. The keys of the Kingdom have been given to the Church. It does not fulfill its mandate by relinquishing those keys but rather by using them to open up the avenues of approach to the Kingdom for all peoples and all population groups at every level of human society. It makes no

---

[2] Edward Schillebeeckx, *Church: The Human Face of God* (New York: Crossroad, 1990), 157.

biblical sense whatever to deny, as many do, that the upbuilding of the Church everywhere in the world is a proper concern of the proclamation of the good news of the Gospel; and it is high time for a forthright repudiation of such nonsense.[3]

In choosing compassion and justice as its principles of action, the community presents itself as a contrast society witnessing to the kingdom as God's ultimate plan of how human society should be restructured. The church community shows what God's kingdom can do when it is accepted and its dominant values become the basis for human society.

The importance of community building in every culture as the major and fundamental goal of mission has been stressed over and over again. In the words of Louis Luzbetak:

> Building Community is a very basic and essential part of the Church's mission. The specific challenge of every Christian Community is none other than to "demystify" the New Testament community model by translating it into the concrete socio-cultural situation and real life here and now. Each society has its way of respecting an individual, its way of bearing another's burden, its way of listening, forgiving, caring, sharing, serving, spending oneself for others—in a word, its way of becoming a true New Testament Christian community, here in the Philippines, Thailand, United States or Italy, and now, two thousand years after the first Pentecost. The building of New Testament Christian communities in our own times is, in fact, one of the most central objectives of mission, if not the very heart of mission.[4]

In building the "local" church the kingdom is brought straight into the midst of the people and finds expression in their own culture and circumstances.

To engage in dialogue with the world and with the other religious traditions

That means, first, *to challenge society as a whole*, to transform itself along the basic principles of the kingdom now present: justice, peace, brotherhood/sisterhood, and human rights. And second, *to engage in dialogue with other religious traditions* in which God's kingdom makes itself present as well. These are constitutive elements of proclaiming the gospel, since the ultimate goal of

---

[3] Johannes Verkuyl, "The Biblical Notion of Kingdom: Test of Validity for Theology of Religion," in *The Good News of the Kingdom: Mission Theology for the Third Millennium,* ed. Charles Van Engen, Dean S. Gilliland, and Paul Pierson (Maryknoll, New York: Orbis Books, 1993), 73.

[4] Louis J. Luzbetak, *The Church and Culture: New Perspectives in Missiological Anthropology* (Maryknoll, New York: Orbis Books, 1988), 391.

the kingdom is the transformation of the whole of creation; the church must understand its mission in the service of the imminent kingdom.[5]

This threefold mission finds its expression in *Redemptoris Missio* as follows:

The Church is effectively and concretely at the service of the Kingdom. This is seen especially in her preaching, which is a call to conversion. Preaching constitutes the Church's first and fundamental way of serving the coming of the Kingdom in individuals and in human society. . . .

The church, then, serves the kingdom by establishing communities and founding new particular churches and by guiding them to mature faith and charity in openness towards others, in service to individuals and society, and in understanding and esteem for human institutions.

The church serves the kingdom by spreading throughout the world the "gospel values" which are an expression of the kingdom and which help people to accept God's plan. It is true that the inchoate reality of the kingdom can also be found beyond the confines of the church among peoples everywhere to the extent that they live "gospel values" and are open to the working of the Spirit, who breathes when and where he wills (cf. Jn 3:8) (*RM*, no. 20).

Redemptoris Missio regards interreligious dialogue also as a constitutive element of the church's evangelizing task. It is "part of the church's evangelizing mission" (*RM*, no. 55); it is one of its expressions and, moreover, "a path toward the Kingdom" (*RM*, no. 57). The document *Dialogue and Proclamation* adds: "Interreligious dialogue and proclamation, though not on the same level, are both authentic elements of the Church's evangelizing mission. Both are legitimate and necessary. They are related but not interchangeable" (*DP*, no. 77).

The importance of these two documents concerning the question of interreligious dialogue cannot be overestimated.

In light of the history of the concept of dialogue over the past century, these documents represent what might be called the complete "domestication" of the previously alien or at least marginal notion of dialogue within the catholic mainstream. From having been a maverick concept less than fifty years ago, interreligious dialogue has now become "an integral element of the church's evangelizing mission."[6]

In *Redemptoris Missio* and *Dialogue and Proclamation* interreligious dialogue is seen in terms of appreciation of the implicit Christian elements discernible within other religious traditions. In this view the basis required for dialogue lies

---

[5] Richard P. McBrien, *Catholicism* (London: Geoffrey Chapman, 1981), 717.

[6] Joseph DiNoia, "The Church and Dialogue with Other Religions: A Plea for the Recognition of Differences, in *A Church for All People,* ed. Eugene LaVerdiere (Collegeville, Minnesota: The Liturgical Press, 1993), 79.

in these commonly shared though implicit elements, and the object of dialogue is to bring these elements to light. The kingdom as God's saving will for all human beings is present anywhere and therefore:

> This respect [for the saving presence of God] in turn impels Christians to engage in dialogue with persons who, while they do not share explicit Christian faith, must be regarded as being touched by the Spirit and striving according to their lights to respond to this grace, although they do not know this. It is in this complex sense that dialogue can be said to be integral to the Church's evangelizing mission: mission and dialogue express the single, though differentiated, Christian participation in the single, though diversely advanced, purpose of the triune God.[7]

Since the coming kingdom of God in the present world always remains a "preliminary" or "proleptic" anticipation of the kingdom, an ideal community will never emerge. Human societies and the church itself need structures, which will always reveal this preliminary aspect as well as the "sinfulness" of all human endeavors. Only when the fullness of the kingdom comes will all structures of the community be done away with, because the kingdom in glory is "anarchy," that is, a community or society that no longer needs structures because perfect love has become the guiding rule. As Walter Pannenberg puts it:

> The Kingdom is not yet the way among men; it is not the present reality. Our present world, with its injustices, brutalities, and wars, demonstrates the gap between itself and the Kingdom. . . . But the future of the Kingdom releases a dynamic factor into the present that kindles again and again the vision of man and gives meaning to his fervent quest for the political forms of justice and love. . . . The function of the Church is a preliminary function. By this we mean that the existence of the Church is justified only in view of the fact that the present political forms of society do not provide the ultimate human satisfaction for individual or corporate life. If the present social structures were adequate, there would be no need for the Church. For then the Kingdom of God would be present in its completeness.[8]

Or in the words of Jürgen Moltmann:

> The Church in the power of the Spirit is not yet the Kingdom of God, but it is its anticipation in history. Christianity is not yet the new creation, but it is the working of the Spirit of the new creation. Christianity is not yet the new humankind but it is its vanguard, in resistance to deadly introversion and in self-giving and representation for man's future.[9]

---

[7] Ibid., 80.

[8] Walter Pannenberg, *Theology and the Kingdom of God* (Philadelphia: Westminster Press, 1977), 80-82.

[9] Jürgen Moltmann, *The Church in the Power of the Spirit* (New York: Harper & Row, 1977), 196.

TWO WAYS OF BEING IN MISSION

The church's ultimate goal is to serve the kingdom and to lead humankind to its final destiny. Wherever the kingdom shows itself in the world, the church must help to promote and to bring it to its fullness. The mission of the church in the service of the kingdom is, therefore, basically twofold: First, as we saw above, we are called to make God's kingdom present by proclaiming its presence in word and sacrament. This happens through the creation of Christian communities in which God's kingdom shines forth like a symbol, a sign, or a parable, where its presence can clearly be discerned and its final goal appears like a foretaste of what is to come in fullness in God's own time.

Second, we can see that neither Jesus nor his Spirit have abandoned the world; they continue to be present and active among people. In us, the community of believers and followers of Jesus, his action, which is present everywhere, acquires a visibility and symbolic reality. Because of this, we are called and sent into the world to serve and to promote the ongoing action of Jesus and the Spirit. From this, the second dimension of our mission follows: to be at the service of and to promote collaboratively God's own continuing action in the world and among people outside the church community. It is our task to discover God's kingdom here, to rejoice over its presence, to learn from it, and to bring it to completion. Our ability to be in mission for the kingdom with joy and authenticity is probably the first and most important criterion for bringing the kingdom into our world.

If the church community feasts on the presence of God's kingdom in its midst most intensely in the eucharistic meal celebration, then there must also be a feast aspect in the church's second missionary task. We are, therefore, called to promote feasts where people of all races, cultures, religious traditions and worldviews come together to enjoy one another's company in life-giving relationships and genuine compassion. It is precisely in these values that God's kingdom makes itself felt outside the periphery of the church community and can be experienced as present in the midst of human affairs.

The two feast aspects are interrelated ways of pursuing the one goal of mission, which is the realization of the new heaven and the new earth that is God's promise to all peoples. In these common feasts we want to celebrate the kingdom already present among these people and to help them to see and to experience in their own way the presence of God, who wants all people to be reached by divine love. We may say that it is in getting actively involved in promoting God's transformative action in the world that the church community will build itself up as an authentic symbol of and witness to that action.[10]

Which is the more urgent mission at the moment: the building up of church communities in all parts of the world or our witness to God's kingdom everywhere in the world? They are of equal importance, since one includes the other. Jacques Dupuis makes this point:

---

[10] Michael Amaladoss, "New Faces of Mission," *UISG Bulletin* 99 (1995), 21-33.

Building the Reign together extends, moreover, to the different dimensions of the Reign of God, which can be called horizontal and vertical. Christians and others build together the Reign of God each time they commit themselves of common accord in the cause of human rights, each time they work for the integral liberation of each and every human person, but especially of the poor and the oppressed. They also build the Reign of God by promoting religious and spiritual values. In the building of the Kingdom the two dimensions, human and religious, are inseparable. In point of fact, the first is the sign of the second. There is, perhaps, nothing which provides interreligious dialogue with such a deep theological basis, and such true motivation, as the conviction that in spite of the differences by which they are distinguished, the members of different religious traditions, co-members of the Reign of God in history, are traveling together toward the fullness of the Reign, toward the new humanity willed by God for the end of time, of which they are called to be co-creators with God.[11]

If the kingdom of God is operative everywhere in the world and not just in the church, then our mission is to witness to this presence, to "sniff it out," to raise people's awareness of it and to celebrate it wherever it becomes tangible. If our mission is that of Jesus, namely, to proclaim and to bring God's kingdom into the world, then that very kingdom calls on us to pursue these two ways.

THE CHURCH, THE UNIVERSAL SACRAMENT OF SALVATION AND MEDIATOR OF THE KINGDOM

With regard to the salvation of non-Christians the following question still arises: If the kingdom as God's universal will to save all people is active outside of the church, is this activity still mediated through the church? or is it independent of the church in some way? The answer varies according to whether or not we identify the kingdom now with the pilgrim church.

Those who maintain a distinction between kingdom and church argue as follows: Pope John Paul in *Redemptoris Missio* asserts that "for those people [non-Christians], salvation in Christ is accessible by virtue of a grace which, while having a mysterious relationship to the church, does not make them formally part of the church, but enlightens them in a way which is accommodated to their spiritual and material situation. This grace comes from Christ" (*RM*, no. 10).

This text is seen as a clear rejection of *ecclesiocentrism*. The necessity of the church for salvation is not to be understood in a way that means access to the kingdom is only possible through the church. One can partake in the kingdom of God without being a member of the church and without passing through its

---

[11] Jacques Dupuis, *Toward a Christian Theology of Religious Pluralism* (Maryknoll, New York: Orbis Books, 1997), 346.

mediation of the kingdom.[12] Theologians who take this stand in no way deny that the salvation of any human being is based on Christ's death and resurrection. For them, all grace is Christocentric. They hold that God's saving grace in Jesus Christ reaches the non-Christian not directly through the church but by circumventing the church in ways only known to God. Rudolf Schnackenburg seems to indicate this indirectly by saying:

> The Kingdom of Christ is . . . a more comprehensive term than "Church." In the Christian's present existence on earth his share in Christ's Kingdom and his claim to the eschatological Kingdom . . . find their fulfillment in the Church, the domain in which the grace of the heavenly Christ are operative. . . . But Christ's rule extends beyond the Church . . . and one day the Church will have completed her earthly task and will be absorbed in the eschatological Kingdom of Christ or of God.[13]

The kingdom of God, God's all-embracing will of salvation inaugurated through Jesus Christ, is present in the other religious traditions as well. Through sharing in the mystery of the universal plan of salvation, the members of other religious traditions are thus members of the kingdom of God already present as a historic reality. By following their religion, they not only achieve their own salvation but contribute also to the construction of the kingdom in the world. By accepting the positive elements of the kingdom in their traditions, and responding to these elements of grace, Jacques Dupuis concludes

> that they find salvation and become members of the Reign of God in history. It follows that the religious traditions contribute, in a mysterious way, to the building up of the Reign of God among their followers and in the world. They exercise, with regard to their own members, a certain mediation of the Kingdom—doubtless different from that which is operative in the Church—even if it is difficult to give a precise theological definition of this mediation.[14]

Theologians who hold to the identification of the kingdom on earth now with the pilgrim church cannot accept this position. For them, all saving grace passes through the church, otherwise the church could not be called the universal sacrament of salvation. Basing their view on a careful reading of the main documents of Vatican II, they maintain that we cannot deduce from these documents that Vatican II distinguished between the kingdom present now in history and the pilgrim church here on earth. Their arguments are the following:

---

[12] Jacques Dupuis, *Jesus Christ and the Encounter of World Religions* (Maryknoll, New York: Orbis Books, 1991), 6.

[13] Rudolf Schnackenburg, *God's Rule and Kingdom* (New York: Herder and Herder, 1968), 301.

[14] Dupuis, *Toward a Christian Theology of Religious Pluralism*, 346.

The Council describes the church as being by its very essence the *universal sign of salvation*. This description, which holds a prominent place in the *Dogmatic Constitution on the Church* (LG 48), is quoted both in the *Decree on the Church's Missionary Activity* (AG 1) and in the *Pastoral Constitution on the Church in the Modern World* (GS 45). When calling the church a sacrament, the Council understands a symbolic reality established by Christ, a sign that contains and confers the grace it signifies. The church, therefore, is not merely a cognitive sign, which makes known something that already exists, but an efficacious sign that brings about the redemption to which it points. Since the church is seen as a universal sacrament, i.e., as *"an instrument for the redemption of all"* (LG 9), we must assume that the salvation of all human beings depends in some way on the church. The church is involved in the salvation of all who are saved (LG 16). Whatever faith or belief people may confess, we must assume that the grace which saves them is in a *mysterious way* linked to the church. They are, in the words of the Council, through this grace *ordered* to the church. That means the saving grace they receive outside the church gives the recipients a positive inclination towards the church, so that all who live by God's grace are in a certain sense affiliated with the church.[15]

The inescapable question is how does the church save if its nature, as *Lumen Gentium* claims, is that of "a universal instrument" of salvation (*LG*, no. 1)? To say this suggests that the church is actively at work in the salvific process; however, it does not explain how the church accomplishes this result. Francis Sullivan puts the question this way: "In what way can the Church be said to exercise an instrumental role in the salvation of all those people who apparently have no contact with the Church?" As at least a partial answer, referring to the encyclical *Mystici Corporis* of Pius XII, the teaching of the Council (*Constitution on the Sacred Liturgy*, no. 83) and the eucharistic prayers of the liturgy, Sullivan sees the church mediating salvation to non-Christians through prayer and intercession. Consequently, we can say that the church, at least by means of intercessions, especially during the eucharist, prays and offers Christ's sacrifice for the salvation of all people. Thus the church's intercessory mediation extends to all who are being saved. In Sullivan's words:

> On the basis of the teaching of the council, and the eucharistic prayers which reflect this teaching, we have sound reason for affirming that because of the church's role as priestly people, offering to the Father with Christ the High Priest the sacrifice from which grace of salvation flows to the whole world, the church is rightly termed the universal sacrament of salvation in the sense that it plays an instrumental role in the salvation of every person who is saved.[16]

---

[15] Avery Dulles, "Vatican II and the Church's Purpose," *Theology Digest* 32 (1985), 344-345.

[16] Francis A. Sullivan, *The Church We Believe In* (New York: Paulist Press, 1988), 128.

The orientation of the church toward the kingdom is most beautifully revealed in the central act of worship, the celebration of the eucharist. Mark's account of the Last Supper closes with Jesus' words: "Truly, I say to you I shall not drink again of the fruit of the vine until that day when I drink it new in the kingdom of God" (Mk 14:25). Thus the eucharist is situated within the context of the eschatological kingdom. In his handing on of the story of the origins of the Lord's supper, Paul also clearly sees its celebration within an eschatological context: "For as often as you eat this bread and drink the cup, you proclaim the Lord's death until he comes" (1 Cor 11:26).

But the link between church and kingdom in the eucharist is still more profound. It is with his blood that Jesus establishes the new covenant (Lk 22:20; 1 Cor 11:25), the divine order of eschatological grace for all humanity. Only by virtue of the universal efficacy of the blood of this covenant (Mk 14:24) is it possible for human beings to be saved. In the celebration of the Lord's supper, the church is clearly presented as belonging to his kingdom; it celebrates this covenant, established by the blood that, according to the Lukan account, is poured out "for us" (22:20). The eschatological benefits of salvation are intended "for us," which must be understood as including those believers in Christ who are actually celebrating the eucharist. But these benefits do not extend to Christians alone; they reach out to all human beings whose salvation is ultimately guaranteed through the death and resurrection of Christ.[17]

The conclusion is that the celebration of the eucharist, as the actual and continuing remembrance of the origin of salvation through Christ's death "for all" effectively made present, remains the fountain of salvation for every human being. It is therefore the church's celebration of the saving event in the eucharist that mediates the kingdom of God to the whole world.

A number of theologians have voiced their reservations concerning the direct mediation of salvation for the non-Christians through the church.[18] The arguments can be briefly summarized as follows: Christ is the only mediator of salvation for all through his life, death, and resurrection. The universal mediation of Christ in the order of salvation concretely refers to the fact that his risen humanity is the obligatory channel, the instrumental cause, of grace for all people. Since Christ in his risen state has acquired a new relationship to all, we can correctly say that the whole human race is already saved in Jesus Christ. It would therefore not be wrong for us to say that the whole human race is already constituted as "people of God."

The church is the sacrament of this universal salvation. However, the meditation of salvation—the church through its prayer of intercession offers to God for all people who do not belong to its community in order that the grace of salvation in Christ may be granted to them—belongs, so to speak, to the *moral order* and can therefore not be put on the same level with the grace that

---

[17] William Henn, "The Church and the Kingdom of God," in *Studia Missionalia* 46 (1997), 130.

[18] Dupuis, *Toward a Christian Theology of Religious Pluralism,* 347-357.

is granted through a sacramental mediation to the faithful belonging to the church.

The church is surely the concrete place where the Spirit is present in order to bring about the final salvation. The church must therefore be understood as the point toward which "non-ecclesial" grace, of which the church is the visible expression in the world, is tending. The church is the sacramental sign of the presence of divine grace in the world. But to conclude that its intercession through prayer and the eucharist is sacramentally effective for the salvation of those outside of it is inappropriate. The church's prayer, as all prayer, is effective but cannot be put on the level of an efficacious sign as mediated through the sacraments.

The same conclusion can be made from the following argument: The church is regarded as the *sacrament of the kingdom*. If the kingdom is broader than the church, then the mediation of the kingdom obviously cannot be limited to the church alone. God is not bound to the sacrament. That means that people can attain to the reality of the kingdom of God without recourse to the sacrament of the church and without belonging to the body of the church. Others can be members of the kingdom of God without being part of the church and without recourse to its mediation.

The presence of the church as a sign and sacrament of the kingdom in the world bears witness that God has established God's kindgom in this world in Jesus Christ. As an efficacious sign the church contains and effects the reality that it signifies through its word and action. Yet it still belongs to the sacramental realm, that is, to the realm of the relative. The necessity of the church is not of such a nature that the access of the kingdom of God would be possible only through the church. Others can be part of the kingdom of God and Christ without being members of the church and without recourse to its mediation.[19] In the words of Jerome P. Theisen:

> The Church as sacrament may mean only that the Church exists in the world as the visible sign of the saving grace that God is effecting through Christ at a distance from the visible Church. The Church mirrors, articulates, and makes intelligible the process of salvation that is being accomplished anywhere in the world. . . . In this sense the Church as sacrament exists to show forth the riches of God's mercy in Christ. It is a universal sacrament of salvation in that it becomes a sign of God's salvific activity in Christ wherever this occurs in the world. The thrust of the sacramental model of the Church leads to an understanding of the Church as a visible event and concrete manifestation of God's grace effecting salvation of people anywhere in the world.[20]

---

[19] Ibid., 354-355.

[20] Jerome P. Theisen, *The Ultimate Church and the Promise of Salvation* (Collegeville, Minnesota: St. John's University Press, 1976), 134.

From this, it also follows that the church will dissolve itself into the kingdom when it comes in fullness. The sacramental function of the church in history indicates its provisional nature and implies that it will disappear when the fullness of the kingdom is achieved, since as a sacrament it was subordinated to the kingdom. When the perfect reality has been achieved, the sign loses its raison d'être. In the words of Karl Rahner:

> The Church, if only she be rightly understood, is living always on the proclamation of her own provisional status and of her historically advancing elimination in the coming Kingdom of God towards which she is expectantly traveling as a pilgrim, because God for his own part is coming to meet her in the Parousia and her pilgrimage, too, is taking place in the power of Christ's coming. The essential nature of the Church consists in pilgrimage towards the promised future.[21]

KINGDOM CONSCIOUSNESS
AND THE MISSION OF THE CHURCH

As the community of those chosen to carry on the vision of Jesus, the church must define itself in relation to the kingdom, which is meant for humankind and the whole of creation. The church's mission is to reveal through the ages the hidden plan of God (Eph 3:3-11; Col 1:26) and to lead humankind toward its final destiny. It must be seen to be entirely at the service of this divine salvific plan for all human beings and all of creation, which is operative and present wherever people live, no matter what religion or faith they may confess.

> The Church is not placed at her own service: she is entirely oriented towards the Kingdom of God that is coming. For only the Kingdom, as the fullness of God's manifestation, is absolute. . . . The abiding vocation of the Church does not consist in the qualitative increase of her members. In dialogue and collaboration with all the people of good will (who may belong to other religions and spiritual families), she is called to manifest and foster the Reign of God which . . . keeps happening through the religious history of humankind, well beyond the visible boundaries of the "People of God."[22]

The identity of the church depends ultimately on its kingdom consciousness based on scripture. It would reveal this in its sensitivity to the priority of the

---

[21] Karl Rahner, *Theological Investigations* 10 (London: Darton, Longman, and Todd, 1969), 298.

[22] Claude Geffre, quoted in Jacques Dupuis, "A Theological Commentary: Dialogue and Proclamation," in *Redemption and Dialogue: Reading* Redemptoris Missio *and* Dialogue and Proclamation, ed. William R. Burrows (Maryknoll, New York: Orbis Books, 1994), 158.

kingdom. According to Howard A. Snyder, such kingdom consciousness includes the following five elements.

1. Kingdom consciousness means living and working in the firm hope of the final triumph of God's reign. In the face of contrary evidence Kingdom Christians hold on to the conviction that God will eventually swallow up all evil, hate, and injustice. They firmly believe that the leaven of the Kingdom is already at work in the dough of creation, to use Jesus' own parable. This gives Christians an unworldly audacious confidence that enables them to go right on doing what others say is impossible or futile.

Looking at the world of today, we have reason to doubt that the human species has the requisite capacity to change. Many view the present world situation with despair. Christian faith has been one important way in which people have lived with hope in the midst of apparently hopeless conditions. But those who open themselves to the Kingdom will discover there is a power at work in us that can transform even our distorted wills. This transformation is not subject to our control but comes as a gift. We call it grace, and we can place no limits on the extent to which grace can make us into new men and new women.

2. Understanding God's Kingdom means that the lines between "sacred" and "secular" do not exist in concrete reality. God's Kingdom means that all things are in the sphere of God's sovereignty and, therefore, of God's concern. All spheres of life are Kingdom topics.

3. Kingdom awareness means that ministry is much broader than church work. Christians who understand the meaning of God's reign know they are busy about the Kingdom, not about the church. They see all activity as ultimately having Kingdom significance.

4. In the Kingdom perspective, concern for justice and concrete commitment to the Word of God are necessarily tied together. An awareness of God's Kingdom, biblically understood, resolves the tension between two vital concerns. First, those committed to the Kingdom want to win people to personal faith in Jesus Christ, since the Kingdom is the ultimate longing of every human heart. Secondly, they are also committed to peace, justice, and righteousness at every level of society because the Kingdom includes "all things in heaven and on earth" (Eph 1:10) as well as the welfare of every person and everything God has made.

5. The reality of the Kingdom of God can be experienced now through the Spirit who gives the believer the first fruits of the fullness of the Kingdom in the here and now. Particularly in their liturgy, Kingdom people anticipate its joy. The different charisms given by the Holy Spirit witness concretely to the Kingdom as present. They are appreciated by all as clear manifestations of the powerful presence of the Kingdom in the midst of their daily life.[23]

---

[23] Howard A. Snyder, *Models of the Kingdom* (Nashville, Tennessee: Abingdon Press, 1991), 154-155.

The church is inseparable from the person of Jesus and has a mission of salvation for the world. As the sacrament of the kingdom, it is God's choice, not ours, and is called to accomplish with the Holy Spirit God's plan for creation: the salvation of the whole world. It exists in the world and for the world as Jesus' chosen agent to carry on his mission to gather all people into the one family of God. Not only does it have to celebrate the kingdom already in its midst and strive to create everywhere communities in which the kingdom is explicitly experienced, but it must also seek out the kingdom present beyond its boundaries. Here it seeks to rejoice in its presence and to help people discover in their own midst the God of the kingdom who wants the salvation of all. It is this last task of the church that can really fully be seen and, with conviction and joy, be taken up in the measure we come to realize that God's kingdom here and now is more comprehensive than the church. The church is in the service of the kingdom, which embraces all of reality, not only the graced reality called church.

CONCLUDING REFLECTIONS ON CHURCH AND KINGDOM

There are many books written about the future of the church. Most of them portray the difficulties and the problems the church will have to face and what changes it will have to make if it wants to remain faithful to its mission. There are often as many proposals as there are books. The problem is that we are standing at a point of history where old, approved solutions to many problems do not seem to work anymore. We are told what is happening at the moment is a major paradigm shift, which introduces such discontinuities into the present that a linear approach will not lead to any solution. We need to see the present reality and the possible future in a way that is different from our usual linear viewpoint. We cannot predict the future, but we have to invent it, based on some insights of linear thinking and on our understanding of the present paradigm shift.

This requires two things of us: (1) to recognize that we are no longer involved in linear change; and (2) a tremendous belief in God, trusting the message we have to offer is God's saving plan for all God's kingdom. The new situation places us almost on the same level at which the early church found itself. The early Christians could not rely on the past, nor did they have clear instructions from the Lord for the future. Reading the signs of the times and trusting in the presence of the Lord in the power of the Holy Spirit, they proclaimed their way of action: "We and the Holy Spirit have agreed" (Acts 15:28). Accordingly, we too have to trust in the presence of the Holy Spirit and yet use our own imagination and reasoning power to find the way. To rely on the past is partially correct, but it will not suffice; more is needed. We need a prophetic imagination to look into the future.

Judging from what we now see before us, the church of the future will have two major issues to deal with if it wants to remain faithful to the kingdom entrusted to it: *inculturation* and *solidarity with the poor* in the process of globalization. To deal with these two issues, this book proposed two models of church that address themselves directly to the relevant problems. To inculturate the Christian message in a way that it can be understood and offer salvation in respective cultural contexts is demanded from all local churches, wherever they may be. The BECs we propose as a model are not the only solution for meeting this challenge, but they definitely offer an answer to many churches in the continents where the future of the church will be found: Latin America, Africa, and Asia.

The second issue, solidarity with the poor and marginalized of the world, refers to the basic root of Jesus' message of the kingdom. If the church puts its concern for these people in second or third place, it will not have much to say in the future. If the church loses the poor, those left out, the ones who do not count, it has betrayed the very purpose for its existence, which is to proclaim the good news of the kingdom to the poor in the way Jesus understood his mission. The model proposed here, the church as a contrast society, focuses on this demand of the kingdom. In a time when we experience what has been called "compassion fatigue," we must make it uncompromisingly clear that the poor remain the first concern of the Christian community. That was Jesus' own concern, and his kingdom will always carry the qualification: good news *to the poor*.

There is only one way to keep these two issues alive at all times in the church: we must return to Jesus' own life principles and to his message of the kingdom. We must embrace all cultures. We must always and primarily preach the good news to the poor. If we do this, then we will know for sure that, when we look at the future church, it will be a world church. As Karl Rahner envisioned it: "Either the Church sees and recognizes the essential differences of other cultures for which she should become a World Church, and with a boldness draws the necessary consequences from this recognition, or she remains a Western Church and so, in the final analysis, betrays the true meaning of Vatican II."[24]

We just finished the Jubilee Year with its motto "Christ yesterday, today, and tomorrow!" We know he will not leave his church. That, however, does not dispense us from courageously searching for new ways of proclaiming the kingdom so that its saving message will reach all human beings in their own cultures and that the poor will know they are not excluded, for it is to them that the good news is first addressed.

---

[24] Karl Rahner, "Towards a Fundamental Theological Interpretation of Vatican II," *Theological Studies* 40 (1979), 724.

Epilogue

Simon Peter's fisherman's net, the church, is not for catching a small select group or some kind of spiritual elite. It is the net for a universal church capable of offering a home to all peoples and every kind of human being.

Throughout its history the church has needed reminders of this again and again. The great demands and challenges of the gospel have led to repeated attempts to establish churches for small groups, elites of specially selected men and women. Such churches were meant to distinguish themselves from the masses through exceptional holiness, special insights into God's mysteries, and a way of life that demanded very high standards. These attempts also witness to the deep longing of those who have the sincere wish to live up to the high expectations of Christ's church.

Yet the image of the net teaches us that the church was not meant to be an elite community. Without taking anything away from the demands of the gospel, its ultimate purpose is to be open and welcoming to ordinary people—the poor, the sick, those who do not count but are able to enkindle a tiny flame of faith and open themselves to the small light of love.

We are talking about a church whose shepherds bear the responsibility of having a "big heart." They need to be endowed with understanding, compassion, mercy, and a broad vision. They need to point to ways that even the weakest and least talented can walk. Only when they do this are they seriously on the way toward a church that resembles Peter's net, filled with the biggest catch ever made.[1]

---

[1] Adapted from Carlo Maria Martini, *Mein spirituelles* (Wörterbuch: Pattloch Verlag, 1998).

Selected Bibliography

Aguirre, Rafael. "Early Christian House Churches." *Theology Digest* 32 (1985), 151-155.

AMECEA Plenary, 1976. "Building Christian Communities." *Afer* 18 (1976), 250.

Arens, Heribert. "Das Prophetische am Ordensleben." *Ordenskorrespondenz* 33 (1992), 8-22.

Ashley, Benedict M. *Justice in the Church: Gender and Participation.* Washington, D.C.: Catholic University Press, 1996.

Auer, J., and Joseph Ratzinger. *The Church: The Universal Sacrament of Salvation.* Vol. 8 of *Dogmatic Theology.* Washington, D.C.: The Catholic University of America Press, 1993.

Azevedo, Marcello, S.J. "Basic Ecclesial Communities: A Meeting Point of Ecclesiologies." *Theological Studies* 46 (1985), 601-620.

Bas van Iersel. "Who according to the New Testament Has the Say in the Church?" *Concilium* 148 (1981), 11-17.

Baum, Gregory. "The Meaning of Church." In Gregory Baum, *The Credibility of the Church Today.* New York: Herder and Herder, 1968.

Bellagamba, Anthony. *Mission and Ministry in a Global Church.* Maryknoll, New York: Orbis Books, 1992.

Bertsch, Ludwig. "Inculturation in Europe's Societal Situation: An Introduction." *Yearbook of Contextual Theologies.* Aachen: Missio Institut, 1993/4.

Boff, Clodovis. "The Church in Latin America: Between Perplexity and Creativity." *Sedos Bulletin* 27 (1998), 131-141.

―――. "The Catholic Church and the New Churches in Latin America." *Sedos Bulletin* 31 (1999), 196-201.

―――. "The Search for Justice and Solidarity: Meeting the New Churches." *Sedos Bulletin* 31 (1999), 202-205.

Boff, Leonardo. *Church, Charism, and Power: Liberation Theology and the Institutional Church.* London: SCM Press, 1985.

―――. *Ecclesiogenesis. The Base Communities Reinvent the Church.* Maryknoll, New York: Orbis Books, 1986.

Bonhoeffer, D. *Gesammelte Schriften.* Vol. 3. München: Kaiser Verlag, 1958.

Borg, Marcus. *Jesus, a New Vision: Spirit, Culture, and the Life of Discipleship.* San Francisco: Harper & Row, 1987.

―――. *The God We Never Knew.* San Francisco: Harper, 1997.

Brown, Raymond. *Priest and Bishop: Biblical Reflections.* New York: Paulist Press, 1970.

―――. *The Community of the Beloved Disicple.* London: Geoffrey Chapman, 1979.

―――. *Biblical Exegesis and Church Doctrine.* New York/Mahwah, New Jersey: Paulist Press, 1985.

―――. "Not Jewish Christianity and Gentile Christianity but Types of Jewish/Gentile Christianity." *The Catholic Biblical Quarterly* 45 (1983), 74-79.

Brueggemann, Walter. *The Prophetic Imagination.* London: SCM Press, 1992.

Casaldáliga, Pedro, and José-Maria Vigil. *Political Holiness: A Spirituality of Liberation.* Maryknoll, New York: Orbis Books, 1994.

Chenu, M.-D. "The New Awareness of the Trinitarian Basis of the Church." *Concilium* 146 (1981), 14-22.

Cobb, John B. *Sustainability: Economics, Ecology, and Justice.* Maryknoll, New York: Orbis Books, 1992.

Congar, Yves. *Lay People in the Church.* London: Bloomsbury Publishing Co. Ltd., 1957.

Covell, Ralph. "Jesus Christ and World Religions." In *The Good News of the Kingdom: Mission Theology for the Third Millennium,* edited by Charles Van Engen, Dean S. Gilliland, and Paul Pierson. Maryknoll, New York: Orbis Books, 1993, 162-171.

Cullmann, Oscar. *Christ and Time.* Philadelphia: Westminster, 1950.

de Lubac, Henri, S.J. *Catholicism: Christ and the Common Destiny of Man,* trans. Lancelot C. Sheppard and Elizabeth England. San Francisco: Ignatius Press, 1988.

DiNoia, Joseph. "The Church and Dialogue with Other Religions: A Plea for the Recognition of Differences." In *A Church for All People,* edited by Eugene LaVerdiere. Collegeville, Minnesota: The Liturgical Press, 1993, 75-89.

Doyle, Dennis M. *Communion Ecclesiology: Vision and Versions.* Maryknoll, New York: Orbis Books, 2000.

Dulles, Avery. "The Succession of Prophets in the Church." *Concilium* 4 (April 1968), 28-32.

——. "Successio Apostolorum." *Concilium* 148 (1981), 61-67.

——. *A Church to Believe In: Discipleship and the Dynamics of Freedom.* New York: Crossroad, 1982.

——. "Ecclesial Futurology: Moving towards the 1990s," *CTSA Proceedings* (1985).

——. "Vatican II and the Church's Purpose." *Theology Digest* 32 (1985), 344-345.

——. *Models of the Church.* Expanded edition. Garden City, New York: Image Books, 1987.

——. "The Church and the Kingdom." In *A Church for All People,* edited by Eugene LaVerdiere. Collegeville, Minnesota: The Liturgical Press, 1993, 13-27.

Dunn, James D. G. *Jesus and the Spirit.* London: SCM Press, 1975.

——. *The Christ and the Spirit.* Vol. 2, *Pneumatology.* Edinburgh: T&T Clark, 1998.

Dupuis, Jacques. "Evangelization and Kingdom Values: The Church and the 'Others.'" *Indian Missiological Review* 14 (1992), 4-21.

——. "A Theological Commentary: Dialogue and Proclamation." In *Redemption and Dialogue: Reading* Redemptoris Missio *and* Dialogue and Proclamation, edited by William R. Burrows. Maryknoll, New York: Orbis Books, 1994, 119-158.

——. "Religious Plurality and the Christological Debate." *Sedos Bulletin* 28 (1996), 229-333.

——. *Toward a Christian Theology of Religious Pluralism.* Maryknoll, New York: Orbis Books, 1997.

Duquoc, Christian. "Charism as the Social Expression of the Unpredictable Nature of Grace." In *Charism and Church,* edited by Duquoc and Floristan. New York: Seabury, 1978.

——. *Provisional Churches: An Essay in Ecumenical Ecclesiology.* London: SCM Press, 1986.

——. "Jesus Christus, Mittelpunkt des Europa von Morgen." In *Das Neue Europa, Herausforderung für Kirche und Theologie* (QD 144), edited by P. Huenermann. Freiburg i. Br., 1993, 100-110.

Dych, William V. *Thy Kingdom Come: Jesus and the Reign of God*. New York: Crossroad, 1999.

Ferguson, Everett. *The Church of Christ: A Biblical Ecclesiology for Today*. Grand Rapids, Michigan: Eerdmans, 1996.

Frankemoelle, Hubert. "The Root Supports You (Rom 11:17-18)." *Theology Digest* 47 (2000), 227-231.

Fuellenbach, John. *The Kingdom of God*. Maryknoll, New York: Orbis Books, 1995.

―――. *Throw Fire*. Manila: Logos Publication, 1998.

Galilea, Segundo. *Following Jesus*. Maryknoll, New York: Orbis Books, 1981.

Gnilka, Joachim. *Jesus of Nazareth: Message and History*. Peabody, Massachusetts: Hendrickson Publishers, 1997.

Granfield, Patrick. "The Concept of the Church as Communion." *Origin* 28 (1999), 753-758.

Grassmann, Günther. "The Church as Sacrament, Sign and Instrument." In *Church—Kingdom—World*, edited by Gennadios Limouris. Geneva: World Council of Churches, 1986, 1-16.

Gunton, Colin. "Church on Earth: The Roots of Community." In *On Being the Church: Essays on the Christian Community*, edited by Colin E. Gunton and Daniel W. Hardy. Edinburgh: T&T Clark, 1989, 48-80.

Haight, Roger. *An Alternative Vision: An Interpretation of Liberation Theology*. New York: Paulist Press, 1985.

Haughey, John C. "Charisms: An Ecclesiological Exploration." In *Retrieving Charisms for the Twenty-First Century*, edited by Doris Donnelly. Collegeville, Minnesota: The Liturgical Press, 1999, 1-16.

Healey, Joseph. *A Fifth Gospel: The Experience of Black Christian Values*. Maryknoll, New York: Orbis Books, 1981.

―――. "Evolving a New Model of Church: A Comparison of the Basic Christian Communities in Latin America and the Small Christian Communities in Eastern Africa." *Verbum SVD* (1985), 211-225.

Hendrickx, Herman. *The Household of God: The Communities behind the New Testament Writings*. Quezon City: Claretian Publications, 1992.

―――. *A Key to the Gospel of Matthew*. Manila: Claretian Publications, 1992.

Henn, William. "The Church and the Kingdom of God." In *Studia Missionalia* 46 (1997), 119-147.

Huntington, Samuel P. "The Clash of Civilizations?" *Foreign Affairs* (Summer 1993), 22-49.

Jeanrond, Werner G. "Community and Authority: The Nature and Implication of the Authority of Christian Community." In *On Being the Church: Essays on the Christian Community*, edited by Colin E. Gunton and Daniel W. Hardy. Edinburgh: T&T Clark, 1989, 81-109.

John Paul II. *Redemptoris Missio*. Vatican City: Libreria Editrice Vaticana, 1991.

Kasper, Walter. *Theology and Church*. New York: Crossroad, 1989.

―――. "The Church as Communio." *New Blackfriars* 74 (1993), 232-244.

―――. "Relating Christ's Universality to Interreligious Dialogue." *Origins* 30 (2000), 321-323, 327.

Kasper, Walter, and Gerhard Sauter. *Kirche Ort des Geistes*. Freiburg: Herder, 1976.

Kehl, Medard. *Die Kirche: Eine katholische Ekklesiologie*. Würzburg: Echter Verlag, 1992.

Kirchschläger, Walter. *Die Anfänge der Kirche: Eine Biblische Rückbesinnung*. Graz: Styria Verlag, 1990.

———. "Plurality and Creativity in Church Structure." *Theology Digest* 45 (1998), 249-253.

Komonchak, Joseph A. "Ecclesiology of Vatican II." *Origin* 28 (1999), 763-768.

———. "The Significance of Vatican Council II for Ecclesiology." In *The Gift of the Church: A Textbook on Ecclesiology in Honor of Patrick Granfield, OSB,* edited by Peter Phan. Collegeville, Minnesota: The Liturgical Press, 2000, 69-92.

Küng, Hans. *The Church.* New York: Sheed and Ward, 1967.

———. "Paradigm Change in Theology: A Proposal for Discussion." In *Paradigm Change in Theology: A Symposium for the Future,* edited by Hans Küng and David Tracy. Edinburgh: T&T Clark, 1989, 3-31.

Kuzmic, Peter. "The Church and the Kingdom of God: A Theological Reflection." In *The Church: God's Agent for Change,* edited by Bruce J. Nicholls. Flemington Markets, Australia: Paternoster Press, 1986, 49-81.

Ladd, George Eldon. *The Present of the Future: A Revised and Updated Version of Jesus and the Kingdom.* Grand Rapids, Michigan: Eerdmans, 1974.

Lambino, Antonio B. "A New Theological Model: Theology of Liberation." *Towards Doing Theology in the Philippine Context.* Manila: Loyola Papers 9, 1977, 2-25.

Lampe, Armando. "The Globalization of Poverty." *Sedos Bulletin* 32 (2000), 131-135.

Lee, Bernard J., and Michael A. Cowan, *Dangerous Memories: House Churches and Our American Story.* Kansas City, Missouri: Sheed and Ward, 1986.

Limouris, Gennadios. "The Church as Mystery and Sign in Relation to the Holy Trinity—In Ecclesiological Perspectives." In *Church—Kingdom—World: The Church as Mystery and Prophetic Sign.* Faith and Order Paper no. 130, edited by Gennadios Limouris. Geneva: World Council of Churches, 1986, 18-49.

Lobinger, Franz. *Like His Brothers and Sisters: Ordaining Community Leaders.* Quezon City, Manila: Claretian Publications, 1998.

Lochman, Jan Milic. "Church and World in the Light of the Kingdom of God," In *Church—Kingdom—World: The Church as Mystery and Prophetic Sign.* Faith and Order Paper no. 130, edited by Gennadios Limouris. Geneva: World Council of Churches, 1986, 58-72.

Lohfink, Gerhard. "Did Jesus Found a Church?" *Theology Digest* 30 (1982), 231-235.

———. *Jesus and Community.* London: SPCK Press, 1985.

———. *Wem gilt die Bergpredigt?* Freiburg: Herder, 1988.

———. *Does God Need the Church?: Toward a Theology of the People of God.* Collegeville, Minnesota: The Liturgical Press, 1999.

Lohfink, Norbert. "Religious Orders: God's Therapy for the Church." *Theology Digest* 33 (1986), 232-244.

———. *Option for the Poor: The Basic Principle of Liberation Theology in the Light of the Bible.* Berkeley, California: Bibal Press, 1987.

———. "Where Are Today's Prophets?" *Theology Digest* 37 (1990), 103-107.

Lonergan, Bernard. "Theology in Its New Context." In *Conversion,* edited by W. E. Conn. New York: Alba House, 1978, 3-21.

Luzbetak, Louis J. *The Church and Culture: New Perspectives in Missiological Anthropology.* Maryknoll, New York: Orbis Books, 1988.

Machinek, Marian. "Die Vieldeutigkeit der Rede von Kirche als Kontrastgesellschaft und ihre moraltheologische Implikationen." *Forum Katholischer Theologie* 15 (1999), 134-146.

McBrien, Richard P. *Catholicism.* London: Geoffrey Chapman, 1981.

Mesters, Carlos. "The Use of the Bible in Christian Communities of the Common People." In *The Bible and Liberation*, edited by N. K. Gottwalk and R. A. Horsley. Maryknoll, New York: Orbis Books, 1993, 119-133.

Metz, Johann B. *Followers of Christ: The Religious Life and the Church*. New York: Paulist Press, 1978.

———. "For a Renewed Church before a New Council: A Concept in Four Theses." In *Toward Vatican III: The Work That Needs to Be Done,* edited by David Tracy with Hans Küng and Johann B. Metz. New York: Seabury, 1978.

Michiels, Robrecht. "Church of Jesus Christ, An Exegetical-Ecclesiological Consideration." *Louvain Studies* 18 (1993), 297-317.

Minar, Paul S. *Images of the Church in the New Testament*. Philadelphia: Westminster Press, 1977.

Moloney, Francis J. *Disciples and Prophets: A Biblical Model for the Religious Life*. London: Darton, Longman, and Todd, 1980.

Moltmann, Jürgen. *The Church in the Power of the Spirit*. New York: Harper & Row, 1977.

Nardoni, Enrique. "Charism in the Early Church since Rudolph Sohm: An Ecumenical Challenge." *Theological Studies* 53 (1992), 646-662.

Neutzling, Inacio. "Celebrationes dans les Communautes de Base." *Spiritus* 24 (1983), 115-155.

Newbegin, Lesslie. *Sign of the Kingdom*. Grand Rapids, Michigan: Eerdmans, 1980.

Nolan, Albert. *Jesus before Christianity*. Maryknoll, New York: Orbis Books, 1978.

Nwagwu, Mary Gerard. "Communion and Self-Reliance: Signs of Church as God's Family in Africa." *Afer* 42 (2000), 18-25.

O'Grady, John F. *The Roman Catholic Church: Its Origin and Nature*. New York: Paulist Press, 1997.

Pannenberg, Wolfhart. *Theology and the Kingdom of God*. Philadelphia: Westminster Press, 1977.

Power, David N. "A Theological Assessment of Ministries Today." In *Trends in Mission toward the Third Millennium*, edited by W. Jenkinson and H. O'Sullivan. Maryknoll, New York: Orbis Books, 1991, 185-201.

Prior, Anselm. *Toward a Community Church*. Gemiston: Lumko Publication, 1991.

Rahner, Karl. *The Church and the Sacraments*. London: Burns and Oates, 1963.

———. *The Dynamic Element in the Church*. New York: Herder and Herder, 1964.

———. *Spirit in the Church*. London: Burns and Oates, 1979.

———. "Towards a Fundamental Theological Interpretation of Vatican II." *Theological Studies* 40 (1979), 716-727.

———. *Concern for the Church*. Vol. 20 in *Theological Investigations*. New York: Crossroad, 1981.

Rahner, Karl, and Joseph Ratzinger. *The Episcopacy and the Primacy*. New York: Herder and Herder, 1963.

Rigal, Jean. "Toward an Ecclesiology of Communion." *Theology Digest* 47 (2000), 117-123.

Rodriguez, Pedro. "Theological Method for Ecclesiology." In *The Gift of the Church: A Textbook on Ecclesiology in Honor of Patrick Granfield, OSB,* edited by Peter Phan. Collegeville, Minnesota: The Liturgical Press, 2000, 129-156.

Rossi de Gasperi, F. "Continuity and Newness in the Faith of the Mother Church of Jerusalem." *Bible and Inculturation*. Inculturation working papers on living faith. Rome, 1983, 17-69.

Schillebeeckx, Edward. *Church: The Human Face of God.* New York: Crossroad, 1990.

Schmaus, Michael. *The Church as Sacrament.* London: Sheed and Ward, 1975.

———. *The Church: Its Origin and Structure.* London: Sheed and Ward, 1977.

Schnackenburg, Rudolf. *God's Rule and Kingdom.* New York: Herder and Herder, 1968.

———. "Signoria e regno di Dio nell'annuncio di Gesu e della Chiesa delle Origini." *Communio* 86 (1986), 41-42.

Schoelles, Patricia. "Liberation Theology and Discipleship: The Critical and Reforming Tendencies of Basic Christian Identity." *Louvain Studies* 19 (1994), 46-64.

Schreiter, Robert J. *Constructing Local Theologies.* Maryknoll, New York: Orbis Books, 1985.

Schüssler Fiorenza, Francis. *Foundational Theology: Jesus and the Church.* New York: Crossroad, 1984.

Schweizer, Edward. *Church Order in the New Testament.* London: SCM Press, 1961.

———. *The Church as the Body of Christ.* Atlanta: John Knox Press, 1976.

———. *The Holy Spirit.* Philadelphia: Fortress Press, 1980.

Shorter, Aylward. "Secularism in Africa." *Sedos Bulletin* 30 (1998), 10-14.

Snyder, Howard A. *Models of the Kingdom.* Nashville, Tennessee: Abingdon Press, 1991.

Sobrino, Jon. *Christology at the Crossroads: A Latin American Approach.* Maryknoll, New York: Orbis Books, 1978.

Song, C. S. *Jesus and the Reign of God.* Minneapolis: Fortress Press, 1993.

Stafford, J. Francis. "The Inscrutable Riches of Christ: The Catholic Church's Mission of Salvation." In *A Church for All People: Missionary Issues in a World Church,* edited by Eugene LaVerdiere. Collegeville, Minnesota: The Liturgical Press, 1993, 31-50.

Sullivan, Francis A. *Charisms and Charismatic Renewal: A Biblical Theological Study.* Dublin: Gill and Macmillan, 1982.

———. *The Church We Believe In.* New York: Paulist Press, 1988.

Tavard, George. *The Church, Community of Salvation: An Ecumenical Ecclesiology.* Collegeville, Minnesota: The Liturgical Press, 1992.

Theisen, Jerome P. *The Ultimate Church and the Promise of Salvation.* Collegeville, Minnesota: St. John's University Press, 1976.

Torres, Sergio, and John Eagleson, eds. *Challenge of Basic Christian Communities.* Papers from the International-Ecumenical Congress of Theology, February 20-March 2, 1980, São Paulo, Brasil. Maryknoll, New York: Orbis Books, 1981.

Twomey, Gerald, ed. *Thomas Merton: Prophet in the Belly of a Paradox.* New York: Paulist Press, 1978.

van Drimmelen, Rob. *Faith in a Global Economy: A Primer for Christians.* Geneva: WCC Publications, Risk Books Series, 1998.

Venetz, Hermann-Josef. "So fing es mit der Kirche an." *Ein Blick in das Neue Testament.* Zürich: Benzinger Verlag, 1981.

Verkuyl, Johannes. "The Biblical Notion of Kingdom: Test of Validity for Theology of Religion." In *The Good News of the Kingdom: Mission Theology for the Third Millennium,* edited by Charles Van Engen, Dean S. Gilliland, and Paul Pierson. Maryknoll, New York: Orbis Books, 1993, 71-81.

Viviano, Benedict T. *The Kingdom of God in History.* Wilmington, Delaware: Michael Glazier, 1988.

Werbick, Jürgen. *Kirche: Ein Ekklesiologischer Entwurf für Studium und Praxis.* Freiburg: Herder, 1994, 76-80.

Wilfred, Felix "Once Again . . . Church and Kingdom." *Vidyajyoti* 57 (1993), 6-24.

————. "No Salvation outside of Globalization." *Euntes-Digest* 29 (September 1996), 135-144.

————. "Church's Commitment to the Poor in the Age of Globalization." *Vidyajyoti* 62 (1998), 79-95.

Wood, S. K. "The Church as Communion." In *The Gift of the Church: A Textbook on Ecclesiology in Honor of Patrick Granfield, OSB,* edited by Peter Phan. Collegeville, Minnesota: The Liturgical Press, 2000, 159-176.

Wostyn, Lode L. *Exodus towards the Kingdom: A Survey of Latin American Liberation Theology.* Manila: Claretian Publications, 1986.

Yoder, John Howard. "A People in the World: Theological Interpretation." In *The Concept of the Believer's Church,* edited by James Leo Garrett. Scottdale, Pennsylvania: Herald, 1969.

————. *The Priestly Kingdom: Social Ethics as Gospel.* Notre Dame, Indiana: University of Notre Dame Press, 1984.

MISCELLANEOUS PUBLICATIONS AND PAPERS

The Nature and Purpose of the Church. Faith and Order paper no. 181, Bialystock, Poland: Ortdruck Orthodox Printing House, 1998.

Ishvani-Kendra Reseach Seminar 2000. "A Vision of Mission for the New Millennium." *Sedos Bulletin* 32 (2000).

International Theological Commission: Text and Document 1969-85, edited by M. Sharky. San Francisco: Ignatius Press, 1989.

Union of Superiors General. *Consecrated Life Today: Charisms in the Church for the World.* Montreal: St. Paul, 1994.

Extraordinary Synod of Bishops. "The Final Report," II,C, 1. *Origins* 16 (1985).

Statistical Yearbook of the Church 1998. Vatican City: Libreria Editrice Vaticana, 2000.

Congregation of the Doctrine of the Faith. "Some Aspects of the Church Understood as Communion." *Origins* 21 (1992).

Medellín Document. *The Church in the Present Day Transformation of Latin America in the Light of the Council.* Washington, D.C.: Catholic Bishops Conference, 1970.

AMECEA Pastoral Institute. *Communities Called Church.* Eldoret: Gaba Publication, 1979.

Towards a Community Church. 2d edition. The Training for Community Ministries Series, no. 28T. Natal, South Africa: Lumko Publications, 1997.

For All the People of Asia: Federation of Asian Bishops' Conferences Documents from 1970-1991, edited by Gaudencio B. Rosales and C. G. Arevalo. Maryknoll, New York: Orbis Books, 1992.

Index

Previously Published in
The American Society of Missiology Series

Protestant Pioneers in Korea, Everett Nichols Hunt Jr.

Catholic Politics in China and Korea, Eric O. Hanson

From the Rising of the Sun, James M. Phillips

Meaning across Cultures, Eugene A. Nida and William D. Reyburn

The Island Churches of the Pacific, Charles W. Forman

Henry Venn, Wilbert Shenk

No Other Name? Paul F. Knitter

Toward a New Age in Christian Theology, Richard Henry Drummond

The Expectation of the Poor, Guillermo Cook

Eastern Orthodox Mission Theology Today, James J. Stamoolis

Confucius, the Buddha, and the Christ, Ralph Covell

The Church and Cultures, Louis J. Luzbetak

Translating the Message, Lamin Sanneh

An African Tree of Life, Thomas G. Christensen

Missions and Money, Jonathan J. Bonk

Transforming Mission, David J. Bosch

Bread for the Journey, Anthony J. Gittins

New Face of the Church in Latin America, edited by Guillermo Cook

Mission Legacies, edited by Gerald H. Anderson, Robert T. Coote, Norman A. Horner, and James M. Phillips

Classic Texts in Mission and World Christianity, edited by Norman E. Thomas

Christian Mission: A Case Study Approach, Alan Neely

Understanding Spiritual Power, Marguerite G. Kraft

Missiological Education for the Twenty-first Century: The Book, the Circle, and the Sandals, edited by J. Dudley Woodberry, Charles Van Engen, and Edgar J. Elliston

Dictionary of Mission: Theology, History, Perspectives, edited by Karl Müller, Theo Sundermeier, Stephen B. Bevans, and Richard H. Bliese

Earthen Vessels and Transcendent Power: American Presbyterians in China, 1837-1952, G. Thompson Brown

The Missionary Movement in American Catholic History, 1820-1980, Angelyn Dries

Mission in the New Testament: An Evangelical Approach, edited by William J. Larkin Jr. and Joel W. Williams

Changing Frontiers of Mission, Wilbert Shenk